IMMANUEL KANT

CRITIQUE
OF
PRACTICAL REASON

IMMANUEL KANT

CRITIQUE OF PRACTICAL REASON

Translated by
H. W. CASSIRER

Edited by G. Heath King and Ronald Weitzman

with an Introduction by
D. M. MacKINNON

MARQUETTE
UNIVERSITY
PRESS

Translation copyright: Olive Cassirer

Library of Congress Cataloging-in-Publication Data

Kant, Immanuel, 1724–1804.
  [Kritik der praktischen Vernunft. English]
  Critique of practical reason / Immanuel Kant ; a new
translation by H. W. Cassirer ; edited by G. Heath King and Ronald
Weitzman ; with an introduction by D. M. MacKinnon.
    p. cm. — (Marquette studies in philosophy ; no. 17)
  Includes index.
  ISBN 0-87462-616-1
  1. Ethics. I. Cassirer, H. W. (Heinrich Walter), 1903– II. King,
G. Heath. III. Weitzman, Ronald, 1945– IV. Title. V. Series:
Marquette studies in philosophy ; #17
  B2773.E5 C37 1998
  170—ddc21

                                                        98 - 9019

Cover sketch: Kant © Michael Nagle,
based on portraits by Kant's contemporaries

Printed in the United States of America
© Marquette University Press, 1998
MARQUETTE UNIVERSITY PRESS
MILWAUKEE

The Association of Jesuit University Presses

This translation is dedicated to

OLIVE CASSIRER

IMMANUEL KANT
CRITIQUE OF PRACTICAL REASON

TABLE OF CONTENTS

INTRODUCTION

The late Dr. H. W. Cassirer (1903–1979) was the elder son of the famous German philosopher and polymath, Ernst Cassirer. The family took refuge in Britain following the Nazi accession to power in 1933, being Jewish and therefore in obvious, ultimate danger. Ernst Cassirer came to Oxford, but not long afterwards he moved to Sweden and then to the U.S.A. His son, Heinz[1], remained in Britain and worked with the distinguished British Kantian scholar, Professor H. J. Paton, then professor of logic and metaphysics in the University of Glasgow. At Paton's suggestion, Heinz Cassirer wrote a commentary on Kant's third Critique, the *Critique of Judgment*, which Methuen published in the late thirties; he also assisted Professor Paton with the last stages of the preparation of the latter's commentary on the first half of Kant's *Critique of Pure Reason*, which he brought out in the autumn of 1936 under the title of *Kant's Metaphysic of Experience*. In 1937 Paton moved to Oxford as White's Professor of Moral Philosophy, and Cassirer was invited there to teach as a refugee scholar, concentrating on Kant's philosophy. In 1946 he secured a permanent appointment in the Department of Moral Philosophy at Glasgow, which in those years was achieving a covetable international reputation in Kantian studies, under the late Professor W. G. Maclagan, remaining there until his retirement. In 1954 he published, in the Muirhead Library of Philosophy series, a study on Kant's *Critique of Pure Reason* under the title: *Kant's First Critique*. But he was already working on the relation of Kant's theory of knowledge to his ethics, and the first draft of the translation of the *Critique of Practical Reason*, which now appears posthumously, was completed in 1945.

Cassirer grew up in the ambience of Marburg neo-Kantian philosophy. Increasingly during his teaching years in the United Kingdom, he concentrated on Kant himself, seeking where the philosopher's theory of knowledge was concerned to present it as a much more subtle, nuanced version of the empiricism fashionable in the Oxford to which he moved in 1937. He had, for instance, a very

---

[1] [Heinz Cassirer had by this time published his commentary on Aristotle's *De Anima* (Tübingen 1932, reprinted 1968), about which the renowned Aristotelian scholar, W. D. Ross, wrote in *The Classical Review* of May 1933 that "it would be hard to name a better account of Aristotle's psychology." Editors]

sure grasp of the quite distinctive emphases of Kant's criticism of transcendent metaphysics, which was by no means unconnected with his awareness not only of the contents of the *Critique of Judgment*, but more importantly of the way Kant treats the themes of God, freedom and immortality in the *Critique of Practical Reason*. The English tendency to confine study of Kant's ethics to the text of the *Grundlegung* (*Groundwork of the Metaphysics of Morals*) led to a failure to face up to the extent to which his profoundly closely argued metaphysical agnosticism provided the foundation for his central doctrine of the primacy of practical reason. This last is a doctrine which could with justice be dubbed profoundly metaphysical, even one with Platonic resonances. Kant's tendency in the work, where Greek philosophy is concerned, is to fasten attention on the Stoa and Epicurus. Yet the myth of Gyges in *Republic* II defining the questions raised by Glaucon and Adeimantus, brings the issues raised by their interrogation of Socrates much nearer to Kant's concern in the *Critique of Practical Reason* than is sometimes realized.

There is no doubt that the *Critique of Practical Reason* is an exceptionally demanding work. The brief introduction to a newly published translation cannot in any sense provide a commentary, even a summary of an argument that is richly complex and extremely subtle. But Cassirer's version excellently conveys the unevenness of the original, the way in which it oscillates between a merely homiletic simplicity and a metaphysical density, experienced chiefly by the reader where treatment of the relation of phenomena to things-in-themselves, and of the closely connected topics of time and causality, is concerned. But of course the density of the exposition is by no means confined to these passages. If freedom is for Kant the pivotal member of the familiar triad, God, freedom and immortality, and everyday awareness of the searching demand of the moral law the *ratio cognoscendi* of freedom's unquestionable reality, the attempt to probe the inward structure of the awareness thrusts the writer to the frontiers of the comprehensible in his exposition. Kant's attempt to reconcile methodological determinism in the exact sciences with moral freedom remains one of the most baffling, and yet most ceaselessly suggestive essays, in European metaphysical speculation. It is a pity of course that in his second Critique Kant ignored what he was to write in the third, on the complementarity of mechanical and teleological explanation. But even if he had taken more account of this important development of his thinking the central difficulty would remain, enticing the student to make his own, if he can, insight that lies on the very frontiers of the intelligible but which yet suggests the reconciliation of apparently inevitable and yet hardly reconcilable assumptions. Cassirer's version of Kant's most important treatment of this theme in the *Critique of Practical Reason* enables the serious student of philosophy to engage with it anew.

Moreover, this version appears at a time when there is a marked increased of interest in Kant's later writings on religious topics, not only his best-known essay in this area — *Religion within the Bounds of Mere Reason*, — but also his opuscula on such topics as evil and eschatology. The *foundation-structure* for these very suggestive later works is laid in the text of the *Critique of Practical Reason*. Anyone who reads them together must see what a great gulf separates Kant from Hegel and how the former's rationalism was of a kind to enable him to enjoy religious perception of the sort that was eventually denied to the bolder, more wide-ranging speculation of his successor. It would be a fitting response to Cassirer's labours in providing English-speaking readers with this provocative, and at times rough-hewn version of one of the acknowledged masterpieces of European moral philosophy, if it encouraged the writing of a comprehensive study envisaging Kant's whole treatment of the relations of God, revealed religion and morality.

It remains my own conviction (confirmed by study of this translation of the *Critique of Practical Reason*) that no other treatment of the topic of man's hope of immortality goes deeper than Kant's, and that if at times he seems to have made it impossible for himself to attach significance to what he says, this very paradox is evidence of the depth to which he has penetrated (with a great simplicity) to the central issues involved. A new evaluation of his whole contribution to theology might prove quite unexpectedly rewarding.

DONALD M. MacKINNON

Donald MacKinnon (1913–94) was Regius Professor of Moral Philosophy at the University of Aberdeen, then Norris-Hulse Professor of Divinity at Cambridge University. He was made a Fellow of the British Academy in 1978.

FOREWORD
by the Editors

The circumstances that helped to prepare the way for the present translation of Kant's second Critique are as important as they are unusual to relate. The manuscript dates from 1976, three years before Cassirer's death. He had prepared a first draft thirty years earlier, for the use of some of his students at Oxford University.

In his lengthy summary of the *Critique of Practical Reason*, which served as part of the preface to his commentary on Kant's third Critique,[1] Cassirer wrote that "the problem of the relation between universals and particulars is one of Kant's fundamental problems [in the second Critique]... it is necessary to emphasize this point because it has been overlooked by many of Kant's interpreters." Later, in the same section, he writes: "I have said again and again that the problem of the relation between the supersensible and the sensible worlds seems to me to be the fundamental problem of Kant's philosophy." Cassirer remained steadfast in upholding these assertions in the midst of the very different philosophical climate which prevailed in Britain for a long time after the second world war. By this time, he was devoting his energies to the writing of his commentary on the *Critique of Pure Reason*.[2] But, even before he had started to correct the proofs of that work, Cassirer had embarked on what to many would appear to be a startling venture for a firm adherent of Kant's philosophy to take upon himself, namely, a study of the Bible, and in particular the letters of St. Paul, along with the moral teaching of the Old Testament prophets. He retired from academic life early so as to devote all his time to these labours, which involved dividing and analyzing the greater part of St. Paul's letters under forty spiritual and emotional categorical headings, and writing a book contrasting both the similarities as well as the forcefully different ethical teachings of Kant with St. Paul's doctrine and personality.[3] (The second chapter of that book is devoted to a study of Kant's ethics, with its focus on the *Critique of Practical Reason* but also delving into passages from *Groundwork of the Metaphysics of Morals* and the later

---

[1] *A Commentary on Kant's Critique of Judgment*, London (Methuen)/New York (Barnes & Noble) 1938 (reprinted 1970).

[2] *Kant's First Critique: an appraisal of the permanent significance of Kant's Critique of Pure Reason* - Muirheard Library of Philosophy, London (Allen & Unwin)/New York (Humanities Press) 1954 (reprinted 1968 & 1979).

[3] *Grace and Law: St. Paul, Kant, and the Hebrew Prophets*, Grand Rapids (Eerdmans)/Edinburgh (Handsel Press) 1988.

Religion within the Bounds of Mere Reason.) It was only then, twenty-one years after he had begun this enterprise, that he decided to translate the whole of the New Testament from the Greek.[4]

As that task was nearing completion Cassirer made it known that he considered there to be an urgent need for an English translation of Kant's *Critique of Practical Reason* that would be technically accurate, attentive to the spirit as well as the letter of Kant's original — and not take misleading shortcuts in the process. He began work on the second Critique as soon as he completed translating the New Testament. Being fully alive to the difficulties to which Kant's blocks of baroque prose give rise, he set out to uncoil these in a manner that would ensure no lessening of the tensions contained within each interlinking part. Most crucial would be the method whereby the translation would show the movement of Kant's thinking in the actual process of its unfolding. Although Kant's expression is often abstract and stilted, the three underlying themes of the second Critique — freedom, God and immortality — body forth, as it were, with an almost tactile impact. Yet the manner in which Cassirer accomplishes this is subtle and measured. The following passage may serve to illustrate this point:

> Wenn wir irgend etwas Schmeichelhaftes vom Verdienstlichen in unsere Handlungen bringen können, dann ist die Triebfeder schon mit Eigenliebe etwas vermischt... [283] (Ak159)

L.W. Beck's translation (1949), which is generally considered the standard, reads:

> Whenever we bring any flattering thought of merit into our actions, the incentive is already mixed with self-love...

M. Gregor's translation (1996) follows suit:

> When we can bring any flattering thought of merit into our action, then the incentive is already somewhat mixed with self-love...

Now Cassirer:

> If anything of a flattering sort, anything which makes us think of merit, is allowed to have a bearing upon our actions, then the motive force is already somewhat mixed up with self-love...

Notice that Cassirer complements the *active voice* of the original by using the verb "think" instead of the noun "thought". If he uses

---

[4] *God's New Covenant: A New Testament Translation*, Grand Rapids (Eerdmans) 1989.

here a passive construction it is in keeping with the active voice so as to bring out Kant's specific intention in employing the modal verb *können* — "If anything of a flattering sort...is *allowed* to have a bearing upon our actions...". The choice of words articulates a process: the continual struggle between *free will* and man's natural inclinations, a struggle that underlies the whole of Kant's moral teaching. This activity of decision is missing in the translations by Beck, Gregor (and the much earlier one by Abbott) who render Kant's *können* innocuous, or omit it altogether. The vigilance and insight evinced, by contrast, in this passage from Cassirer permeates his version in countless variations.

All this we had to keep firmly in mind when preparing the translation for publication. On carefully examining the manuscript, which Cassirer had left untouched at the time of his death, it was our policy, whenever an editorial hand appeared to be necessary, to make a minor adjustment only after we had made certain that the translator's intended construction or emphasis of a clause or sentence would in no way be weakened. It is our belief that Cassirer's version affords an at once deeper and more lucid access to Kant's thought than has as yet been achieved.

G. HEATH KING
RONALD WEITZMAN
March 1998

G. Heath King received his doctorate in philosophy at the University of Freiburg, Germany, and is the author of Existence, Thought, Style: perspectives of a primary relation portrayed through the work of Søren Kierkegaard (*Marquette 1996*). *Ronald Weitzman writes music criticism for national newspapers and musical journals in Britain, and was entrusted by Cassirer with preparing the manuscripts of his later years for publication.*

Figures embedded in the text and appearing in square brackets indicate the start of a page in the First Edition (1788); those prefixed with the letters "Ak" closely correspond with the paging in vol. 5 of the German Academy edition (de Gruyter, Berlin 1900–). The translator worked from the text edited by Benzion Kellermann in Ernst Cassirer's *Kants Werke* (Vol. 5, Bruno Cassirer, Berlin, 1912–1922), referring also to the editions by Paul Natorp (Preussische Akademie der Wissenschaften, Berlin, 1900–1942), and Karl Vorländer (Meiner Verlag, Hamburg, 9th edition 1967). Words and phrases in italics (and bold italics) follow Kant's own emphases.

Dr. Timothy Kircher, who acted as contact between the publishers and editors, was asked to prepare an index, which in turn owes a great debt to that which appeared in the German edition of Karl Vorländer but which is modified and at times extended so as to follow some of the differences in Cassirer's version. The supplements, *Kant's criticisms of the present age* and *Examples and illustrations used by Kant*, underscore the timeless quality of the philosopher's thought.

CRITIQUE
OF
PRACTICAL REASON

[3] (Ak3) PREFACE

The present enquiry bears the title simply of a Critique of Practical Reason in general, not that of a Critique of *Pure* Practical Reason, and does so notwithstanding the fact that the parallelism with the speculative Critique would seem to require the latter designation. The reason why this should be so will be made sufficiently evident in the course of the present investigation, the sole purpose of which is to establish the fact *that there is* such a thing as *pure practical reason*, while, at the same time, with this end in view, making the entire *practical faculty* of that reason subject to criticism. Should the Critique be successful in this enterprise, there is no need for the *pure faculty itself* to be made subject to criticism by it, so as to ensure that reason did *not*, in making such a claim, act in a merely presumptuous manner, and *transcend* its proper limits (this being the very position in which speculative reason might easily find itself). For if reason, as pure reason, is actually efficacious in practice, it furnishes proof of its own reality as well as that of its concepts through what is accomplished by it in deed, and any attempt on the part of a reasoner of the over-subtle sort, with a view to arguing against the possibility of reason's having practical efficacy, is condemned to futility.

[4] In establishing the reality of the faculty in question, the reality of transcendental *freedom* is established along with it — and that, in that absolute signification of freedom of which speculative reason stood in need in its employment of the concept of causality, so as to secure itself against the antinomy into which it inevitably falls, as it sets out, while dealing with the nexus of causal connection, to conceive in thought a cause *unconditioned* by anything else. Still, speculative reason could do no more than exhibit the concept in question in a problematic sense, that is to say, as something not inconceivable. As for the objective reality of the concept, it was unable to secure it; and all it could accomplish was to prevent it that it should not, through the alleged impossibility of that which, in fact, it is obliged to allow to be at least conceivable, find its very being threatened, and be plunged into an abyss of scepticism.

This is what constitutes the character of the concept of freedom, inasmuch as proof of its reality is furnished by an apodeictic law issuing in practical reason. The concept of freedom is the *coping stone* of the entire edifice of a system of pure reason, even of reason taken in its speculative sense. (Ak4) As for the remaining concepts, those of God and of immortality, which, having the status of mere Ideas, are incapable of gaining a firm foothold in the sphere of speculative reason, they now attach themselves to the concept of freedom, acquiring their stability and their objective reality, along with the concept of freedom and by means of it. [5] In other words, *proof* of the *possibility* of the concepts in question is supplied by virtue of the fact that freedom has actual existence, the Idea of freedom, for its part, being made manifest through the instrumentality of the moral law.

Moreover, among all the Ideas arising from speculative reason, freedom is the only one the possibility of which is *known* to us in an *a priori* manner, even though we are incapable of comprehending it, and it is thus known to us on the ground that freedom is the condition[1] of the moral law which *is* known to us.

As for the Ideas of *God* and *immortality*, on the other hand, they are not conditions of there being a moral law but conditions only of there being a certain [6] object necessarily to be postulated by a will determined by that law. That is, they refer solely to the practical employment of our pure reason. And this is why, where the Ideas in question are concerned, we cannot make the claim that we *know* or *comprehend* even their possibility, let alone their actuality. Still, they are conditions subject to which alone a will determined by morality is capable of being applied to its object—the *summum bonum* [the highest good]—, an object with which it finds itself provided in an *a priori* manner. And from this it follows that, with reference to the realm of practice which is here under consideration, we can and, in fact, must, *postulate* the possibility of these Ideas, even though, theoretically speaking, we have no knowledge or comprehension of them.

---

[1] In the present place I call freedom the condition of the moral law, while later, in the treatise itself, I contend that the moral law is the condition subject to which we are first enabled to *become conscious* of freedom. Now, to prevent someone from imagining that there was something *inconsistent* about this way of proceeding, I would merely make the following observation. While it is indeed true that freedom is the *ratio essendi* of the moral law, it is true likewise that the moral law is the *ratio cognoscendi* of freedom. And indeed, but for the fact that our reason came to frame, first of all, the notion of the moral law—and doing so with distinctness—, we should never believe ourselves to be entitled to *presuppose* such a thing as freedom, even though there is nothing contradictory about it; while, on the other hand, it is true that, if freedom did not exist, the moral law would *not be met with* in us at all.

Indeed, as regards the demand that we should be satisfied on this latter point, it is sufficient from a practical point of view that no inner possibility — i.e. no self-contradiction — is to be met with in these Ideas. What occurs, then, is this: that that which, in reference to speculative reason, was a merely *subjective* ground for taking something to be true, is *objectively* valid from the point of view of a reason of the same purity but which is concerned with practice, and that in such a way, as regards the Ideas of God and of immortality, that — by means of the concept of freedom — objective reality is provided for them and also a right to make use of them. In fact, what is provided here is a subjective necessity (arising from a need on the part of pure reason) to postulate these Ideas. At the same time, reason is not extended in this manner, where its theoretical knowledge is concerned. (Ak5)And what happens is that the possibility, which formerly was nothing more than a *problem*, is here [7] turned into an *assertion*, into something given, with the result that the practical employment of reason is being brought into connection with the elements of its theoretical employment. Moreover, as regards the need under consideration, it is not hypothetical in character. It does not serve as an *arbitrary* purpose of speculation, to the effect that if, while engaged in speculation, one's *intention* was to mount up, so as to bring the employment of reason to completion, one was as such under the necessity of postulating something or other. No, the need here is one that *accords with law*. And what it demands is that something is to be postulated in the absence of which there is no possibility that there should happen the very thing which, what we do or leave undone being under consideration, we have been strictly enjoined that we *ought* to do.

From the point of view of our speculative reason, it would indeed be a more satisfactory state of affairs if, no such circuitous route having to be taken, it were in a position to solve the problems in question by itself, preserving them for practical employment as something into which it had insight. However, the truth is that our power of speculation does not find itself in so favourable a position. Those who vaunt of such profound insights should not keep them to themselves but instead should exhibit them publicly, so that they may be examined and their value assessed. Their aim is to furnish *proof.* Well, then, let them furnish proof — and, with them as the victors, the critical philosophy places its entire armour at their feet. *Quid statis? Nolint. Atqui licet esse beatis.*[2] — But since they do not, in fact, want

---

[2] What makes you hold back? They choose not to go through with it. Yet there is nothing to stop them from being happy. Horace, *Satire*, i.i.19 [Editors' tr.]

to do this, presumably because they do not [8] have the power, we ourselves must take matters in hand, our aim being that the concepts of *God, freedom* and *immortality*, regarding the *possibility* of which speculation could not provide a sufficient guarantee, should be looked for in the field of reason's moral employment, and that they should be founded on that employment.

What has been said serves likewise to provide, for the first time, an explanation of the enigmatic contention found in the Critique that, while, in the field of speculation, objective *reality* had to be *denied* to the *categories* when they are *employed* in reference to the supersensible, it was still possible to *grant* this *reality* to them in application to the objects of pure practical reason. Originally, such a point of view was bound to have the appearance of *lacking in consistency*, so long, that is, as the employment in question was known only by name. However, through a thorough-going analysis of that employment, one is now made aware of this fact: that the reality in question does not, in the present case, have for its aim any theoretical *determination* of the *categories*, or any extension of knowledge into the field of the supersensible. All that is meant, as regards the relationship which is being considered, is that *an object* does, in fact, appertain to the categories. Such objects are of the kind that either they are contained, in an *a priori* manner, in the necessary determination of the will, or else, are inseparably bound up with the object of the determination in question. [9] In this way the alleged inconsistency is made to disappear, because the concepts under consideration are employed in a way different from the one that is required by speculative reason. (Ak6) On the other hand, confirmation hardly to be expected hitherto, and also most gratifying, is now supplied by the *consistent way of thinking* characteristic of the speculative Critique, evidence of this being that, while the Critique would not allow the objects of experience, including our own selves, to be anything more than *appearances*, it nevertheless asserted that things-in-themselves had to be presupposed as underlying them. In other words, the speculative Critique was insisting that the supersensible was not all a fiction, and that the concept of the supersensible was not to be looked upon as being empty of content. And now the position is that practical reason, by itself and without having made any arrangement with speculative reason, provides objective reality for a supersensible object bound up with the category of causality, that is to say, it provides objective reality for *freedom*, although, the concept in question being practical, it does so only with a view to its practical employment. In other words, what in the other field was merely something allowing of being *conceived of in* *thought*, now finds itself confirmed by virtue of a fact. Hence, in the Critique of Practical Reason, full confirmation is at the same time provided for the strange, though incontestable, assertion made by the speculative Critique, that even *the thinking subject, **in the inner intuition** which it has *of itself*, is *nothing more than an appearance*. In fact, it all fits so well that [10] such a thesis was bound to occur to one, even though the speculative Critique had furnished no proof of that proposition.[3]

As this is the true state of affairs, I have also come to comprehend why the most convincing objections brought forward against the Critique that I have so far encountered centre on these very points which are of cardinal significance, namely that, *on the one hand*, the objective reality of the categories, as applied to noumena, is denied within the field of theoretical knowledge, while it is affirmed within the field of practice, and *on the other hand* there is this paradoxical demand: that man was to look upon himself as noumenon, inasmuch as he was the subject of freedom, while at the same time looking upon himself in his own empirical consciousness as a phenomenon in respect of the natural realm. And indeed, so long as one has not found any determinate conceptions of morality or freedom, there was no way of [11] guessing what one meant the character of the noumenon to be, upon which the alleged appearance was to be founded. Neither was it clear whether it was still possible at all to form a conception of such a noumenon, seeing that, as regards the theoretical employment, all concepts of pure understanding had already been restricted to mere appearances. Only a detailed Critique of practical reason is in a position to remove all such misconceptions, while at the same time throwing a clear light upon the consistent way of thinking which, in fact, constitutes the greatest asset of such a Critique.

(Ak7) So much by way of justifying the fact that in the present work concepts and principles of pure speculative reason, which have already had their own particular critical enquiry applied to them, are here, from time to time, made once again subject to examination. True enough, the adoption of such a procedure is by no means well suited

---

[3] There is only one way of reconciling causality as freedom with causality as natural mechanism, the former being established by the moral law and the latter by natural law, and both being met with in one and the same subject, i.e. in man. This cannot be done unless man is represented as a being in himself in the former character, while an appearance in the latter — the one with regard to *pure*, the other with regard to *empirical*, consciousness. Apart from the adoption of such a procedure, there is no way in which reason can avoid getting involved in self-contradiction.

in other cases, if one's purpose be that a science to be established is to take a systematic course, seeing that matters already judged upon should in fairness merely be referred to, as distinct from being raised once again. However, in the case *here* under consideration, the adoption of such a procedure was permissible, and indeed necessary, on the ground that reason, as regards the way it deals with the concepts in question, is being considered in the transition it makes to an employment of them which is quite different from the one it made of them in the *former* case. And it is the very fact that [12] such a transition is made which makes necessary a comparison between the course newly adopted and the original one, while at the same time making evident the connection existing between them. One should not, therefore, look upon such considerations — which include, among others, the consideration that has here been directed once again towards the concept of freedom, although only in respect of the practical employment of pure reason — as insertions serving merely to fill in gaps to be found in the critical system of speculative reason, for this system is complete, so far as its own purposes are concerned. Otherwise the position would be as it is with a building constructed in haste, its props and buttresses having to be added at a later time. For the considerations in question deal with what are true members of the system, serving to make evident the connectedness exhibited by it, with the aim that concepts which were originally incapable of being presented other than in a problematic sense should now become comprehensible as exhibiting something real. This reminder concerns chiefly the concept of freedom regarding which one cannot fail to observe how surprising it is that there are still so many men who boast that they are perfectly capable of comprehending it and accounting for its possibility, while at the same time considering that freedom merely in reference to what it signifies psychologically. As against this, had they first embarked upon a thoroughgoing consideration of the concept in its transcendental reference, [13] they would have become aware, first of all, of the *indispensability* of the concept as a problematic one, serving to bring the employment of speculative reason to completion; and secondly, they would have become aware of the entire *incomprehensibility* of the concept. And then, if, at a subsequent stage, they had proceeded to concern themselves with the concept's practical employment, they could not have failed to realize of their own accord that the employment in question had, in respect of the principles underlying it, to be accounted for precisely in the way to which otherwise they are so loath to give their assent. The concept of freedom is a stone of stumbling for all *empiricists*, while, at the same time, it is the key to the most sublime practical principles for *critical* moralists who, in this way, are made aware that (Ak8) *rationalism* is the method they must necessarily adopt. And in view of all this, I would appeal to the reader not to pass over lightly what is said about this concept at the end of the Analytic.

It may be asked whether the development of such a system of pure practical reason, by way of subjecting the latter faculty to a Critique, is something that has cost a great effort, or merely a little one, especially as regards the question of not missing the right point of view to be adopted if there is to be a possibility that this system, taken as a whole, should be correctly delineated. I must leave it to those who have expert knowledge of this kind of work to pronounce judgment upon the point in question. [14] The *Groundwork of the Metaphysics of Morals* is indeed presupposed in what is undertaken here, but only inasmuch as that work provides the reader with a pre-liminary acquaintance with the principle of duty, while at the same time setting forth a determinate formula in respect of duty.[4] In every other respect the present undertaking is independent of anything else. A *classification*, for the sake of *completeness*, of all practical sciences has not been added here — a task corresponding to what was accomplished in the Critique of speculative reason. The valid reason for this not being done is to be found in reason's practical faculty which we are here considering. And indeed, the specific determination of duties as duties of man, [15] for the purpose of their being classified, is possible only on condition that the subject of the deter-mination in question — i.e. man — has first become known in re-spect of his actual constitution, although, on the other hand, the only knowledge relevant here is that which has reference to duty as such. But then, man's constitution is of no concern to a Critique of practical reason in general. The task of such a Critique is that it should set forth in their completeness the principles underlying the possi-

---

[4] A certain reviewer who meant to say something by way of censuring the said work has, in fact, hit upon the truth more effectively than he himself may have intended by his assertion that in that work no new principle of morality was set forth but only a *new formula* of it. But then, is there anyone who would propose to introduce a new principle underlying all morality, thus, as it were, inventing mo-rality for the first time? This would imply that, until he came, the world had been ignorant of the nature of duty, or else had found itself in a state of perpetual error about it. But anyone who knows what a *formula* means to a mathematician, a formula which determines with complete accuracy what is to be done if a certain problem is to be correctly pursued, any failure in this respect thus being excluded, will be far from looking upon a formula that will do this very thing for all duties in general as something unimportant or capable of being dispensed with.

bility of practical reason as well as the extension and the limits of that reason, taking no special account of human nature. Classification, then, belongs in the present case to the system of the science, as distinct from the system of the Critique.

A certain reviewer of the *Groundwork of the Metaphysics of Morals*, a truth-loving and penetrating man, and who is thus worthy of all respect, has brought forward the objection *that, in that work, the concept of the good had not been determined antecedently* to the determination of *the moral principle* (Ak9) (a thing which, in his opinion, necessarily ought to have been done.)[5] As regards [16] this man, I

---

[5] There is another objection which might be brought forward against me, namely, that I did not first supply an explanation of the concept of the *faculty of desire* or the *feeling of pleasure*. However, [16] such a reproach would be unfair, because one has the right to suppose in all fairness that the explanation in question was supplied by psychology. On the other hand, there remains the possibility that, in psychology, the definition under consideration should be arranged in such a way that the feeling of pleasure is taken to be that upon which the determination of the faculty of desire is founded. (And that, in fact, is the procedure which is generally adopted.) But then, this would have the inevitable result that the supreme principle of practical philosophy must turn out to be *empirical* in character, this being the very point of view which remains to be proved, and which, in fact, is being altogether repudiated in the present Critique. In consideration of all this, I propose to supply the explanation here, in the form it must have, if, as is only fair, the controversial point in question is at the beginning left undecided. — **Life** is the faculty present in a being capable of acting in conformity with laws issuing from the faculty of desire. The **faculty of desire** in such a being is the *faculty* it has of becoming, *through its representations*, the *cause of the reality of the objects of these representations*. **Pleasure** is the *representations of the agreement of an object* or of an action with the **subjective** *conditions of life*, i.e. its agreement of the faculty of the *causal efficacy of a representation in respect of the actuality of its object* (or else, agreement with the way in which the forces present in the subject are determined towards action in such a way as to produce the object). This is all I need say by way of criticizing concepts borrowed from psychology. The remainder is accomplished by the Critique itself. One [17] will easily become aware that the present exposition leaves undecided the question whether pleasure is in every case that upon which the faculty of desire is founded, or whether, under certain conditions, pleasure is subsequent to the determination of the faculty of desire. And the reason for this being so is that such an exposition is made up of nothing but of what are criteria pertaining to the pure understanding, i.e. made up of categories which contain nothing empirical. A careful procedure such as we have had recourse to here is greatly to be recommended throughout the entire field of philosophy, yet in a good many cases it is neglected. What is required is that one should not make oneself guilty of prejudging matters prior to the complete analysis of a concept — which is often achieved only at a very late stage — , and that one should not anticipate matters by having recourse to venturesome definitions. Moreover, throughout the course of the Critique, of theoretical as well as of practical reason, notice is being taken of the fact that there is many an opportunity of making good defects such as

hope to have satisfied him in the second chapter of the Analytic. In the same way I have taken into account a number of objections which have reached [17] me from men who give evidence of their good will and who have at heart the discovery of the truth. But then, those who have nothing before their eyes except their own [18] old system, and with whom it is a foregone conclusion what is to be approved of and what disapproved, do not desire a discussion which might be contrary to their own purposes. (Ak10) And as for myself, I shall deal with these matters in the same way as I have done up to now.

If one is called upon to provide a detailed determination of a particular faculty of the human soul, in respect of its sources, its contents and its limits, there is (human nature being what it is) indeed no other way of proceeding than that one should begin with the *parts*, exhibiting them completely, in so far as the acquaintance one has already made with the elements renders this possible. However, there is another way of attending to the matter, a way more philosophical and *architectonic* in character, namely, that one should seek to acquire a correct grasp of the *Idea of the whole* and should set oneself the task to make comprehensible all those parts, in the mutual relation in which they stand to one another, by way of deriving them from the whole in question. The means of accomplishing this is by bringing them within the compass of a faculty issuing in pure reason. This way of examining things, along with justification of what one does, [19] is possible only on condition that one is most intimately acquainted with the system; and those who looked upon the first kind of enquiry as something vexatious, not thinking it worth the trouble to become acquainted with it, are not in a position to take the second step, namely, to gain a general survey of things such as implies a synthetic return to that which previously was given merely analytically. And this being so, it is indeed small wonder that these men should find inconsistencies everywhere, notwithstanding the fact that the gaps in the system, suspected because of there being inconsistencies, are, in truth, attributable not to the system itself but merely to the incoherent way of thinking characteristic of these men.

The reproach that my intention is to introduce a *new language* is not something of which I am afraid in the case of the present treatise, because the type of knowledge here in question lends itself to popular treatment by its very nature. As a matter of fact, a reproach of this kind would, even in the case of the first Critique, occur to no one

are met with, if the old dogmatic course of philosophizing is adopted, as well as of correcting mistakes not detected until the time one employs concepts in such a way that reason's concern is with these *concepts taken in their entirety*.

who had done more than simply turn the pages of that work. The artificial invention of new words in cases where the language has no lack of terms adequate to express given [20] concepts is a childish endeavour, the aim being that, if one cannot distinguish oneself among the multitude through giving expression to thoughts both new and true, one can, after all, do so by putting a new patch upon the old garment. Hence, if the readers of the work under consideration are familiar with modes of expression which, while more popular, are just as adequate to the thought as I believe those others to be, or should they venture to demonstrate the *futility* of the thoughts themselves, and with it, the futility of any expression by which such a thought is signified, the result will be as follows. As to the first point, they would put me under a considerable obligation; for the sole obligation I have is that I should be understood. And as to the second point, they would well deserve of philosophy. As against this, my own position is that (Ak11) I have grave doubts whether, so long as the said thoughts retain their former standing, it will be possible to discover expressions which, though adequate to them, are yet in more current use.[6]

[21] (Ak12) It is in this way, then, that the *a priori* principles underlying two faculties of the mind, the [22] faculty of knowledge

---

[6] What I am more afraid of in the present case than the incomprehensibility of which I have spoken is that occasionally certain expressions should be misinterpreted, even though I have selected them with the greatest care, so that the conception to which they point should not be missed. To take an example: in the table of categories of *practical* reason, there appear, under the title of *modality*, the expressions the *permitted* and the *forbidden* [21] (that which, in the field of practice, is objectively possible or impossible). Now, as to the way in which language is ordinarily used, these expressions have almost the same meaning as the expressions *duty* and *contrary to duty* which appear under the next category. Here, however, the *first* is to signify that which agrees or conflicts with a practical precept which is no more than *possible* (this is the sort of thing which happens whenever the solution of a problem in geometry or mechanics is in question), while the *second* signifies that which stands in such a relation to a law to be met with, in *actuality*, in reason as such. This distinction of meaning is, in fact, not altogether foreign to the common use of language, although it is somewhat out of the ordinary. For example, it is *forbidden* for an orator as such to coin new words or phrases, while this is to a certain extent *permitted* to a poet. In neither case is there any question of duty, for if a man is ready to incur the loss of his reputation as an orator, there is no way of preventing him. What we are here concerned with is solely the distinction between *imperatives* according to whether their determining grounds are *problematic, assertoric* or *apodeictic*. In the note where I have contrasted the [22] moral Ideas concerning practical perfection to be found in the various schools of philosophy, the position is similar. I have here made a distinction between the Idea of *wisdom* and that of *holiness*, and have done so notwithstanding the fact that I myself have contended, at the same time, that, fundamentally and objectively considered, they are one and

and the faculty of desire, have been ascertained and have been deter-minately fixed with regard to the extent and the [23] limits of the use to be made of them. And the result of this procedure is that a secure foundation has been laid for a systematic philosophy — theoretical phi-losophy as well as practical — which has the character of a science.

Is there a worse fate that could befall these labours than for some-one to make the unexpected discovery that *a priori* knowledge nei-ther exists at all nor could exist? However, there is no risk of this happening, since it would amount to somebody's setting out to fur-nish proof, by means of reason, that there was no such thing as rea-son. For the truth of the matter is this: if we say of something that it is by means of reason that we have knowledge of it, we do so only if we are conscious of the fact that, even though we had not become familiar with the said circumstance by way of coming across it in experience, we could still have known it. [24] In other words, knowl-edge by means of reason and *a priori* knowledge are one and the same thing. To seek to extract necessity from an empirical proposi-tion (*ex pumice aquam*)[7], and to provide, along with this necessity, true universality for a judgment, is plainly a self-contradictory pro-cedure. (And no rational inference is without this universality, not even an inference by analogy, for analogy implies that universality and objective necessity are at least presumed, and thus, after all, pre-suppose their existence.) To substitute subjective necessity, i.e. cus-

the same. But then the wisdom I have in mind in that place is the one to which man (the Stoic) makes an arrogant claim, which, in other words, by a figment of the imagination, he takes to be a property of man, *subjectively* speaking. (The ex-pression "virtue" of which the Stoics likewise made such great display might per-haps be said to signify even better what is characteristic of their school.) However, it is the expression "*Postulate* of pure practical reason" which could most easily give rise to misinterpretation. And this would happen if we confused it with the signifi-cation which appertains to the postulates in pure mathematics which carry apodeictic certainty with them. But then, what these postulates postulate is the *possibility of an action* which has antecedently been recognized as *possible*, with complete cer-tainty, in an *a priori* theoretical manner. As against this, it is the *object* itself (God and the immortality of the soul) which is postulated by the other kind, this being done on the basis of laws that are apodeictic but *practical* — in other words, solely on behalf of a reason concerned with practice. Thus the certainty of the postulated possibility is not [23] theoretical at all, and consequently also not apodeictic, i.e. not a known necessity, having references to an object. But instead it is a necessary presupposition having reference to the subject, the aim being to secure obedience to laws of reason which, while indeed objective, are yet practical in character. In other words it is nothing more than a necessary hypothesis. And as regards this rational necessity, subjective yet true and unconditioned, "postulate" was the best expression I could discover for it.

[7] Draw blood from a stone (*lit.* trying to extract water from a pumice-stone). [Editors]

tom, for the objective one which pertains only to *a priori* judgments, amounts to denying to reason the power of judging the object, that is, to thinking reason incapable of having knowledge of the properties that belong to the object. To take an example: it implies that, if something often, and indeed always, follows upon a certain antecedent state, one is not entitled to say that one may draw an *inference* from one to the other (for this would signify objective necessity and imply the concept of an *a priori* connection). All that one was entitled to say would be that, after a manner not unlike that of the animals, one was in expectation of the occurrence of similar cases. And in taking such a view, this amounts to one rejecting the concept of a cause that, strictly speaking, is *false*, and [25] nothing more than the result of allowing oneself to be deceived in one's thinking. As for the efforts made to remedy this lack of objective validity and of the universal validity following from it, by arguing that there was, after all, no reason why we should attribute to rational beings other than ourselves a different way of representing things; if that were a valid inference, it would imply that our ignorance did us greater service in extending our knowledge than could be accomplished by any thinking of our own. For what it would entail is that, by reason of the fact that rational beings other than man are unknown to us, we had the right to presuppose that they were such as we know ourselves to be. In other words, the position would be that we really knew these beings. (Ak13) There is a further circumstance I need not even mention here: if a judgment is universally assented to as true, this does not establish proof of its objective validity (that is to say, of its validity as a piece of knowledge). On the contrary, even though it should happen accidentally that there was such universal agreement, this would furnish no proof of a correspondence of the judgment with the object, the truth of the matter being that objective validity is what constitutes the sole ground for there being necessary universal agreement.

[26] In the face of such a *system of universal empiricism* with regard to principles, Hume would indeed find himself in a perfectly comfortable position. After all, as is generally known, he demanded nothing more than that, as regards the concept of a cause, necessity, in the objective sense, should be altogether discarded, and that, instead of this, a merely subjective necessity, i.e. custom, should be presupposed. His aim was to deny to reason any power of pronouncing judgment concerning God, freedom and immortality, while at the same time he had undeniably great skill, provided only that his principles were granted to him to draw his conclusions with the

greatest logical cogency. Still, Hume did not conceive of empiricism in such universal terms as to include in it mathematics. He took mathematical propositions to be analytic in character; and if that were the true account of the matter, they would indeed be apodeictic, while, at the same time, no inference could be drawn from this circumstance concerning a power of reason to be the source of apodeictic judgments in philosophy also — synthetic ones, I mean — as is the case with the proposition about causality. On the other hand, if empiricism with regard to principles is taken as something *universal*, mathematics would likewise become implicated.

[27] Now, if mathematics gets involved in a conflict with reason, inasmuch as it allows of no principles except empirical ones — certain proof of this being inevitable when furnished by the antinomy which arises on the occasion when mathematics supplies incontestable proof of the infinite divisibility of space, while empiricism can on no account admit of such a possibility — it follows that there is a palpable contradiction between, on the one hand, the greatest possible demonstrative evidence, and on the other hand, the alleged inferences basing themselves on principles of experience. Hence, one cannot help asking, like the blind man mentioned by Cheselden, "What is it that deceives me: sight or feeling?" (For empiricism has its foundation in a necessity which is *felt*, while rationalism has it in one which is *comprehended*.) And what becomes manifest in this manner is that empiricism, in its universal sense, is in fact genuine *scepticism* which, in so unqualified a manner, was falsely ascribed to Hume[8], [28] who, through the way in which he dealt with mathematics, retained at least one reliable criterion of experience, (Ak14) whereas scepticism does not admit of any criteria (which can never be found anywhere except among *a priori* principles), and that notwithstanding the fact that experience does not consist of feelings merely but of judgments as well.

Since, however, during this philosophical and critical age of ours, it is barely conceivable that anyone should take such an empiricism seriously, and since, if it is put forward for consideration, this is presumably with a view to training the faculty of judgment and — by

---

[8] Names by which the followers of a sect are designated have at all times been used in such a way as to carry with them a good deal of distortion of the correct facts. It is as though somebody made the following assertion, "N. *is an idealist*"; for although he not merely concedes but insists that our representation of external things have real objects corresponding to them, having the character of [28] external things, he will still hold that the form in which they are intuited does not appertain to them by themselves but appertains solely to the human mind.

way of contrast — to bringing the necessity of *a priori* rational principles more clearly to light, we may, after all, be thankful to those who are prepared to undertake a task by which they will find themselves but little instructed in other respects.

INTRODUCTION

THE IDEA OF A CRITIQUE OF PRACTICAL REASON

The sole concern of the theoretical employment of reason was with the objects of the faculty of knowledge, while the Critique of reason, in respect of this employment, did, strictly speaking, concern itself exclusively with the *pure* faculty of knowledge, because the suspicion was aroused — a suspicion subsequently confirmed — that such employment might easily go beyond the limits set to it, losing itself among inaccessible objects or even among self-contradictory concepts. As against this, the practical employment of reason is quite different. What reason is occupied with, so far as this employment is concerned, is the grounds determining the will, will being the faculty of producing objects which correspond to representations, or at least, the faculty of determining oneself, i.e. one's causality, with a view to carrying such objects into effect, no matter whether [30] or not one's physical power is adequate for this. This being the true state of affairs, it is at least possible for reason to be sufficient in determining the will, objective reality appertaining to it inasmuch as it is the willing alone that matters.

So the first question to be asked in the present case is this: is pure reason by itself sufficient to determine the will, or is it only as empirically conditioned that reason is capable of being a ground of the determination of the will? Now what makes its appearance here is a concept of causal efficacy, that of *freedom*, which, notwithstanding the fact that it is incapable of being exhibited empirically, has been justified by the Critique of pure reason. And should we now be in a position to discover grounds which furnish proof of the circumstance that the property in question is, in fact, to be assigned to the human will (and in the same way to the will of all rational beings), what has been made evident in this way is not merely that pure reason is capable of having practical efficacy, but that pure reason alone, not the empirically conditioned one, actually has a practical efficacy which is unconditioned in character. (Ak16) It is, therefore, not a Critique of *pure practical* reason but one of *practical* reason in general to which we shall have to devote our labours. For pure reason, once it has been demonstrated that it exists, does not require a Critique, seeing that the conditions adequate for a Critique of its entire employment is contained within pure reason itself. [31] This, then, is the obligation which rests upon the Critique of practical reason in general: it should cause the empirically conditioned reason to cease from making the arrogant claim that it alone, to the exclusion of everything else, was capable of playing the part of being a determining ground of the will. The employment of pure reason, once it has been shown to exist, is seen to be the one which alone is immanent, while the empirically conditioned employment, which arrogates exclusive dominion to itself, is transcendent, this circumstance expressing itself, as it does, in its making claims and giving orders in which it goes entirely beyond its proper territory. Such a state of affairs is indeed the very reverse of what could rightly be said of pure reason in its speculative employment.

However, since it is, after all, pure reason from which there derives the knowledge which here forms the foundation of reason's practical employment, the division of the Critique of practical reason will have to be arranged, in its general structure, in conformity with what was done in the Critique of speculative reason. So there must be found in this Critique a *Doctrine of Elements* and a *Doctrine of Method*, the former containing as its first part an *Analytic*, serving as a rule of truth, and then a *Dialectic*, being an exposition of the illusion to be met with in judgments of practical reason and the removal of that illusion. On the other hand, the arrangements made regarding the sub-division [32] of the Analytic will be the reverse of what was found in the Critique of pure speculative reason. For in the case of the present Analytic we shall begin with *principles*, proceed to *concepts*, turning only then, if possible, to the senses, whereas in the case of speculative reason, we began with the senses and had to end up with principles. The reason why we have to proceed in this way is, in turn, that our concern in the present case is with a will, and because we are considering reason not in its relationship to objects but in relationship to that will and its causal efficacy. That being so, we must begin with the principles governing the causal efficacy in question, which is not conditioned by anything empirical. And it is only then that the attempt can be made to give a definite account of how concepts concerning the determination of such a will find their application to objects and, last of all, to the subject and those of its powers which fall within the domain of sensibility. Causal efficacy by virtue of freedom, that is to say, some practical principle exhibiting purity, is inevitably the point where we must start here, such a principle, for its part, serving to determine what are the objects to which it alone is capable of being applied.

[33] CRITIQUE OF PRACTICAL REASON

PART I

DOCTRINE OF THE ELEMENTS
OF
PURE PRACTICAL REASON

THE ANALYTIC OF PURE PRACTICAL REASON

CHAPTER I

THE PRINCIPLES
OF PURE PRACTICAL REASON

§1. – EXPLANATION

Practical *principles* are propositions in which a universal determination of the will is contained, such as comprehends under
it a plurality of practical rules. They are subjective, or *maxims*,
if the condition on which they rest is looked upon by the subject as
valid only for its own will, while they are objective principles, or
practical *laws*, if the said condition is recognized as objective, i.e. as
valid for the will of every rational being.

Observation

If we suppose that *pure* reason is capable of containing within
itself a practical ground, that is to say, one sufficient for the determination of the will, [36] practical laws exist; while, in the contrary
case, all practical principles will be nothing more than maxims. In
the event that the will of a rational being is such that it is liable to be
affected in a pathological manner, then there is the possibility that
there should be encounterable here a conflict between maxims, on
the one hand, and, on the other, practical laws recognized by that
will itself. For example, a man lays it down as a maxim that he will
tolerate no insult without taking revenge, while being aware, at the
same time, that it is not a practical law which is here in question but
merely his own maxim, there being no possibility, on the other hand,
if it be taken to be a rule holding good for every rational being, of
embodying it in one and the same maxim without this giving rise to
self-contradiction. The principles which determine what happens to
the knowledge we have of nature (e.g. the principle which lays it
down that, in the communication of motion, action and counter-

action are equal) are, at the same time, laws of nature; for in that case the employment of reason is theoretical, being determined by the nature of the object. (Ak20) As for knowledge concerned with practice, that is, the knowledge whose sole concern is with the grounds determining the will, the position is this: that principles which one lays down for oneself are not, on that account, laws to which one is inevitably subject. This is because, in the field of practice, reason is concerned with the subject, that is to say, with the faculty of desire, there being the possibility here that the rule should have to conform in many respects to the special constitution of that subject. Any and every practical rule is a product of reason, because what it does is prescribe an action as a means for bringing something into effect, that is to say, as something intended. On the other hand, such a rule is for a being, in which reason is not the one and only determining ground of the will, an *imperative*, that is to say, a rule which is signified by an "ought" which, for its part, expresses the objective compulsoriness of the action. In this manner it is indicated that, if the will were determined solely by reason, the action would inevitably take place in conformity with that rule. In other words, imperatives are objectively valid [37] and are wholly different from maxims which have the character of subjective principles. On the other hand, there are two alternatives regarding imperatives. They determine either the conditions of causality to be met with in a rational being, inasmuch as it is an efficient cause, while taking account only of the effect and whether it can be adequately attained, or else, it is only the will they determine, no matter whether or not it is adequate to accomplishing the effect. The first kind of imperative would be hypothetical and would contain nothing but precepts of skill, while the second kind would be categorical, they alone being practical laws. Maxims, then, have the character of *principles* but they are not *imperatives*. Imperatives, on the other hand, if they are conditioned in character, not determining the will absolutely as a will, but only in reference to a certain effect — in other words, if they are hypothetical imperatives — then they are indeed practical *precepts*, while yet they are not *laws*. As for laws, they must provide an adequate determination of the will as a will, no previous account being taken of the question whether I have the power of carrying into effect something which I desire, or what I have to do to bring about the effect. The said imperatives, then, have to be categorical. Otherwise they do not have the character of laws, because they lack the necessity which, if it is to be a practical necessity, must be independent of pathological conditions, those conditions, that is, which attach to the will in a merely accidental manner. To take an example, suppose one says to someone that he must work and save while he is young, so that he should not suffer want in his old age: that is a practical precept addressed to his will which is correct and, at the same time, important. Still, it will be immediately perceived that the will is here referred to something *else* with regard to which it is presupposed that the man desires it. And as regards the desire in question, it must be left to the agent himself to decide whether he is counting on other resources, over and above a fortune acquired by himself, whether perhaps he does not, after all, have any hope that he will reach old age, or whether his idea is that, in the event of his being in distress in the future, it will be possible for him to scrape through. Reason, from which alone [38] any rule which is to contain necessity can spring, does, it is true, impart necessity also to the precept under consideration (for, apart from this, that precept would not be an imperative). Still, that necessity is conditioned in a purely subjective manner, and there is no way of presupposing that it should exist in all subjects to the same degree. (Ak21) What is required by the legislation issuing in reason, on the other hand, is that reason should stand in no need to presuppose anything but *itself*, because the rule laid down is objective and universally valid, only on condition that it holds good, apart from any reference to contingent subjective conditions whereby one rational being is distinguished from another. Let us suppose, for instance, that we say to a man that he must never make a lying promise, then the rule here in operation is one that exclusively concerns his will, there being no consideration of the question whether or not any purposes a man may have are attainable by that will. It is merely the willing which is supposed to be determined by that rule, and this in a wholly *a priori* manner. Now, should it turn out that this rule was correct, from the point of view of practice, then it is a law which, because it is an imperative, is categorical. Practical laws, then, refer exclusively to the will, no account being taken of what is accomplished by the will's causal efficacy. And as regards this efficacy, one is entitled to abstract from it (as something belonging to the world of sense), so as to have the said laws before one in all their purity.

§2. – THEOREM I

Practical principles which presuppose an *object* of the faculty of desire (something partaking of the nature of "matter") as a determining ground of the will are, one and all, empirical and are incapable of yielding practical laws.

What I understand by "matter of the faculty of desire" is an object desired to be brought into reality. But then, if the fact that we are desirous of an object of this kind [39] is something that precedes the practical rule, and is the condition subject to which that rule is adopted as a principle, then my contention is, *first of all*, that the said principle is never anything but empirical in character. The ground by which the choice is determined in such a case is the representation of an object, and concerns that relation of the representation to the subject by virtue of which the subject's faculty of desire is prompted to bring the object into reality. Now such a relation to the subject is what is called *pleasure* taken in the reality of an object. It would be necessary, therefore, to presuppose this pleasure as being the condition whereby the determination of the choice is made possible. But then, as regards the representation of some object or other, whatever it may be, there is never the possibility that it should be known in an *a priori* manner whether *pleasure* or *pain* will be accompanying it, or whether such an object will be a matter of *indifference*. It follows that, in a case such as this, the ground which determines the choice must always be empirical, and accordingly holds good for the material practical principle which presupposed that ground as its condition.

Secondly, since a principle which bases itself solely on what is a subjective condition, namely, susceptibility to pleasure or pain (this being something that can never be known in any other way except empirically, and which can never be valid for all rational beings alike), it is indeed possible that the principle should serve as a *maxim* for the subject having that susceptibility; while, on the other hand, it cannot serve as a [40] (Ak22) *law*, not even for the subject itself (because it lacks objective necessity, which can never be known except in an *a priori* manner.) And it will thus be perceived that a principle of this sort can in no circumstances supply a practical law.

§3. – THEOREM II

Practical principles of the material type are, in virtue of their nature, one and all, of the same kind and come under the general principle of self-love and private happiness.

The pleasure arising from the representation of a thing, inasmuch as it is to be a ground determining that a thing should be desired, is based upon the *susceptibility* of the subject, being so on the ground that what it *depends* on is whether or not a certain object has actual existence. And accordingly, the said pleasure belongs to the domain of sense, or feeling, not to that of the understanding which, for its part, expresses the relation of representations to an *object* in conformity with concepts, not a relation to the subject in conformity with feelings. Pleasure thus has practical efficacy, only inasmuch as the feeling of pleasantness which the subject expects to receive from the actual existence of the object is that which determines the faculty of desire. But then, if in a rational being there be present a consciousness of the pleasantness of life, a pleasantness accompanying it through the whole of its existence, it is *happiness* which is signified here, while the principle laying it down that happiness is to become the supreme determining ground of [41] choice is the principle of self-love. From this it can be seen that "material" principles which assign the ground determining choice to pleasure or pain to be felt because of the actual existence of some object or other, are entirely of the *same kind*, inasmuch as they come, one and all, under the principle of self-love or private happiness.

Conclusion to be drawn

The place assigned to the determining ground of the will by all *material* practical principles is that of the *lower faculty of desire*, and if there were no *merely formal* laws by which the will was adequately determined, there would be *no* way of conceding the existence of a *higher faculty of desire*.

Observation I

It must be a matter of surprise that men otherwise acute should have found it possible to entertain the belief that the distinction between the *lower* and the *higher faculty of desire* was dependent on whether the **representations** accompanied with (Ak23) the feeling of pleasure had their source in the *senses* or the *understanding*. For if one is enquiring into the grounds determining the desire, saying that they are attributable to the expectation of a feeling of pleasantness arising from some object or other, then the question where the *representation* of the object engendering the delight comes from is a matter of complete indifference, and all that counts is to what extent it does *delight*. If a representation, no matter whether it has its origin in the understanding, is incapable of determining choice in any other way than by presupposing the presence of a feeling of pleasure in the subject, then the capability of the representation for becoming a ground of determining choice is entirely dependent on the condition in which the subject's inner sense finds itself, that is to say, dependent on whether the object can affect inner sense in such a way as to give rise to a feeling of being pleased. [42] No matter how different in kind representations of objects may be from one another — whether they arise in the understanding, or even in reason, in contradistinction from representations arising in sensibility — the fact remains that it is the feeling of pleasure on the strength of which alone, if the matter be considered in strictness, these representations become grounds determining the will, the expected pleasantness and delight being what stirs up the activity for the production of the object. Moreover, as regards the said feeling of pleasure, not only is it invariably of the same kind, in so far as it can never be known in any other way except empirically, but also in so far as it is one and the same vital power that is affected by it, the faculty of desire being the orbit within which it expresses itself, and in view of this, there being no possibility that the difference between it and some other ground of determination — whatever it may be — should be anything more than a difference in degree. And indeed, were it otherwise, what way would there be of instituting a *quantitative* comparison between grounds of determination wholly different from one another, in respect of their mode of representation, so as to give preference to the one which affects the faculty of desire with the greatest intensity? Let us suppose a man has succeeded, but only for a single occasion, in obtaining a book from which he may learn a very great deal. Yet he returns it unread on account of a hunt which he does not wish to miss. Someone may take his departure in the middle of a fine speech, so as not to be late for a meal. He may take his leave of a company providing entertainment by way of rational conversation, a thing which at other times he greatly values, and he may do so for the purpose of occupying his seat at the gaming table. He may even turn away a poor man, whom to benefit he rejoices on other occasions, on the ground that just at present he has no more money in his pocket than he needs to pay his entrance fee for seeing a comedy. The fact is that, so long as what determines the will is the feeling of pleasantness or unpleasantness which he expects some cause or other to arouse in him, it is a matter of complete indifference to him what kind of representation it is by which he is affected. What alone matters to him, for the purpose of making his choice, is how intense the feeling of pleasantness is, how long it lasts, the ease with which it is obtained, and how often it can be repeated. Just as it is [43] a matter of complete indifference to the man who needs gold for the defraying of an expense whether the material in question is gold dug out of a mountain or gold washed out of the sea, as long as it is accepted by everyone at the same valuation, so no man, if it is life's pleasantness which alone is of interest to him, asks the question whether what is at play are representations arising in the understanding or representations arising in the sensibility. What he enquires into is solely the *quantity* and *intensity* of the *delight* which these representations provide for the longest possible time. Indeed, the very men who would gladly deny that pure reason had the power of determining the will (Ak24) — no feeling of any kind being presupposed — are the very men who are capable of deviating from the explanation they themselves have provided to such an extent as to declare afterwards, with regard to what they had previously brought under the same principle, that it was entirely heterogeneous in character. For example, we find that pleasure may be taken merely in *exertion of strength*, in the consciousness of the power one's mind has in the overcoming of obstacles which oppose themselves to our intentions. Or pleasure may be taken in the cultivation of one's intellectual talents, etc. And here we quite rightly speak of *more refined* joys and delights, because they are more within our control than others are, and because they do not become stale but, on the contrary, strengthen the feeling we have for them in such a way as to enable us to derive even greater enjoyment from them. Thus, while giving delight, they serve at the same time to cultivate us. Still, if on that account we seek to make out that they determine the will in a way different from what happens when it is determined merely through sense, we ought to consider that what is, after all, presupposed here is that, if the pleasures in question are to be possible, there must exist in us a feeling predisposing us in that way, as the first condition of that delight. And thus the true state of affairs is seen to be very much like this. It is as though ignorant men desirous of dabbling in metaphysics conceived of matter as being so fine, so super-fine, that they go on with this to the extent of being liable to be seized by a feeling of giddiness, and were thus led to the belief that what they had achieved by their way of proceeding was to devise a being that is *spiritual*, and at the same time, extended in space. If, as Epicurus does in his treatment of virtue, [44] we make everything dependent on the pleasure which it promises, where its capacity for determining the will is concerned, we cannot subsequently censure him for taking this pleasure to be of exactly the same kind as that arising from the coarsest of the senses. For there is no reason whatever for imputing to him the view that the representation whereby the feeling in question is excited has to be assigned exclusively to the bodily senses. In many cases, he also sought (as far as one gathers) the source of these representations in the employment of the higher faculty of desire. But that neither did nor could prevent him from taking the view, in accordance with the aforesaid principle, that the pleasure itself which these representations afforded us might quite possibly be intellectual in character — that this pleasure, I say, by virtue of which alone the representations are capable of being grounds determining the will, is in every case entirely of the same kind.

To be *consistent* is the highest obligation incumbent upon a philosopher; and yet it is that which is met with least frequently. The schools of ancient Greece supply us with a larger number of examples of the said consistency than are to be met with in this *syncretistic* age of ours where the fashion is artificially to devise a *system of compromise*, comprising principles which contradict one another, and displaying everywhere a spirit of dishonesty and superficiality, such a course being taken because it commends itself more highly to a public well content for a man to know a little of everything, while, truth to tell, knowing nothing at all: the role being played in thus proceeding is that of a Jack of all trades. The principle of private happiness, no matter to what extent understanding or reason might be made use of in association with it, would still fail to contain any determining grounds of the will except such as are suitable for the *lower* faculty of desire, and the inevitable conclusion to be drawn from this is as follows. Either there is no such thing as a higher faculty of desire at all, or else *pure reason* has the power of having practical efficacy by itself. In other words, pure reason, without the presupposition of any feeling, that is, without any reference to the representations of the pleasant or the unpleasant (which make up the element of matter in respect of the faculty of desire, this matter never supplying any condition for principles except one which is empirical in character) — pure reason, I say, must be capable of determining the will, solely [45] by virtue of the form exhibited by the practical rule. Only in such a case does reason, inasmuch as it determines the will by itself — not being at the service of the inclinations — (Ak25) occupy the place of a faculty of desire, to be entitled a *higher* faculty, in the true sense of that word. This faculty, to which the pathologically conditioned faculty of desire is subordinate, is *specifically* distinguished from the latter to the extent that even the slightest admixture of impulses which come of this lower faculty have the effect of undermining its strength and its position of superiority, just as whenever anything in the least empirical is allowed to enter in as the condition of a mathematical demonstration, this has the effect that its dignity and its impressiveness are lessened, and indeed brought to nought altogether. When it is a practical law that is in question, reason determines the will directly, not by means of an intervening feeling of pleasure or pain, not even pleasure taken in that law, and it is only the fact that reason is capable of having practical efficacy, as pure reason, which makes it possible for it to play the part of the *legislator*.

Observation II

To be happy is necessarily the wish of a being which, while rational, is yet finite, and is thus inevitably a ground determining its faculty of desire. For as regards the property of finding contentment in the *whole* of one's existence, this condition is not an original possession or state of blessedness which would presuppose a consciousness of its independence and self-sufficiency. No, the condition of finding oneself happy has, in the case of such a being, the characteristic of a problem imposed upon it by the finiteness of its nature, by the circumstance, that is, that it is a being which has needs. And such a need is concerned with that which stands for the element of matter, in respect of the being's faculty of desire. In other words, its concern is with something that has reference to a feeling of pleasure or pain which underlies it subjectively, and it is, by virtue of the said feeling, that it is decided what the being stands in need of so as to be contented with its state. On the other hand, for the very reason that the material ground of determination here in question cannot be known by the subject in any other way than empirically, it is impossible to look upon the task to be undertaken here as having the character of a law, because a law, being objective, would have to contain (as valid in all cases and for all rational beings) [46] *one and the same determining ground* of the will. And indeed, although it is *invariably* the concept of happiness which forms the foundation when what is in question is the practical relation of *objects* to the faculty of desire, the fact remains that the concept of happiness is nothing more than the general title for subjective grounds of determination, that it determines nothing specifically (this being the very thing which alone matters concerning the practical task here being considered), and that, without such determination, there is no way of providing a solution. If the question be where each man is to find his happiness, everything turns upon the particular feeling of pleasure or pain in each man, and even as regards one and the same subject, upon the varying needs it has, in conformity with the way in which the said feeling suffers alteration. Hence what, as a law of nature, is a *subjectively necessary* law, is, *objectively* speaking, a practical principle of a very *contingent* character which, seeing that it can be very different in different subjects, and indeed, must be, can never be the source of a law. And all this is so because, where the desire for happiness is concerned, what is decisive is not the form of the legislation but merely that which constitutes the element of matter, namely, whether I may expect pleasure from obeying the law, and the degree of that pleasure. Principles of self-love can, it is true, contain general rules of skill (i.e. ways of discovering the means for carrying out a design).(Ak26) But in that case they are principles[9] which are merely theoretical in character, signifying (to take an example) what [47] means are to be used for designing a mill by a man who desires to eat. As for practical principles based upon self-love, on the other hand, they can never be universal in character, seeing that the ground determining the faculty of desire has its foundation in the feeling of pleasure or pain regarding which it can never be assumed that it is universally directed towards the same objects.

Yet even though there actually was complete agreement between finite rational beings as to what objects they were to take to be objects of their feelings of pleasure or pain, and they were agreed likewise what were the means to be employed for attainment of the former and avoidance of the latter, it would *by no means* entitle them to make out that the *principle of self-love* was a *practical law*; for the uniformity in question would, after all, be merely contingent in character. It would still remain true that the ground of determination was only subjectively valid and was merely empirical, being devoid of that necessity which is invariably conceived of whenever it is a law that is in question, *viz.* objective necessity resting on *a priori* grounds. An alternative would be that one sought to make out that the said necessity was not practical at all but merely physical, an inclination compelling us to perform the action with the same inevitability as yawning is when we see others yawn. As a matter of fact, one could maintain with a better right that there were no practical laws at all but only *recommendations* made on behalf of our appetites, this view being preferable to raising merely subjective principles to the rank of practical laws. It is emphatically required that such laws should carry

[9] Propositions which, in mathematics or natural science, are called *practical* propositions, should, properly speaking, be given the name of *technical* propositions, for the reason that the tenets in question have nothing whatever to do with the determination of the will. All they signify is the manifoldness of possible actions which are sufficient for accomplishing a certain effect. And so they are theoretical in the same way as are all propositions enunciating something about the connection between a cause and an effect. But then, the truth of the matter is that he who is desirous of accomplishing an effect must accept likewise that he should play the part of the cause.

objective necessity with them and not a merely subjective one, and that they should be known by reason in an *a priori* manner, not by virtue of experience (however universal it may be, empirically speaking). And indeed, even rules concerned with uniform appearances are called natural laws only if, as with mechanical laws, they are actually known in an *a priori* manner, or else, [48] as with chemical laws, if it is assumed that they would be known to us in an *a priori* manner and on the basis of objective grounds, were our insight to go further than it does. On the other hand, it is expressly laid down that it must be subjective, not objective, conditions which underlie the choice in the case of merely subjective practical principles - in other words, they ought to be represented as having the character of mere maxims and never that of practical laws.

This last observation does, at first sight, appear to amount to nothing more than a juggling about words. In truth, however, it is the definition of the most important distinction which can ever come up for consideration within the field of practical investigations.

§4. – THEOREM III

(Ak27) If a rational being is to conceive of its maxims as practical universal laws, it can do so only by conceiving of them as principles which contain the determining ground of the will, not in respect of its matter but solely in respect of its form.

It is the object of the will which is the matter of a practical principle. Such an object is either the ground which determines the will, or it is not. In the event of its being a determining ground of the will, the rule governing the will would be subject to an empirical condition, i.e. to the relation in which the determining representation stands to the feeling of pleasure or pain, and, in consequence, the rule would not have the status of a practical law. But then, as regards a law, once all matter, i.e. every object of the will as its determining ground, has been separated from it, there is nothing that remains [49] but the mere *form* of a universal legislation. And from this it follows that there is either no possibility at all that a rational being should conceive of its subjectively practical principles, i.e. of its maxims, as being, at the same time, universal laws. Or else, it must suppose that the mere form of these maxims, by virtue of which they *acquire their suitability for a universal legislation*, is that which alone bestows upon them the character of practical laws.

Observation

Even a man equipped with the most ordinary understanding is capable, without receiving any instruction, of distinguishing what form a maxim must have so as to make it suitable for a universal legislation, and what form it cannot have. To take an example, let us suppose that I have adopted it as my maxim to increase my capital by every secure means at my disposal. Now my present position is that I have in my hands a *deposit*, the owner of which has died, without having left anything in writing concerning the matter. This is plainly an instance of my maxim. But then, what I wish to find out is whether that maxim allows of being thought of as being valid as a universal practical law. Applying it, therefore, to the present case, I ask myself whether it is capable of taking the form of a law, in other words, whether there is the possibility of my laying down, by virtue of my maxim, a law such as this, that everybody is entitled to deny the existence of a deposit, with regard to which no one is in a position to furnish proof against the recipient that it has been given. What I immediately become aware of is that such a principle, conceived of as a law, would destroy itself, because the effect it would have would, in fact, be that there was no such thing as a deposit at all. A practical law, if I am to acknowledge it as such, must qualify as suited to a universal legislation. This is an identical proposition and is thus self-evident. If, therefore, my contention is that I am subject to a practical *law*, there is no possibility of my referring to my inclination (in the present instance, my greed) as a [50] (Ak28) determining ground suitable for a universal practical law. And indeed, the said inclination is far from being fitted for a universal legislation. On the contrary, the truth is that, if it is given the form of a universal law, the inevitable effect must be that it will gradually wipe itself out altogether.

The desire for happiness is universal, and so is the *maxim* by virtue of which that desire is made by each man a determining ground of his will. Still, it must be a matter of surprise, in view of what has been said, how it could have occurred to men of discernment to make out that, on that account, the desire for happiness was to be thought of as a universal *practical law*. And indeed, while in other cases a universal law makes everything harmonious, the effect of one's wishing to bestow upon the said maxim the universality of a law would be the very opposite of harmony, with the most flagrant contradictions resulting as well as the complete annihilation of the maxim itself and of its purposes. And that would be so, on the ground that, in the supposed case, it would not be the one and the same object towards which the will of all was directed. On the contrary, each man would have an object private to him (his own well-being), a state of affairs, where there can be an accidental agreement with other men's purposes which are likewise directed towards themselves, but which is by no means sufficient to give rise to a law, seeing that the exceptions one is justified in allowing for, as opportunity serves, are, in fact, endless and quite incapable of being comprehended in a determinate manner, under a universal rule. The harmony this results in resembles that encountered in a certain satirical poem which describes the harmony subsisting between two marriage partners bent on each other's ruin in the following words, "*Oh, what wondrous harmony, whene'er he wants a thing, so does she...*". Or else, one is reminded of the story we are told about the arrogant claim made by King Francis I against the Emperor Charles V, where it is said, "What my brother Charles wants [*viz.* Milan] I want too." Empirical grounds of determination are unsuited to form the basis of a universal legislation which is external; and they are just as little suited to an internal one. For what happens here is that each man takes his own subject as that upon which the inclination is founded, [51] one man one subject, another man another subject, and that even as regards each one of them, it is now one inclination and then another which has the preponderating influence. To discover a law, while laying down this condition — that is, to govern them, one and all, in such a way as to produce universal harmony — is absolutely impossible.

§ 5. – PROBLEM I

Supposing it is merely the legislative form of maxims which by itself alone is a sufficient determining ground of the will, the task set is to discover the character of a will capable of being determined solely in this manner.

Since the mere form of the law can be represented only by reason and in no other way, and, since it is thus not an object of the senses, and, in consequence, is not to be assigned to the realm of appearances, the conclusion to be drawn is as follows. The representation of that form, as a determining ground of the will, differs from all those determining grounds which deal with events in nature, in conformity with the law of causality, by reason of the fact that in their case the determining grounds must themselves have the character of appearances. (Ak29) But then, if the position be that, apart from the universal legislative form aforementioned, there is no other determining ground of the will capable of serving that will as a law, the conclusion to be drawn is that such a will is to be conceived of as entirely independent of the law of nature, that is to say, the law of causality, the concern of which is with appearances and the relation in which they stand to one another. But then, such independence is what is called *freedom*, taken in the strictest, i.e. the transcendental, sense of that word. It thus follows [52] that a will to which nothing can serve as a law except only the mere legislative form of the maxim is a free will.

§6. – PROBLEM II

Supposing that a will is free, we are to discover that law which alone is suited to determine it in a necessary manner.

Since what constitutes the element of matter in the practical law, that is to say, any object towards which the maxim is directed, is incapable of ever being given to us in any other way except empirically, while, on the other hand, the free will (being independent of empirical conditions, that is to say, those which belong to the world of sense) must yet allow of being determined, it is necessary that a free will, being independent of what constitutes the element of *matter* in the law, should none the less come across a ground of determination in that law. But then, with the exception of the matter of the law, there is nothing contained in it except the legislative form. And from this it follows that the legislative form, in so far as it is contained in the maxim, is that which alone is capable of playing the part of a determining ground of the will.

Observation

Freedom and an unconditioned practical law thus refer to one another reciprocally. Now the question I wish to raise here is not whether they actually differ from one another, or, on the contrary, whether the position is that an unconditioned law is nothing else than the consciousness which pure practical reason has of itself, reason, for its part, being wholly identical with the positive concept of freedom. Instead I wish to raise the question: where does our *knowledge* of that which is unconditioned in the field of practice have its *starting-point* — [53] does it start from freedom or from the practical law? Freedom cannot be the starting-point of that knowledge, since we are incapable of having immediate consciousness of it — and that on the ground that our original conception of it is negative in character. Neither are we capable of inferring freedom from experience, seeing that experience gives us knowledge only of the law governing the appearances — in other words, gives us knowledge of the mechanism of nature, which is the precise counterpart of freedom. It is the *moral law*, therefore, of which we become immediately conscious, as soon as we set about the task of designing maxims for ourselves. It is the moral law which offers itself to us, *first of all*, reason exhibiting it as a determining ground (Ak30) which cannot be prevailed upon by any sensible condition, as a ground, that is, which is, in fact, entirely independent of any conditions of this kind. It is in this way, then, that we are led directly to the concept of freedom. But then, how is it that consciousness of that moral law is rendered possible? We can become conscious of pure practical laws in the same way as we have consciousness of pure theoretical principles, by attending to the necessity with which reason prescribes them to us, and by eliminating all empirical conditions, which is what reason directs us to do. The concept of a pure will arises from the way in which the practical laws are dealt with, just as consciousness of there being a pure understanding arises from the way in which the theoretical principles are dealt with. That this is the true subordination of our concepts, that it is morality by which the concept of freedom is first disclosed to us, in other words, that it is *practical reason* by virtue of which speculative reason finds itself, through the said concept, presented, for the first time, with the most insoluble of problems, being placed in a most embarrassing position — all this is made sufficiently evident by the following considerations. Nothing belonging to the field of appearances can be explained by way of having recourse to the concept of freedom. On the contrary, it is the mechanism of nature which must here serve as our sole guide. Moreover, the antinomy of pure reason which arises, when reason, in dealing with the series of causes, sets out to make its way upward, so that it may attain to the unconditioned, has this result: that reason, whichever alternatives it adopts, becomes implicated in [54] incomprehensibilities, while, where mechanism is concerned, it at least has its utility in providing an explanation of appearances. And so it would never have occurred to anyone to undertake the bold enterprise of introducing freedom into science were it not for the fact that the moral law, and practical reason with it, had taken up their stand, obtruding the concept of freedom upon us. Moreover, as regards the order to be assigned to offer concepts to be met with in us, experience likewise serves to offer confirmation of what has been said. Let us suppose that there is a man who alleges that he finds his lustful desire wholly irresistible, when presented with the object of his favour as well as with an opportunity of enjoying it. Now ask him whether he would not master his desire if, on encountering such an opportunity, a gallows were set up in front of his house, and that, immediately after the gratification of his lustful craving, a rope were to be tied round his neck. Surely, there would be no need to spend much time guessing what reply he would make. But then, ask him what the position would be if his sovereign, while threatening instantaneous execution, as was done in the other case, made the demand on him that he was to bear false testimony against an honourable person whom that prince would fain bring to ruin, by way of having recourse to specious subterfuges. Now let your man be asked this question: whether in such a case, however great his love of life may be, it would still be possible for him to gain the mastery over it. Whether or not he would master it is a matter about which he will perhaps not be so bold as to assert anything with certainty. But that it is possible for him to do so is something he must concede without hesitation. His way of judging, then, is this: that he is able to do a certain thing, by virtue of the fact that he is conscious that he ought to do it; and he recognizes the presence of freedom within himself, a circumstance which otherwise, in the absence of the moral law, would have remained unknown to him.

§7. – The Fundamental Law Issuing in Pure Practical Reason

Act in such a way that the maxim of your will can always be thought of as being, at the same time, a principle underlying a universal legislation.

[55] (Ak31) Observation

Within the field of pure geometry postulates are to be found which have the character of practical propositions. However, there is nothing contained in these beyond the presupposition that we are *able* to do a certain thing, in the event of its being demanded that we *should* do it. These are the only propositions occurring in geometry which are concerned with something existing, and, being what they are, they are to be regarded as practical rules that are subject to a condition of the will which is problematic in character. However, what happens in the case that concerns us here is that the rule lays it down absolutely that we are to proceed in a certain manner. The practical rule is thus unconditioned, i.e. it is to be thought of as a categorical practical proposition which is *a priori* in character, a proposition by virtue of which the will is objectively determined in a manner both absolute and immediate: this takes place by virtue of the practical rule itself which has thus the character of a law. Indeed, pure *reason* having *of itself practical* efficacy is, in the present case, the immediate source of law. As for the will, it is thought of as being independent, in other words, as a pure will, which is determined *by the mere form of the law*, while the determining ground in question is looked upon as being the supreme condition to which all maxims are subject.

This state of affairs is startling enough, and nothing resembling it can be found anywhere within the whole field of practical knowledge. The *a priori* thought of a possible universal legislation, a thought merely problematical in character, is being commanded unconditionally as a law, nothing being borrowed either from experience or from any external will. But then, we should keep in mind that what we are dealing with here is not a precept, in accordance with which it is laid down that an action is to take place by virtue of which a certain desired effect is to be rendered possible; for if that were the case, the rule would invariably be dependent on physical conditions. No, the rule which concerns us here determines merely the will, doing so in an *a priori* manner, in respect of the form exhibited by the maxims arising from that will. And in such a case it is at least not inconceivable that a law doing service on behalf of the *subjective* form appertaining to principles should be thought of as being a determining ground — and that by virtue of the *objective* form pertaining to a law in general. [56] The consciousness of this fundamental law may be given the name of a fact of reason, because there is no possibility of extricating it, by some sort of specious reasoning, from any data antecedently supplied to us by reason, no possibility, for instance, of extricating it from our consciousness of freedom, for no such consciousness is, in fact, antecedently given to us. On the contrary, if the law in question can be called a fact of reason, that is because it impinges upon us by itself as a synthetic *a priori* proposition, not founded upon any intuition, whether pure or empirical. True enough, if freedom of the will were presupposed, the proposition in question would be analytical. However, the assertion of freedom of the will, taken as a positive *concept*, would require the possession of a power of intellectual intuition which can on no account be assumed in the case we are here considering. On the other hand, if the law under consideration is to be looked upon as *given*, without this giving rise to misconception, we shall do well to note that it is not an empirical fact which is here in question but a fact arising from pure reason — the only one of its kind. In this way reason proclaims that it is the original source of legislative power (*sic volo, sic jubeo*).[10]

Conclusion from the Above

Pure reason has by itself practical efficacy, and provides man with a universal law which we call the *law of morality*.

Observation

(Ak32) It is impossible to call in question the fact referred to above. All one has to do is analyze the nature of the judgments made by men concerning the law-abidingness of their actions, and one will invariably find the position to be this. No matter what protests may be uttered by the inclinations, their reason, when dealing with the maxim of the will, operative in an action, finds itself, without being corrupted in any way, invariably compelled, in virtue of its very nature, to take the pure will for its standard. In other words, the standard to which it appeals is itself, and, in doing so, it looks upon itself as having practical efficacy in an *a priori* manner. Now, by virtue of the universality of the legislation through which the principle of morality becomes a determining ground of the will — formal in character and occupying the first place of all, no account being taken of whatever subjective differences there may be [57] — , reason declares it to be a law which holds good, at the same time, for all rational beings, inasmuch as they are endowed with a will at all, i.e. endowed with a power of determining their causal efficacy through representing rules to themselves, and as a result are capable of acting in accordance with principles, and as a consequence of this, also, in accordance with *a priori* practical principles. It is these alone which carry with them that necessity which reason demands if it is to acknowledge anything as a principle.

The law of morality is thus not limited to human beings but applies to all finite beings endowed with reason and a will. And indeed, even the infinite being, to be thought of as the supreme intelligence, falls within the scope of that law. On the other hand, in the case mentioned first, that of finite beings, the law takes the form of an imperative. This is so on the ground that, although one may indeed presuppose the presence of a *pure* will, when a rational being is in question, one is not entitled, in the case of a being affected by its

---

[10]As I will, so I command. [*Cf.* Juvenal, *Satire*, vi. 223. Editors]

needs and by moving causes deriving from sensibility, to presuppose the presence of a *holy* will, that is to say, of a will such as would be incapable of adopting maxims contrary to the moral law. With these beings, therefore, the moral law takes the form of an *imperative* which lays down a command, and which is categorical because of the unconditional character of the law. The relation in which such a will stands to the law in question is one of *dependence*, going by the name of *obligation*, a certain kind of *compulsion* to perform an action being signified in this manner, although, on the other hand, the compulsion is one having its source solely in reason and its objective law.

Such an action is given the name of one done from *duty*, on the ground that a choice affected by pathological influences (although, on the other hand, it is not invariably determined by them, and thus still remains a free choice), implies the presence of a desire which derives from *subjective* causes and can thus in many cases be contrary to the pure and objective ground of determination. What is needed, therefore, is a resistance offered by practical reason, this resistance, which partakes of the nature of moral necessitation, deserving the name of an inner yet intellectual constraint. As for the intelligence endowed with all-sufficiency, the choice is rightly represented as being such that there can be no possibility of adopting a maxim except one which could, at the same time, function objectively and be a law. [58] And as regards the concept of *holiness* which, by virtue of this being so, is rightly assigned to it, what it signifies is that such an intelligence, although indeed not exempt from all practical laws, is yet exempt from all practical laws which imply limitation, in other words, exempt from obligation and duty. Moreover, the said holiness of will has none the less the status of a practical Idea which must necessarily serve as an *archetype*. The only thing that suits the position of all finite rational beings is that they should approximate to that archetype by way of a procedure going on *ad infinitum*. The pure law of morality, which on that account is itself called holy, constantly fixes this procedure before their eyes in a manner that accords to the true facts. To feel certain of this progress continuing *ad infinitum*, in respect of one's maxims and one's unchangeable determination to (Ak33) adhere to them, with a view to advancing continually, is what is called virtue. A practical reason which is finite is incapable of accomplishing anything higher than the possession of this virtue which, being a faculty acquired in the natural course of events, can never be brought to complete perfection, on the ground that, in a case like this, assurance never turns into apodeictic certainty, while, when it is mere persuasion which is present, that is a very dangerous state of affairs.

§8. – THEOREM IV

The one principle which underlies all moral laws, as well as the duties in conformity with them, is that of the *autonomy of* the will. *Heteronomy* of choice, on the other hand, is not only incapable of serving as the basis of any obligation, but, in fact, is opposed to the principle of obligation and to the morality of the will. The principle of morality consists solely in this: that there is independence of everything bound up with what, as regards the law, constitutes the element of matter — independence, that is, of any desired object — while yet there is a determination of the choice, by virtue merely of the universal legislative form of which a maxim must be supposed to be capable. Now *the said independence* [59] is *freedom*, in the *negative* sense of that term, whereas the *legislation of its own* which derives from pure reason's having practical efficacy, precisely by virtue of its being pure reason, is freedom in the *positive* sense of that term. The only thing, therefore, which is expressed by the moral law is the *autonomy* of pure practical reason, i.e. autonomy arising from freedom, and freedom itself is, as regards all maxims, the formal condition subject to which alone they are capable of being in agreement with the supreme practical law. If, then, what in willing constitutes the element of matter, which cannot possibly be anything else but the object of a desire which is being brought into connection with the law — if, as I say, this "matter" finds entry into the sphere of the practical law, being regarded *as the condition of its possibility*, there results heteronomy of choice, that is to say, dependence on natural law, its being laid down that some impulse or inclination is to be pursued. In such a case the will does not lay down a law for itself, and all that emerges is a precept which tells us in what way laws appertaining to the pathological aspect of our nature can be obeyed in a reasonable manner. As for the maxim which, if such a procedure is adopted, can never contain within itself that form which is universally legislative, it is not merely that no obligation arises from it but that it is opposed to the very principle of *pure* practical reason, and thus opposed likewise to moral disposition. And this remains true, even though the action resulting from the maxim should be in conformity with the law.

Observation I

(Ak34) A practical precept which carries with it a material, that is to say, an empirical [60] condition, should, therefore, never be counted as having the status of a practical law. And indeed, the law governing the pure will, which is a free will, transfers the will into a sphere quite other than the empirical one, while the necessity expressed by that law, seeing that it is not to be a material necessity, can consist in nothing else but in formal conditions concerned with the possibility of a law in general. As regards what constitutes the element of matter in practical rules, it always rests on subjective conditions, no universality (one holding good for rational beings) being provided in this way, but merely a conditional universality, laying it down, for instance, what, in the event of my *desiring* one thing or another, I should have to do to bring it into existence. Moreover, these rules all centre on the principle of *private happiness*. Now it is indeed undeniable that all willing must have its object, in other words, that which stands for the element of matter. However, it does not follow from this that the element of matter should be the ground which determines the maxim. Indeed, should that be the case, the result would be that the maxim did not allow of being exhibited in a universally legislative form. And this is so because the expectation of the object's existence would then be the cause determining the choice, and one would have to presuppose that the dependence of the faculty of desire on the existence of some object or other was that which formed the basis of the willing. But then, as far as this matter is concerned, our search would have to be wholly among empirical conditions, and there could never be anything which formed the basis of a necessary and universal rule. It is possible that the happiness of others should be the object of the will of a rational being. If, however, such happiness were to be the determining ground of the maxim, it would have to be presupposed not merely that we took a natural delight in the well-being of others, but that this was something which had the character of a need. And this is what actually happens in certain men as a consequence of their sympathetic disposition. But then, we have no right to presuppose the presence of such a need in all rational beings, while in God's case we cannot presuppose it at all. That which stands for the element of matter, in respect of the maxim, may, therefore, remain what it is. [61] It must not, however, be its condition because, if it were, the maxim would be unsuited to form the basis of a law. What is necessary, therefore, is that the mere form of a law, which imposes limitations upon the element of matter, should, at the same time, be a reason why the said "matter" is joined to the will. On the other hand, it must not be treated as a presupposition. For example, let us assume that it is my own happiness which plays the part of "matter". Now, if I presume that everyone aims at happiness (as indeed I have a right to do with regard to every finite rational being), it can become an *objective* practical law, only on condition that I include the happiness of others. The law, therefore, that we are to promote the happiness of others does not have its source in the presupposition that to do so is the object of everybody's choice. It arises solely from the fact that the form of universality becomes the determining ground of the will, this being the condition which reason requires, if it is to bestow upon a maxim arising from self-love the objective validity of a law. Thus it was not the object, i.e. the happiness of others, which was the determining ground of the pure will, but the mere legislative form alone, by virtue of which my maxim founded upon inclination had a limitation imposed upon it, (Ak35) with a view to bestowing upon it the universality of a law, thus making it conformable to pure practical reason. And it was the said limitation, and not the adding of any external spring of action, which alone was able to give rise to the concept of an obligation, the *obligation*, that is, that my maxim springing from self-love was to be extended in such a way as to include the happiness of others.

Observation II

If *private* happiness is made out to be the determining ground of the will, that is the precise opposite of the principle of morality, while — as I have shown above — such must invariably be reckoned to be the case whenever the determining ground, which is to serve by way of playing the part of a law, is assigned to anything other than to the legislative form of the maxim. [62] The said opposition is, however, not merely logical in character, as would be the position with empirically conditioned rules which one nevertheless sought to raise to the status of necessary principles of knowledge. It is a practical opposition. And were it not for the fact that reason speaks with so clear a voice, as regards the relation in which it stands to the will, so as to make it impossible to shout it down—a voice audible even to the most ordinary of human beings — the effect would be that morality had been brought to ruin altogether. As things are, however, the appeal to happiness is one which by now can be maintained only in the philosophical schools where recourse is had to speculations serving only to confuse the mind, men having the audacity to make themselves deaf to that divine voice, for the purpose of being able to hold on to a theory which requires but little racking of the brain.

Let us suppose an acquaintance of yours, for whom in other respects you had a liking, sought to justify himself for having borne false testimony, and did so in the following manner. His first plea is to refer to what he alleges to be a sacred duty, that of promoting one's own happiness. He then proceeds to enumerate all the advantages he has gained by his conduct, and makes mention of the prudence he has exercised, so as to secure himself against all discovery, even against being discovered by yourself, to whom he is revealing the secret, with the sole intention that he might deny it whenever he so pleased. And he then goes on to pretend, in all seriousness, that what he has done is to perform the true duty of man. Now, as regards yourself, you would, if he spoke in this way, either laugh straight in his face, or you would shrink back in horror, notwithstanding the fact that, if someone has regulated his principles, taking his own advantage for his sole standard, you would not wish to bring forward any objection as regards the measures which your man has adopted. Or let us suppose there is someone who is seeking to recommend a man to you as a steward to whom you can blindly entrust all your affairs. To inspire you with confidence, he gives praise to him, saying that he is a prudent man, a taskmaster in pursuing his own advantage. Moreover, he describes him as a man of indefatigable activity who never lets an opportunity go by for gaining his ends. Lastly, [63] to remove any anxiety lest vulgar self-seeking on his part might prove an obstacle, he gives praise to him, pointing out how well he understands how to conduct his life in a refined manner, that he takes his pleasure not in the amassing of money or crude luxury but in the extension of his knowledge and in well-chosen and instructive social intercourse, indeed, even in showing beneficence to the needy. On the other hand, as to the means adopted (means which, after all, derive their worthiness or unworthiness solely from the end pursued), he draws attention to the circumstance that he has no scruples in this matter, treating other people's property and possessions just as though they were his own, (Ak36) provided only he can be certain that he can act in this manner without being discovered or having any obstacles put in his way. Now, if that were the line taken by the man making the recommendation, you would suppose either that he was trying to make a fool of you, or else, that he had taken leave of his senses. And indeed, the border-line between morality and self-love is so clearly and distinctly marked that, if the question be whether a thing belongs to the domain of the one or the other, it is impossible that a mistake should be made even by the most ordinary of observers. The few remarks that follow may appear superfluous, seeing that we are dealing here with so obvious a truth. Still, they may at least serve to impart a somewhat greater distinctness to the judgments made by man's ordinary reason.

The principle of happiness can give rise to maxims, but never to maxims such as would be suited to function as laws for the will, and this would remain so, even if *universal* happiness were singled out as the object of the will. And indeed, seeing that, as regards knowledge of happiness everything rests upon empirical data, on the ground that, whatever judgment is made, it depends altogether on the opinion held by each man — while that opinion is, at the same time, extremely variable — it follows that, although *general* rules are possible in the case under consideration, there can never be any *universal* rules. Or to put it another way, there can be rules which apply on an average and in the majority of cases, but there can never be rules which have to be valid at all times and necessarily. Hence there is no way of founding practical *laws* upon them. Moreover, for the very reason that, in the case under consideration, it is an object of choice that is taken to be the presupposition of the rule which is to determine that choice, [64] the object thus having to precede the rule, it is impossible that the rule should be referred to anything other than to the object and the course recommended by it. In other words, the reference in the rule is to experience and it is founded upon experience, the variety of judgment having necessarily to be endless, in a case such as this. The said principle, then, does not prescribe the same practical rules as applying to all rational beings (even though these rules come under the common title of happiness), whereas the moral law is thought of as one which is objectively necessary, solely on the ground that it is to be valid for everyone endowed with reason and a will.

The maxim deriving from self-love, that of prudence, *merely gives advice*, while the law of morality *gives a command*. But then there is, after all, a great difference between that which we are *advised* to do and that which is *obligatory* upon us.

What is to be done, so as to be in conformity with the principle of the autonomy of choice, is something which can be comprehended, quite easily and without there being any need to hesitate, even by a person equipped with a power of understanding of the most ordinary sort. On the other hand, if what forms the basis is heteronomy of choice, it is difficult to decide what is to be done so as to be in conformity with the principle. What is required for this is knowledge of the world. In other words, as to the question of what one's *duty* is, the correct answer presents itself of its own accord to every one. Yet, if the question be what brings true and lasting advantage with it, here is something — especially if this advantage is to extend to the whole of one's existence — enveloped in impenetrable obscurity. And a great deal of ingenuity is required if the rule of practice adapted to such an end is, by way of skilfully allowing of exceptional cases, to be made tolerably conformable to life and its purposes. None the less, as regards the moral law, it requires of every one that it should be obeyed, and obeyed in all strictness. To be in a position, therefore, to judge what is to be done so as to be in conformity with that law, must not be so difficult as to debar the most ordinary and unpractised understanding from knowing how to proceed upon the task assigned to it, even in the absence of all worldly wisdom.

To satisfy the categorical command of morality is in everybody's power at all times; whereas to satisfy the empirically conditioned [65](Ak37) precept directed towards happiness is something but rarely possible, and, in fact, far from possible for everyone, even with re-gard to a single purpose. The reason for this being so is that what alone matters, in the first case, is the maxim, which must be genuine and pure, while what is also to be taken into consideration in the second case is one's capacities and the physical powers one possesses for bringing a desired object into existence. Besides, as for giving a command which lays it down that every person ought to seek to make himself happy, this would be a foolish way of proceeding, on the ground that one never commands that a man should do what, of his own accord, he inevitably wishes to do. What alone could be commanded to a man in such a case, or rather, presented to him by way of suggestion, are the measures to be adopted, seeing that he is not in the position to accomplish everything which he desires. On the other hand, to command morality, under the general title of duty, is a perfectly reasonable procedure on the following grounds. In the first place, to obey the precept enjoining morality is by no means everyone's wish, were the precept to come into conflict with the in-clinations. And secondly, there is no need that a man should be taught the measures which lay down for him in what way he will be enabled to render obedience to the law in question; for what a man wills to do in this respect he likewise has the ability to do.

He who, in playing a game of chance, has made a *loss*, may well get *annoyed* at himself and his folly. If, on the other hand, he is con-scious of having *cheated*, although he has made a *profit*, he must necessarily come to *despise* himself the instant he measures himself by the standard set up by the moral law. So this law must, after all, signify something other than private happiness. And indeed, if a man is compelled to say to himself, "I am a *villain*, notwithstanding the fact that I have filled my purse", the standard of judgment must plainly be different from the one which would be operative if a man applauded himself, saying, "I am a *clever* fellow, for I have increased my cash".

Finally, there is something else bound up with the Idea of our practical reason, something which is a concomitant of the transgression of a moral law, namely, that such transgression is *deserving of punishment*. But then, there is no way at all [66] of establishing a connection between the concept of punishment as such, on the one hand, and partaking of happiness, on the other. And indeed, although he who punishes may, at the same time, have the benevolent purpose of directing the punishment likewise to the said end, that of partaking of happiness, it is essential, first of all, that the punishment should be justified in itself, i.e. as a mere evil, with the result that the man who is being punished, even though things were left as they are — there being no prospect of any favour concealed behind such harsh treatment — would have to confess that he had received only what he deserved, and that there was a complete correspondence between his conduct and his lot. Whenever it is punishment as such which is in question, what is necessary, first of all, is that there should be justice which constitutes the essential feature of that concept. Justice and kindness are indeed capable of being connected with one another. Yet it is true, at the same time, that the man who deserves punishment has no right whatever to count upon such kindness, considering what his conduct has been. Punishment, then, is a physical evil which, even though it was not, in fact, connected with moral evil as its *natural* consequence, yet ought to be its consequence, and that in conformity with principles underlying a moral legislation. If, then, whenever the question be one of crime, such crime is of itself liable to punishment, even though the physical consequences for the agent be left out of account; if, in other words, crime signifies a forfeit of happiness — to a certain extent, at any rate — it would be plainly absurd to argue that crime consisted in the very fact that the agent had brought punishment upon himself, thus diminishing his own happiness. (Ak38) (And indeed, if the principle of self-love was to be adopted, this would be the concept properly applicable to all crime.) On this view, punishment would be the reason for calling something a crime, while, as for justice, it would consist in this: that all punishment was to be done without, and that even the punishment coming about in the ordinary course of events was to be prevented. And indeed, on such a supposition the action would no longer contain anything evil, on the ground that the evil consequences which followed in different circumstances, and for the sake of which alone that action had been called evil, had now been kept in check. [67] Finally, there is the

whenever there is reward or punishment, this is to be looked
ely as a mechanical contrivance at the disposal of a superior
:rving to set rational beings in motion so that they might
ᴉeir final goal, i.e. happiness. But then, it is evident enough
that we are here confronted with a mechanism governing the will of
rational beings, a mechanism destructive of all freedom. And that
being so, there is no need for us to detain ourselves with such a view.

There is more subtlety, although just as little truth, in the pre-
tension resorted to by those who assume the existence of a certain
special moral sense, and that it is this sense — not reason — which
determines the character of the moral law. On this view, an immediate connection would exist, by virtue of this sense, between virtue
and a feeling of contentment and pleasure, between vice on the one
hand, and a feeling of disquietude and pain on the other. And so
everything would be made to turn on the desire the agent has for his
own happiness. Now without referring, in this connection, to the
remarks I have previously made, I should wish to draw attention to a
certain illusion which is operative here. To be able to represent the
vicious man as tormented by perturbation of mind, in consequence
of his consciousness of the trespasses he has committed, the uphold-
ers of such an opinion are obliged to represent him, where the principal foundation of his character is concerned, as already morally
good — to some extent, at any rate — while they are obliged from
the outset to represent the man who finds delight in his consciousness of actions done in accordance with duty as already virtuous.
The position, then, is this: that the concept of morality did, after all,
have to take first place, no regard being paid to the said contentment, and that there is no way at all of deriving that concept from it.

Now, as for the importance to be attached to what we call duty,
as for the authority of the moral law and the dignity which obedience to it immediately bestows upon a man in his own eyes, all this
has to be valued, first of all, if, as the result of one's being conscious
of being in accordance with the law, one is to come to feel the said
contentment, or conversely, is to feel the bitter reprimand which one
has incurred, should one have to reproach oneself with a transgression of the law. [68] It is impossible, therefore, that the contentment
or disquietude of which we have spoken should be felt prior to one's
having knowledge of obligation, and there is no way of making out
that these feelings are those upon which obligation is based. Indeed,
one must already have proceeded — half way, at any rate — towards
being an honourable man, if one is to be in a position even to imagine the sentiments we have described. On the other hand, as to the

circumstance that the human will has the power, by virtue of freedom, of being directly determined by the moral law, and the further circumstance that frequent practice, in accordance with the ground of determination, can, at long last, engender, on the subjective side, a feeling of contentment with oneself — as regards all this, I have no intention of calling anything into question. On the contrary, it is part of duty that we should add strength to this feeling and cultivate it, as it is the only feeling which, strictly speaking, deserves to be called moral. Still, the fact remains that the concept of duty is incapable of being derived from it. Otherwise, we should have to entertain the notion of a feeling for the law itself, (Ak39) thus treating as an object of sentiment that which, in truth, can never be anything else than something conceived of reason. And such a procedure, if followed up so as to escape plain self-contradiction, would bring complete destruction upon the concept of duty, putting in its place a merely mechanical interplay of the more refined inclinations with the coarser ones, these two kinds coming at times into conflict with one another.

If, then, we wish to institute a comparison between, on the one hand, the principle of pure practical reason which we are advocating (that of the autonomy of the will, a principle which is *formal* in character), and, on the other hand, all "*material*" principles of morality which men have advocated hitherto, we are in a position to exhibit all the rest (in the character which belongs to them as "material" principles) in a table which deals with them exhaustively and covers all possible cases, the formal principle being the only exception. Hence clear evidence is supplied of the circumstance that it is futile to look out for any principle other than the one recommended here. As for the grounds determining the will, these are the only possible alternatives. They are either merely *subjective*, and therefore empirical, or else they are *objective* and rational; and in both cases they are either *external* or *internal*.

[69] (Ak40) *Grounds of the "material" type determining us in the field of practice which are taken to be operative in the principle of morality are as follows:*

SUBJECTIVE		OBJECTIVE	
EXTERNAL	INTERNAL	INTERNAL	EXTERNAL
Education	Physical Feeling	Perfection	Will of God
(according to	*(according to*	*(according to*	*(according to*
Montaigne)	*Epicurus)*	*Wolff and*	*Crusius and other*
		the Stoics)	*theological moralists)*
Civil Constitution	Moral Feeling		
(according to	*(according to*		
Mandeville)	*Hutcheson)*		

[70] (Ak41) All the principles set out on the left are empirical, and are thus in no way suited to play the part of a universal principle of morality. As against this, the principles set out on the right are founded in reason, seeing that what they deal with is perfection looked upon as a *property* of things. and secondly, supreme perfection as inhering in a *substance*, that is to say, in God, and that it is impossible that either of these should allow of being conceived of except through the instrumentality of concepts which originate in reason. Now the former concept, that of *perfection*, can be taken in its *theoretical* sense, and in this case it signifies nothing else than the completeness of each thing in its kind (transcendental perfection), or else it is merely the completeness of a thing as a thing in general which is in question (metaphysical perfection). Both of these are matters which have no bearing upon the present investigation. On the other hand, as regards the concept of perfection taken in its *practical* sense, what it signifies is the suitability or adequacy of a thing in respect of ends of various kinds. This perfection thought of as a *property* of man (and accordingly, as an internal perfection) is nothing other than what we call *talent*, and what strengthens or supplements such talent, *viz. skill.* The supreme perfection conceived as inhering in a *substance*, i.e. God (and accordingly, an external perfection, when considered from the point of view of practice) signifies the suitability of that being in respect of all ends in general. Therefore, ends must first be given to us, and it is only in reference to these that the concept of *perfection* is capable of becoming a determining ground of the will (internal perfection, when it is ourselves that are in question, and external, when it is God). But then, an end must be con-

ceived of as an *object* which has to precede the determination of the will through a practical rule, and accordingly, has to contain the ground through which such determination is rendered possible. In other words, it is the *matter* of the will which is here being taken as the ground determining it — and this can never be anything but empirical in character. And thus, although it may be of service to the Epicurean principle which forms the basis of the doctrine of happiness, it can never be of any service to the purely rational principle of morality and duty. And indeed, if what is taken to be the objects of the will are talents and their promotion, [71] solely because of what they contribute to life's advantages, or else, if it is the will of God which is taken to be the object of the will, in the sense that conformity to it is demanded, no recourse being had to any antecedent practical principle devoid of all reference to the Idea of God, then it can only be the *happiness* expected by us, as the result of what is done by us, which is capable of becoming a cause moving the will.

The conclusion to be drawn from what has been said is, *first*, that all the principles set out in the present table are *material* principles, and *secondly*, that the table contains all possible material principles. And finally, there follows this further conclusion. Seeing that material principles are wholly unsuited to form the basis of the supreme law of morality — and this is a matter which we have established by way of proof — this role must be played by the *formal practical principle* which has its origin in pure reason. According to it, it is the mere form of a universal legislation, rendered possible through the instrumentality of our maxims, which must constitute the supreme and immediate ground determining the will: this is the *only possible* principle suited to give rise to categorical imperatives, that is to say, to practical laws (which bestow upon actions the character of being in accordance with duty), or to put it in more general terms, suited to the principle of morality, both in pronouncing judgment and in its having applicability to the human will, in respect of the manner in which it finds itself determined to action.

[72] (Ak42) I. DEDUCTION OF THE PRINCIPLES DERIVING FROM PURE PRACTICAL REASON.

What the present Analytic demonstrates is that pure reason is capable of having practical efficacy, that is to say, is capable of determining the will independently of anything empirical. This demonstration takes place by reference to a fact through which the proof is furnished of the circumstance that, with beings such as ourselves, pure reason actually has practical efficacy, this fact being the autonomy appertaining to the principle of morality by virtue of which the will is determined to action. The Analytic shows, at the same time, that consciousness of the freedom of the will is inseparably bound up with the said fact, and indeed, is identical with it. And the result of this circumstance is that the will of a rational being which recognizes that, belonging to the world of sense as it does, it is necessarily subject to causal laws in the same way as other efficient causes — that such a being, I say, is yet conscious at the same time that, where the life of practice is concerned, there appertains to it, in the character belonging to it as a being in itself, an existence which is determinable in accordance with the intelligible order of things. It is not a special kind of intuition of itself possessed by the rational being which here plays a part. What happens is that the causal efficacy exerted by that being within the world of sense allows of being determined in accordance with certain dynamical laws which become operative here, while sufficient proof has been supplied elsewhere to show that when freedom is attributed to us, it places us within an intelligible order of things.

[73] If we compare the analytical part of the Critique of pure speculative reason with the present undertaking, it becomes evident that there is a remarkable contrast between the two. In the former case it was not principles but pure sensible *intuition* (i.e. space and time) which supplied the first *datum*, making *a priori* knowledge possible — and that only in reference to the objects of the senses. Synthetic principles deriving from mere concepts, apart from intuition, were not possible. On the contrary, if such principles were to arise, this could only happen by virtue of their being referred to that intuition, which was sensible in character. In other words, the reference had to be solely to the objects of a possible experience, because it is only in virtue of their being brought into connection with the said intuition that the concepts of the understanding render possible the type of cognition which we entitle experience. Any positive *knowledge* beyond the objects of experience — knowledge, that is, of things conceived of as noumena — was denied to speculative reason, and perfectly rightly so. On the other hand, speculative reason accomplished this much: it provided a secure basis for the concept of noumena, by demonstrating the possibility, and even necessity, of conceiving of such objects in thought. For example, it was shown that to assume freedom, conceived of in negative terms, was perfectly compatible with the aforesaid principles as well as with the

limitations imposed upon pure theoretical reason; thus it provided security against any kind of objection to it. On the other hand, it was shown that we were without any definite information about such objects, and that (Ak43) there was nothing at our disposal which could serve to extend our knowledge, the truth being, on the contrary, that we are cut off altogether from all prospect of achieving this.

[74] As for the moral law, on the other hand, even though it does indeed hold out no such *prospect*, it yet supplies us with a fact which is wholly inexplicable on any data pertaining to the sensible world, and inexplicable likewise, as regards the entire scope of the theoretical employment of our reason. This fact not only points to a purely intelligible world but *determines* it in a *positive* manner, permitting us to come to know something which belongs to that world, this something being a law.

What the said law is supposed to do, where rational beings are concerned, is to impart to the world of sense, which is a *sensible realm of nature*, the form of an intelligible world, the form that is, of a *supersensible realm of nature*, while, at the same time, the mechanism governing the said nature is not to be impeded in any way. But then, what is signified by "nature", taken in its most general sense, is the existence of things as subject to laws. The sensible nature of rational beings, conceived of generally, is their existence as subject to empirically conditioned laws, and thus, from the point of view of reason, it has the character of *heteronomy*. The supersensible nature of the same beings, on the other hand, is their existence in accordance with laws which are independent of any empirical condition, and thus it belongs to the *autonomy* of pure reason. Now it is practical laws which are in question, if they are such that, according to them, it is things being known which bring them into existence. And so it is that supersensible nature, in so far as we are capable of forming any conception of it, is nothing else but a realm of *nature subject* to the *autonomy of pure practical reason*. Moreover, the law pertaining to the said autonomy is the moral law which is the fundamental law governing a supersensible realm of nature, or purely [75] intelligible world, the sensible world being its counterpart while, at the same time, the laws governing the latter are not to be infringed in any way. One might call the first the *archetypal* world (*natura archetypa*), the knowledge of which resides solely in reason, while the second world might be called the *ectypal* world (*natura ectypa*), containing as it does the effect to be made possible through the instrumentality of the Idea pertaining to the other world, an Idea that is to be thought of as the determining ground of the will. And indeed, the truth of the matter is this: the moral law transfers us, ideally speaking, into a realm in which pure reason, provided only the appropriate physical power accompanied it, would bring the *summum bonum* into existence, our will being determined by the moral law in such a way as to impart to the form exhibited by the sensible world the characteristic of making up a totality of rational beings.

One need only pay attention to oneself in a perfectly ordinary way to have confirmation of the fact that the said Idea actually underlies the determinations of our will playing the part of a delineation, as it were, which serves as a pattern.

(Ak44) If the maxim, in accordance with which I propose to bear testimony, is examined by practical reason, my consideration is invariably what the position would be, on the supposition that the maxim was to have validity as a universal law of nature. It is evident that, if the matter were looked at from such a point of view, this would result in a demand being made upon everyone that they should tell the truth; for it is inconsistent with the universal character of a law of nature that statements should, on the one hand, be held to serve by way of furnishing proof, while yet allowing that they might be deliberately untrue. In the same way, [76] if the question be whether I have the right to dispose of my life freely, the maxim is definitely determined the moment I ask myself what characteristic it would need to have, so that a realm of nature, obeying this maxim as a law, should be in a position to maintain itself. It is evident that, within the compass of such a realm of nature, there would be no way for anyone to terminate his life *arbitrarily*, seeing that an arrangement allowing this would, in fact, fail to be an abiding natural order. And the same applies in all other cases. But then, in actual nature — in nature that is, inasmuch as it is an object of experience — the free will is not of its own accord determined to action in such a way as to adopt maxims which would be capable of founding, of their own accord, a realm which was in conformity with universal laws, or else, would be suited, of their own accord, to a realm arranged in conformity with such laws. On the contrary, what is operative here are private inclinations which, it is true, constitute a natural whole in conformity with pathological, i.e. physical laws, but which do not constitute a realm such as would be rendered possible solely by virtue of the fact that our will was in conformity with pure practical laws. Nevertheless, we are conscious — and this through the instrumentality of reason — of a law to which all our maxims are subject, just as though it were necessary that, by virtue of our will, a certain order of things must be brought into existence. The position, then, must be this: that what is in operation here is the Idea of a realm of nature which is not empirically given, while yet it is rendered possible in virtue of freedom, the Idea, in other words, of a supersensible realm of nature, to which we assign objective reality — in respect of the practical life, at any rate — , doing so in consideration of the fact that we look upon that Idea as the object of our will, inasmuch as we are beings determinable by pure reason.

[77] So, on the one hand, there are laws governing a realm to which the *will is subject*, and, on the other, laws governing a *realm* which is *subject to a will*, in respect of that aspect of willing, that is, which has reference to the free actions arising from the will. And the difference between the two cases consists in this. In the former case, it is objects which must be the cause of the representations determining the will, while, in the latter case, it is the will which is to be the cause of objects. The conclusion to be drawn from this is that the causal efficacy pertaining to these objects has its determining ground solely in the purely rational faculty. Accordingly, it is possible to entitle the latter pure practical reason.

There are thus two problems very different from one another, namely: how, *on the one hand*, pure reason is capable of having knowledge of objects in an *a priori* manner, and, *on the other hand*, how it is capable of being a ground determining the will directly, the ground that is, of the causal efficacy which the rational being exerts, in respect of (Ak45) making objects actual, this being supposed to be accomplished solely by virtue of the universal validity of reason's own maxims in their character as laws.

The former problem, as pertaining to the Critique of pure speculative reason, requires that it should first be explained how intuitions (apart from which no object can be given to us all, and consequently, none can become known to us synthetically) are capable of having an *a priori* status. As for the solution offered, it amounted to this: that since these intuitions were, one and all, sensible in character, it was impossible that they should give rise to any speculative knowledge going beyond the compass of possible experience. [78] In consequence, no principles arising from pure speculative reason could ever accomplish any more than render experience possible, experience either of objects given, or else, of objects which, although they may be given *ad infinitum*, are yet never given in their entirety.

As for the second problem, it does not (seeing that it pertains to the Critique of practical reason) require any explanation as to how the objects of the faculty of desire are possible; for, since that is a problem which concerns the theoretical knowledge of nature, this matter must be left to the Critique of speculative reason. What must be made clear is merely in what manner reason is capable of determining the will, whether this can happen solely on the strength of empirical representations playing the part of determining grounds, or whether a practical efficacy can, in addition to this, be exerted by pure reason giving rise to a law, a law the concern of which would have to be with an order of nature to be rendered possible, an order of such a kind that it could in no way become known to us through the instrumentality of experience. As for establishing the possibility of there being such a supersensible realm (the concept of which is, by virtue of our free will, to be capable of being, at the same time, the ground of its actuality), this does not require the possession of a power of an *a priori* intuition directed towards an intelligible world, a power of intuition which, since it would have to be supersensible in character, in the case we are here considering, could not conceivably be at our disposal. And indeed, what alone matters regarding the point under discussion is the ground by which the willing is determined, in respect of the maxims adopted by the will, whether that ground is empirical in character, or else a concept having its source in reason and investigating the question whether or not maxims are in accordance with the general principle in conformity to law. And then there is this further question, how it is that the said concept is capable of playing such a part. Whether or not the causal efficacy of the will is sufficient to bring the objects towards which it is directed into actual existence, this is a matter of [79] judgment which must be left to the theoretical principles of reason: the concern of such an investigation is to account for the possibility of the objects of volition. And so the question as to how these objects are intuited plays no part whatever within the scope of an enquiry which deals with problems pertaining to the field of practice. What alone matters is the way in which the will is determined to action, and what is the determining ground informing the maxim arising from it, inasmuch as it is a free will. As for the question of being successful in one's object, it does not enter into consideration, the actual position being this. Supposing only that the *will* is in accordance with the law, from the point of view of pure reason, it makes no difference how matters stand with its *power* of execution. (Ak46) Now whether or not, in conformity with the maxims in question which are occupied with legislating for a realm of being to be rendered possible, such a realm does actually arise, this is of no concern to the Critique which examines the question whether, and in what way, pure reason is capable of having practical efficacy, capable, that is, of determining the will directly.

In performing this task, the Critique can, and in fact must, without incurring any reproach, start out from pure practical laws and their actuality. However, in place of intuition, it takes as their foundation the concept of the type of existence which appertains to them as members of the intelligible world, the concept, that is, of freedom; for this is precisely what is signified by the said concept. But these laws are possible only if they are made to have reference to the freedom of the will, while, freedom being supposed, they are necessary laws. Or conversely, freedom is necessary, by virtue of the fact that these laws are necessary in the character appertaining to them as practical postulates. As to the question how this consciousness of the moral law is possible, or, what amounts to the same thing, how freedom is possible, [80] no further explanation of this can be given, while, on the other hand, it was perfectly possible to argue in defence of the admissibility of freedom. Indeed, that is what was done in the Critique which dealt with questions of theory.

The *exposition* of the supreme principle originating in practical reason has now been brought to a close, that is to say, it has been shown, first, what it contains, that it stands by itself in a wholly *a priori* manner and independently of any empirical principles; and, in addition to this, it has been shown in what way it differs from all other practical principles. As regards the *deduction* of the principle, i.e. the justification of its objective and universal validity, and as regards the question what insight we have at our disposal to account for the possibility of such a synthetic *a priori* proposition, there is no way of our entertaining the hope that we shall make as much progress in this matter as was the case when we were considering the principles which have their source in the theoretical power possessed by the pure understanding. This is because these principles have reference to the objects of possible experience, i.e. to appearances, and we were in a position to furnish proof of the circumstance that it was only on condition that these appearances were made subordinate to the categories, in conformity with the laws in question, that they allowed of becoming *known* as objects of experience, and that, as a consequence of this, all possible experience was under the necessity of being in accordance with these laws. As against this, if the task to be undertaken is that of providing a deduction of the moral law, it is impossible that we should adopt such a course; for the concern of the moral law is not with providing knowledge about the constitution of objects, such as may, in some way or other, be supplied to reason from a source other than itself. On the contrary, the knowledge relevant here is one occupied with reason, inasmuch as it is capable of being of itself the ground of the existence of objects, [81] reason exhibiting, by virtue of that knowledge, causal efficacy in a rational being. In other words, what is in question is pure reason permitting to be looked upon as a faculty capable of determining the will directly.

But then, all human insight is brought to an end as soon as we have arrived at fundamental powers or faculties, (Ak47) seeing that there is nothing about these which would serve to make their possibility comprehensible, while, on the other hand, we have no right to invent or assume them arbitrarily. And so it is that, with the theoretical employment of reason, it is by reference to experience alone that we can be justified in assuming their presence. However, such a substitute, namely, that of adducing empirical proofs, in the place of a deduction from *a priori* sources of knowledge, is likewise denied to us in the present case, where our concern is with the power which pure reason exerts in the field of practice. And indeed, that which is under the necessity of making an appeal to experience, if it is to be in a position to adduce a proof establishing its reality, must be dependent on principles pertaining to experience, as regards the grounds establishing its possibility. On the other hand, that there should be such dependence on empirical principles is wholly inconceivable in the case of a power of reason supposed to have practical efficacy, notwithstanding its operating purely by itself, and indeed, the very concept of such a power precluding any such possibility. Besides, the moral law is given to us as a fact, as it were, which issues from pure reason, a fact of which we have consciousness in an *a priori* manner, and which is apodeictically certain. And this remains true, even though it should turn out to be impossible to adduce a single instance, within the field of experience, of strict obedience having been paid to the moral law. So the conclusion to be drawn from what has been said is this: that the objective reality of the moral law is incapable of being established by way of providing a deduction of it, and that this cannot be brought about by any effort on the part of theoretical reason, no matter whether it confines itself to the field of speculation, or relies upon empirical support. [82] And as regards the latter point, the fact remains that, even though one might be prepared to dispense with apodeictic certainty, it is impossible that any experience should serve by way of providing confirmation of the moral law, and thus furnishing proof of its existence in an *a posteriori* manner. However, in spite of it all, the moral law remains an indisputable fact, solely on the strength of its own nature.

Now a feature of a different kind makes its appearance here, and it is a feature truly paradoxical in character: namely, the position is reversed, the moral law itself doing service by way of providing the principle for the deduction of an inscrutable power of the mind, a power the existence of which no proof whatever can be furnished by anything coming within the compass of experience. Speculative reason, on the other hand, was under the necessity of granting at least the possibility of such power. And this happened when, in order to escape self-contradiction, it was called upon to find, among the cosmological Ideas to which it gives rise, that which could have assigned to it the characteristic of being unconditioned in respect of its causal efficacy. The power here in question is that of freedom; and the moral law, which itself does not stand in any need of grounds being brought forward so as to vindicate it, establishes not merely the possibility but the actuality of freedom in respect of beings which acknowledge this law to be binding upon them. Indeed, the moral law is the law which pertains to that causal efficacy which operates by virtue of freedom. And in so doing it pertains to the possibility of there being a supersensible realm, just as, over and against this, the metaphysical law, which occupied itself with events occurring in the world of sense, was a law pertaining to the causal efficacy governing the realm of sensibility. The true position, then, is this: the moral law determines that which speculative philosophy had to leave undetermined, the law, that is, which has application to a causal efficacy whose concept had to remain purely negative in character, where speculative philosophy was concerned. Thus objective reality is, for the first time, bestowed upon the concept pertaining to this causal efficacy.

[83] (Ak48) The moral law, then, is here set forth as being itself a principle supplying a deduction of freedom, thought of as a causal efficacy taking its rise in pure reason, while at the same time it is pointed out that theoretical reason was under the necessity of *presupposing at least* the possibility of there being some kind of freedom. And this kind of credential allowed to the moral law, namely, that it serves by way of supplementing a need arising on the part of theoretical reason, is quite sufficient to take the place of any *a priori* justification, the actual state of the case being this. The moral law furnishes proof of its reality in a manner which is satisfactory also from the point of a Critique of speculative reason. It takes the following course. There was a certain causal efficacy, conceived of in purely negative terms, the possibility of which was incomprehensible to speculative reason, while, at the same time, it was obliged to presuppose it. Positive determination is now secured for the said causal

efficacy, through bringing in, in addition to this, the concept of a reason which determines the will directly (the condition laid down being that the maxims which the will adopts are to exhibit the form of a universal legislation). And this is the result following from it all. Reason, which invariably got lost in a transcendent sphere whenever it sought to employ its Ideas for the purposes of speculation, is enabled, for the first time, to bestow upon these Ideas objective reality (although, on the other hand, it is a reality pertaining solely to the field of practice), with the result that the *transcendent* employment of reason is being transformed into an *immanent* one (this being brought about by virtue of the circumstance that reason itself does, through the instrumentality of Ideas arising from it, become an efficient cause within the field of experience).

When we were called upon to determine the character of that causal efficacy which is exerted by beings within the world of sense, there was, by virtue of the very nature of that world, never any possibility of our attributing to it the property of being unconditioned, while yet it is true, at the same time, that, as regards any series of conditions, something unconditioned must exist, over and against it, and accordingly, that there must exist also a causal efficacy determined solely by virtue of itself. [84] And so it was that the Idea of freedom, conceived of as a faculty of initiating something with absolute spontaneity, did not have the characteristic of being a thing which reason stood in need of. On the contrary, the assertion that *freedom* must be *possible* rested upon an analytic principle having its source in pure speculative reason. However, since it is wholly inconceivable that one should be in a position to supply, anywhere within the field of experience, a single instance that would be in accordance with the Idea in question, on the ground that, among the causes assignable to things in their character as appearances, there is no possibility at all of our encountering any determination of causal efficacy exhibiting the property of being absolutely unconditioned, the position was found to be as follows. All we were able to do at that stage was to offer a *defence* of the *notion* of a freely acting cause, arguing that such a notion allowed of being applied to a being belonging to the world of sense, inasmuch as that being was, at the same time, being considered in the character appertaining to it as a *noumenon*. It was shown that there was nothing self-contradictory about looking upon all the actions of such a being as physically conditioned, in so far as they had the character of appearances, while, at the same time, looking upon the causal efficacy exerted by it as physically conditioned, in so far as the being that acts is an intelligible being. In this way, then, the concept of freedom has bestowed upon it the status of a regulative principle of reason, the position thus being the following. It is true enough that, by proceeding in this manner, I do not acquire any knowledge of the object to which a causal efficacy of this sort is being attributed, coming to know what the nature of that object is. Still, there is a certain obstacle which is being removed. While, in my explanation of the events occurring in this world — and thus also in my explanation of the actions proceeding from rational beings — I do justice to the mechanism of (Ak49) natural necessity, which lays it down that I am to proceed *ad infinitum* from the conditioned to its condition, [85] I still leave open the place kept empty, where speculative reason is concerned, i.e. the intelligible realm, my intention being to locate the unconditioned in that realm. There was, however, no way of my imparting any *real content* to the *notion* in question, that is to say, I was unable to modify it in such a way as to provide myself with *knowledge* of a being acting in the said manner, not even with knowledge of the possibility that there is such a being. Still, the position is found to be that pure practical reason fills the empty place, doing so in virtue of a definite law pertaining to a causal efficacy which is in operation in a world to be thought of as being intelligible in character (i.e. causality through freedom), in virtue, that is, of the moral law. Admittedly, speculative reason gains nothing by this. Yet there is a gain which is made, namely, that the problematic concept of freedom, to which it gave rise, is placed in a position of *security*, with *objective reality* (which, although applicable only to the field of practice, is none the less undeniable) being procured for that concept. Even the concept of causality which, properly speaking, is applicable, and thus meaningful, solely in reference to appearances, with a view to connecting them into empirical cognitions (a circumstance of which proof has been given in the Critique of pure reason), is not enlarged in such a way as to extend it beyond the limits set down in that work. Indeed, if reason proposed to accomplish this, its purpose would have to be to show how the relation of ground and consequent could be employed synthetically with reference to an intuition other than sensible intuition. In other words, it would have to explain how a *causa noumenon* was possible. But reason is quite incapable of achieving this, while, on the other hand, in its character as practical reason, it does not take the least account of any of this. All it does is to locate [86] the *ground determining* man's causal efficacy (an efficacy which is something given to us) *in pure reason* which, on account of this, is entitled practical reason. As for applying the concept of a cause itself to objects, for the sake of obtaining theoretical knowledge, that is something from which practical reason can abstract altogether, seeing that the said concept is to be met with in the power of understanding, wholly irrespective of the presence of any *a priori* intuition. And so it comes about that it employs the concept, not for the purpose of coming to know objects, but so as to determine, in general terms, the nature of a certain causal efficacy in respect of objects. In other words, reason employs the concept under consideration solely for the purposes of practice. This being so, it is entitled to locate the ground determining the will in the intelligible order of things, while freely confessing, at the same time, that it does not in the least comprehend what role may have to be assigned to the concept of a cause in respect of gaining knowledge of such things. As for causal efficacy, in respect of actions proceeding from the will and occurring within the world of sense, it is indeed necessary that this should become known to reason in a determinate manner, for otherwise it would be actually impossible for practical reason to produce any action at all. On the other hand, there is no need that reason should be in a position to determine, in a theoretical sense, the concept which it comes to form regarding its own causal efficacy in its character as a noumenon, (Ak50) embarking upon such an enterprise, for the purpose of having knowledge of its supersensible existence, and thus imparting significance to the concept in the sense described. And indeed, through the instrumentality of the moral law, significance is acquired by the concept in any case, although it is true enough that the significance which it acquires pertains solely to reason's practical employment. Moreover, even considered from a theoretical point of view, the concept of a cause remains, after all, a pure concept of the understanding, supplied in an *a priori* fashion, and [87] capable of being applied to objects, whether sensibly or non-sensibly given, although, in the latter case, the concept is devoid of any definite significance or application, and is nothing more than a merely formal, though essential, notion, issuing from the understanding, and being concerned with the character pertaining to an object as such. The significance, on the other hand, which reason imparts to the concept, by virtue of the moral law, is exclusively practical in character, the assumption being that the Idea of a law which governs a certain type of causal efficacy (i.e. that exerted by the will) has itself causal efficacy, or — putting it a different way — is the ground by which that efficacy is determined.

II. PURE REASON HAS, IN ITS PRACTICAL EMPLOYMENT, A RIGHT TO AN EXTENSION OF ITS SCOPE WHICH IT IS INCAPABLE OF OBTAINING FOR ITSELF WITHIN THE COMPASS OF ITS SPECULATIVE EMPLOYMENT.

In concerning ourselves with the moral principle, we have set it forth as a law which pertains to a causal efficacy which assigns to the ground determining that efficacy a place lying beyond all conditions to be met with in the world of sense. Where the *will* is concerned, we have *conceived* of it in thought, merely inasmuch as it belongs to an intelligible world, and inasmuch as it is capable of being determined to action in the sense specified. In other words, as regards the subject of that will, i.e. as regards man, we have *conceived* of him in thought, merely in so far as he belongs to a purely intelligible world. More-over, we have taken such a course, notwithstanding the circumstance that we have no knowledge of man, looked upon in this way. [88] (On the other hand, we were entitled to proceed in this manner, in view of what the Critique of pure speculative reason has to declare upon the point in question.) Yet we have done more than this. We have *determined* the character of the will, in respect of the causal efficacy exerted by it, and we have done so by placing reliance upon a law which in no way allows of being classed with the natural laws governing the world of sense. Our knowledge has thereby been made out to *extend* beyond the world of sense, this being an arrogant claim which was, after all, declared to be null and void, in respect of any speculative endeavour, by the Critique of pure reason. What, then, is to be done here where we are called upon to reconcile the practical employment of pure reason with the theoretical one deriving from the same reason, the point at issue being to fix the limits set to the said faculty?

David Hume — who one can rightly say was, strictly speaking, the first to contest the rights of pure reason, thus making it necessary that a thoroughgoing investigation of that faculty should be under-taken — argued in the following manner. The concept of a *cause* is (Ak51) a concept which contains the idea of a *necessity* of connection, in respect of existence, between things that differ, and inasmuch as they differ, with the result that, *A* being posited, I come to have knowledge of the fact that something quite different from it, i.e. *B*, has necessarily likewise to exist. But then, necessity can be assigned to a connection only inasmuch as it is known in an *a priori* manner, seeing that, as regards experience, there is only one thing it can possibly give us knowledge of, as regards a connection, namely, that it exists, not that it exists necessarily. However, he argues, it is impossible that the connection between one thing and another (or one attribute and another, the latter being [89] quite different from the former) should — these not being given to us in perception — be known in an *a priori* manner as something which is necessary. It follows that the concept of a cause must itself be fraudulent and deceptive. To put it at its mildest, the illusion is excusable only inasmuch as what occurs is that the *custom* of perceiving certain things, or their attributes, to be frequently beside, or to succeed one another, being associated with one another in respect of their existence (a *subjective* necessity), is, unawares, being taken for an *objective* necessity, as it is presupposed that such a connection attaches to the objects themselves. It is in this way, then, that the concept of a cause has been surreptitiously obtained, as distinct from being legitimately acquired. And, in point of fact, it can never be so acquired, nor can any valid credential be found for it, on the ground that the connection which the concept demands is nugatory and chimerical, and that it is unable to stand up to the test of any rational criterion, there never being any possibility that any object should correspond to it.

And so it came about that, in respect of all knowledge concerned with the existence of things (mathematics remained so far exempted from this), *empiricism* was introduced as the sole source of principles. And along with this empiricism, the most rigid *scepticism* was introduced, one extending so far as to be applied to the whole of natural science (looked upon as a branch of philosophy). And indeed, if the said principles are adopted, there is never any possibility of *drawing* any *inference* from the attributes pertaining to things, in respect of their existence, to something else following as a consequent (for this would require the concept of a cause which contains the idea that such a connection should have the characteristic of necessity. [90] All that we should be entitled to do is that, under the guidance of a rule having its source in the imagination, we might expect cases similar to what we had encountered on other occasions, an expectation which can never be certain, however often it may have been confirmed. As a matter of fact, it would be impossible to assert with regard to any event that something *must* have preceded it upon which it followed *necessarily* — in other words, that it must have a *cause*. Consequently, however frequent the cases may have been in which things happened in a certain manner, its being possible, accordingly, to draw forth a rule from circumstances as they have been, we should still not be entitled to presume that things must always, and necessarily, happen

in this particular manner. And instead one would have to allow for
the possibility that blind chance may have been in operation, any
employment of reason being brought to an end in this way. (Ak52)
The result of all this is that, as regards inferences ascending from
effects to causes, scepticism comes to be firmly established, there
being no longer any possibility of its being refuted.

As for mathematics, it had so far come off tolerably well, for
Hume's opinion was that mathematical propositions were, one and
all, analytic, i.e. they progressed by virtue of identity from one property to one coming next; in other words, they did so in conformity
with the law of contradiction. (This, however, is a wrong opinion,
the truth being that these propositions are all synthetic. For example,
although geometry is not concerned with the existence of things, but
solely with determining the *a priori* properties exhibited by things
within the framework of a certain type of intuition which it is possible to supply for them, the fact remains that, just as when causal
concepts are employed, geometry makes a transition from one property, *A*, to another, *B*, the latter being quite different from the former,
[91] while yet it is necessarily connected with it.) However, the final
outcome is that this science, so highly praised because of its apodeictic
certainty, must none the less fall victim to the idea that, as regards
principles, it is *empiricism* which rules. The reason for this coming
about is the very same as it was when Hume, while dealing with the
concept of a cause, put custom in the place of objective necessity.
Hence geometry suffers a defeat and, notwithstanding all its pride, it
finds itself compelled to tone down the bold claim it makes, namely,
that it may demand an *a priori* assent to what it does. The applause it
receives because of the universal validity of the propositions it enun-
ciates results from the favourable disposition of the observers who,
playing the part of witnesses, would not wish to deny that what the
geometricians propounded as fundamental principles was something
they had likewise perceived to be the case at all times. Consequently,
even though this was indeed not a matter of necessity, it would surely
be conceded to them that they might expect things to remain the
same in the future. In this way, then, Hume's empiricism, as regards
fundamental principles in the realm of mathematics, inevitably leads
to scepticism, and consequently also, in the realm of any theoretical
enterprise which employs reason in a *scientific* manner (such employment belonging either to philosophy or to mathematics). I leave
it to everyone to decide for themselves whether the employment of
reason in man's ordinary affairs would fare any better (in view of so
terrible an overthrow as is here seen to befall those who are leaders in

the various branches of knowledge), or whether such employment will become implicated even more inextricably in the very same destruction of all knowledge — in other words, that the adoption of *universal* scepticism [92] is bound to be the consequence of resorting to the principles in question, (although, to be sure, it is only the learned who would be affected by it).

The labours I undertook in the Critique of pure reason were indeed occasioned by Hume's doctrine of doubt which I have outlined. Yet it is true enough that, in my work, I went much further that he did and comprehended in it the whole field of pure theoretical reason, in its synthetic employment, and consequently also, that branch of knowledge given the general title of metaphysics. (Ak53) As for the doubts which the philosopher from Scotland expressed concerning the concept of causality, my argument proceeded in the following manner. Hume was quite right if, while taking the objects of experience to be *things-in-themselves* (as is, after all, done by nearly everybody), he declared the concept of a cause to be deceptive and the work of sheer delusion. And indeed, as regards things-in-themselves and the properties attributable to them, there is no way of comprehending how, because A is posited, something different from it, i.e. B, must likewise be posited, and that necessarily. Hume was thus altogether precluded from conceding the existence of such *a priori* knowledge concerning things-in-themselves. Still less was this man, endowed with great acuteness as he was, in a position to admit of the possibility that the concept in question might have its origin in experience, seeing that such an assumption is clearly contrary to the idea of a necessary connection, which is of the very essence of the concept of causality. And so it came about that the concept was repudiated as null and void, its place being taken by custom emerging from the course our perceptions have taken, and the observations we have made as a result of this.

[93] But then, what resulted from the investigations I undertook was that the objects with which we are concerned in experience are by no means things-in-themselves, but are, in fact, nothing more than appearances. And there followed a further result, namely, that, although, in the case of things-in-themselves, it was indeed hard to see, and in fact impossible to comprehend, on what grounds, A being posited, there should be a *contradiction* in not positing B, and that in spite of its being quite different from A (and this is what is signified by necessity of connection such as subsists between A as the cause, and B as the effect). On the other hand — it was argued — it was perfectly conceivable that things, in their character as appear-

ances, must, *within the one experience*, be necessarily connected with one another in certain ways (e.g. in respect of time-relations), and that they are incapable of being separated from one another, without a *contradiction* arising between this and the presence of that connectedness, by virtue of which there is made possible their experience within the context of which they are objects, this being the only way they are knowable to us. And so it turned out to be, with the result that I was in a position to furnish proof of the concept of a cause as having objective reality in respect of the objects of experience. But more than this, I was able to *deduce* it as an *a priori* concept by virtue of the notion of a necessity of connection which the concept carries with it. In other words, I was able to demonstrate the possibility of the concept as arising in the pure understanding and irrespective of any empirical sources. And so it happened that, empiricism having been eliminated as a way of accounting for the origin of the concept, the inevitable consequence of empiricism, *viz.* scepticism, was likewise overthrown. I succeeded in establishing my point, first of all, in the realm of natural science, and secondly, by virtue of the fact that the inference to be drawn rested on precisely the same [94] grounds, in the realm of mathematics, both being sciences which have reference to objects of possible experience. (Ak54) And so it was that, as regards the principle of universal doubt, in respect of everything theoretical reason professes to comprehend, I was in a position to shake that doubt to its foundations.

Now what happens when the category of causality is made to have application to things which are not objects of possible experience but lie beyond the confines of that experience? (And the same question arises in connection with all the other categories, in the absence of which no knowledge of anything that exists can be accomplished at all). After all, it was only in reference to the *objects of possible experience* that I was able to deduce the objective reality of the concepts in question. On the other hand, my success in coming to the rescue of the categories depended on a certain expectation being fulfilled, namely, that I was in a position to show that, although the categories were indeed incapable of bestowing *a priori* determinacy upon objects, in the end they were the means of our being able to *conceive* of objects *in thought*. Now this very circumstance secures for the categories a place within the domain of the power of pure understanding, bestowing upon them a reference to objects in general (whether sensible or non-sensible). If something is still lacking, it is the condition subject to which these categories (principally that of causality) come to have *application* to objects, with intuition as its condition. If no intuition is forthcoming, the application of the category is rendered impossible, and no purpose is served in gaining *theoretical knowledge of the object* in its character as a noumenon. Should such application be ventured upon, this must, as has been done in the Critique of pure reason, be strictly forbidden. [95] Yet there remains the fact of the objective reality of the concept, and that it is capable of being employed even in reference to noumena. Still, when this happens, no determinacy whatever is bestowed upon the concept; and accordingly, there is no possibility that any theoretical knowledge should arise in this way. For the truth is that the concept under consideration (even when it is employed in reference to an object) contains nothing inconceivable: its proof is furnished by the fact that, whenever it was applied to the objects of the senses, there was assigned to it a secure place within the domain of the power of pure understanding. Moreover, it might subsequently turn out that, while it was true enough that the concept, when referred to things-in-themselves (which cannot be objects of experience), was indeed incapable of being determined in such a way as to give rise, for the purpose of gaining theoretical knowledge, to the representation of a *determinate object*, the possibility was yet left open that it might, after all, allow of being determined, and acquiring applicability, in the interests of some other purpose, perhaps that of practice. This could not be the case if, as Hume alleges, the concept of causality contained something which was not conceivable at all.

Now if we are to be in a position to discover the condition responsible for the fact that the said concept should be supposed to have application to noumena, we need only call to mind the reason *why we are not content with the concept's having application to the objects of experience*, but would rather employ it likewise in reference to things-in-themselves. And indeed, if we ask ourselves why that should be so, it will soon become apparent that what makes this a necessity for us is not a theoretical interest but a practical one. Where speculation is concerned, the position would be this: [96] (Ak55) that, even though we succeeded, we should not make any true gain in respect of our knowledge of nature — or, to put the matter in more general terms, in respect of any objects capable of being given to us from some source or other. At best, we should be able to take a wide step from that which is sensibly conditioned to that which is supersensible. (But surely we are sufficiently occupied, even though we remain within the former sphere, industriously tracking down the series of causes.) Our purpose then would have to be, in the searching out of grounds, to bring our knowledge to perfection and to determine its boundaries. Yet the truth of the matter is that an infinite gap would remain unfulfilled between that limit, on the one hand, and that which is known to us, on the other. Our attitude would thereby amount to this: that we had lent our ear to an idle curiosity rather than to a desire for thorough knowledge.

However, apart from the relation in which the *understanding* stands to objects (in the field of theoretical knowledge), there is likewise a relation in which it stands to the faculty of desire: accordingly, this relation is entitled the will, and when the pure understanding (which in this case is entitled reason) has practical efficacy, it is entitled pure will, this coming about solely by virtue of the representation of a law. The objective reality of a pure will, or what amounts to the same thing, of pure practical reason, is supplied, and that in an *a priori* manner, through the moral law, by virtue of a fact, as it were, for this is the proper description of a determination of the will which is inevitable, even though it does not rest on *a priori* principles. But then, the concept of a causal efficacy is already contained in the concept of a will; and accordingly, contained in the concept of a pure will is the concept [97] of a causal efficacy attended with freedom, that is to say, of one which is not determinable in conformity with natural laws, and consequently, incapable of relying upon any empirical intuition by way of establishing its reality. Still, the objective reality of the concept is none the less completely vindicated through the instrumentality of the pure and *a priori* law operative within the field of practice (although this holds good, as will be readily understood, in reference solely to the practical employment of reason, as distinct from the theoretical one). Now the concept of a being endowed with a free will is that of a *causa noumenon*, and sufficient security against the supposition of whether it contains anything self-contradictory is provided by the following considerations.

The concept of a cause is one which has its origin solely in the pure understanding, while the objective reality it has in reference to objects in general is something which, through the deduction which has been undertaken, has likewise been secured for it. Seeing then that the concept of a cause is, in respect of its origin, independent of all sensible conditions, it follows that, considered by itself, it is not restricted to phenomena (unless, that is, one proposed to employ it in a determinate manner, with a view to gaining theoretical knowledge); and thus it is indeed capable of being applied to things thought of as purely intelligible entities. But then, considering that when the concept is given such an application, no intuition is available which could serve as a basis — intuition never being anything but sensible in character — , it follows that *causa noumenon*, although a possible and thinkable concept, is yet an empty one, so far as the theoretical employment of reason is concerned. (Ak56) On the other hand, the desideratum in question in the case I am at present considering is not that, by resorting to the concept, I should obtain *theoretical knowledge* of a being, *inasmuch* as it is endowed with a *pure* will. I am [98] content merely to signify it as a being having such a characteristic, and to connect the concept of causality with the concept of freedom (and with what is inseparably bound up with this, i.e. the supposition that it is the moral law that operates as the ground determining the causality which takes place by means of freedom). And in virtue of the pure and non-empirical origin of the concept of a cause, I have indeed the right to adopt such a course, seeing that I employ it in no other way than in reference to the moral law which, in its turn, determines the reality appertaining to the concept; seeing, in other words, that what I believe myself justified in doing is that, in resorting to the concept, I should employ it solely for the purposes of practice.

If, with Hume, I had denied to the concept of causality its objective reality, not merely in respect of things-in-themselves (i.e. in respect of that which is supersensible), but also in respect of the objects of the senses, it would have resulted in losing all its meaning, and that, as a theoretically impossible concept, it had to be declared altogether useless. And indeed, since no employment whatever is possible in a case where nothing, in fact, is there, it would have been entirely absurd to presuppose that there could be a practical employment of a *theoretically futile concept*. But then, the actual state of the case is this: that the concept of an empirically unconditioned causality, although empty, in the theoretical sense (there being no intuition appropriate to it), is yet a possible concept, referring to an indeterminate object. And so, leaving aside the theoretical procedure, significance is imparted to the concept by means of the moral law, i.e. in reference to practice, the position thus being as follows: Although I do indeed have no intuition at my disposal such as would serve to determine the concept's objective reality in the theoretical sense, [99] it none the less has a real application exhibited *in concreto* in dispositions of the mind and the maxims which are adopted. In other words, there belongs to the concept a practical reality, which allows of being signified in definite terms. And this is sufficient to vindicate the concept even as having reference to noumena.

However, once admissibility has been conceded to the idea that objective reality, in respect of the realm of the supersensible, is to be ascribed to a certain pure concept of the understanding, this has the effect that objective reality is acquired by all the other categories as well, although this is the case, only in so far as they stand in a *necessary* connection with that ground by which the pure will is determined, that is to say, with the moral law. An objective reality they do indeed have, although, on the other hand, it is one which has no applicability except for the purposes of practice, while, as regards theoretical knowledge of the objects under consideration — thought of as an insight into their nature by virtue of pure reason — no influence whatever is exerted such as would have the effect of enlarging that insight. Accordingly, we shall find in the sequel that it is only inasmuch as beings are thought of as *intelligences* that the categories refer to them, in this case, and that, even where this aspect of their nature is concerned, the reference is solely to the relation subsisting between *reason* and the *will*. In other words, the reference is never to anything but the field of *practice*, (Ak57) with no claim to knowledge of things going beyond this. As for further properties of things which, in connection with the categories, might be brought in, properties which pertain to the theoretical mode in which such supersensible things are represented — all this should not be counted as knowledge but merely as a right conceded (from the practical point of view it is even a necessity) to postulate and to presuppose them. [100] And even when supersensible beings (such as God) are presupposed, this being done by way of analogy (*viz.* by virtue of the fact that a relationship, which is purely rational, is, in the interests of practice, used in reference to sensible relationships), the truth of the matter is that, when pure theoretical reason is thus applied to the supersensible (but only with a practical end in view), this does not in the least serve to encourage theoretical reason to give itself up to sentiments of exaltation and to make its entry into the region of the transcendent.

THE ANALYTIC OF PRACTICAL REASON

CHAPTER II

THE CONCEPT OF AN OBJECT OF PURE PRACTICAL REASON.

By the concept of an object of practical reason I understand that representation of an object by which it is looked upon as an effect rendered possible in virtue of freedom. Accordingly, when it is said of something that it is an object of practical knowledge as such, this signifies nothing else than that a relationship subsists between the will, on the one hand, and, on the other, that action which, on its being performed, would have the result that the object (or alternatively, its contrary) was carried into effect. Moreover, as to pronouncing judgment upon the question whether or not something is an object of *pure* practical reason, everything turns upon making a distinction between the possibility or impossibility of *willing* a certain action which, on being done, would bring a certain object into being (supposing, that is, that we had the power requisite for performing the action, this being a matter which only experience can decide). [101] If the assumption be that it is the object which is the ground determining our faculty of desire, what has to be considered, first of all, is the *physical possibility* of bringing that object into being through the free exercise of the powers at our disposal; and it is only subsequently to this that judgment can be pronounced as to whether it is an object of practical reason. If, on the other hand, it is the *a priori* law which permits of being thought of as the ground which determines the action — if, in other words, the action permits of being thought as being determined by pure practical reason, (Ak58) then the judgment as to whether or not something is an object of pure practical reason does not in the least depend on bringing in our physical power as the standard by which things are to be measured. And there is only one question that remains, as regards an action directed towards bringing an object into existence, namely, whether we are permitted to *will* it in the event of its being in our power to perform the action. In other words, it is the *moral possibility* of the action which must take precedence in the present case, seeing that it is not the object of the will which provides the ground by which it is determined but the law by which it is governed.

Thus the *good* and the *evil* are the sole objects of practical reason, the former signifying a necessary object of the faculty of desire, while the latter signifies a necessary object of the faculty of detestation. And this happens in both cases in conformity with a principle of reason.

If the concept of the good, instead of being derived from an antecedent practical law, is, on the contrary, resorted to, with a view that it should serve as the foundation of such a law, then it is made possible [102] that it should be anything else but the concept of something the existence of which promises pleasure. The conclusion to be drawn from this is that, when what is in question is the promotion of the good, it is reference to the said pleasure which must determine the character of the causal efficacy exerted by the subject (or, to put it more exactly, by the subject's faculty of desire). But then, seeing that there is no way of comprehending in an *a priori* manner which representation will be accompanied by *pleasure*, and which, on the contrary, will be accompanied by *pain*, experience would have to be our sole guide, when we were called upon to discern what was to be regarded as inherently good or inherently evil. Now the property to be met with in the subject, in reference to which alone the said experiment is capable of being conducted, is the property of *feeling* pleasure or pain, this having to be looked upon as a certain kind of receptiveness appertaining to inner sense. Thus the consequence here would be that the exclusive concern of the concept laying it down what was thought of as inherently good would have to be the sensation of *pleasure* immediately connected with it, whereas the concept of the absolutely evil referred exclusively to that which immediately excited *pain*. However, apart from anything else, this is clearly contrary to the established use of language which distinguishes between the *pleasant* and the *good*, the *unpleasant* and the *evil*, and which makes the demand that the good and the evil should never be judged otherwise than by virtue of reason, that is to say, through the instrumentality of concepts (which allow of being universally communicated), not through mere sensation which is limited to particular subjects and the receptivity to be met with in them. As against this, no representation of an object is ever such as to make it possible to rely upon an *a priori* reasoning, showing that, in virtue of its very nature, pleasure or pain are immediately connected with it. And so a philosopher who, in his account of practical [103] judgments, should find himself obliged to consider a feeling of pleasure to be that upon which they were founded, would be compelled to call *good* that which was the *means* of achieving the pleasant, and call *evil* that which was the *cause* of unpleasantness or pain; for, as regards pronouncing judgment upon the relationship subsisting between means and ends, it is indeed reason to which this task is assigned. However, although it is reason alone which has the power of grasping the connection between means and that which is aimed at by these means, so that one might define reason as the faculty directed towards ends (Ak59) (these ends never being anything other than grounds which determine the faculty of desire in accordance with principles), it is essential to take proper account of the following circumstance. The practical maxims resulting from the aforementioned concept of the good would be such that they never contained anything which was good in itself, as an object of the will, but only that which was good for achieving *some other purpose*. The good would invariably be that which was merely useful, and as regards that which it was useful for, it would in every case have to reside in something having its place outside the will. Now, in being called upon to denote the distinction to be drawn between the said sensation as a pleasant one, and on the other hand, the concept of the good, it would turn out that, on the principles here adopted, nothing inherently good existed at all, and that the true nature of the good has to be looked for simply in its providing the means for accomplishing something else, *viz.* some pleasantness or other.

"*Nihil appetimus, nisi sub ratione boni; nihil aversamur, nisi sub ratione mali.*"[11] This is a formula of great age current in the philosophical schools which, on many occasions, is used correctly enough. Yet it frequently happens that it is used in a way most injurious to philosophy, this coming about by virtue of the fact that the expressions *boni* and *mali* contain an [104] ambiguity, owing to certain limitations inherent in the language, which makes it possible for them to bear a double meaning. And the inevitable result of this is that, in discussing practical laws, one has to proceed in a most tortuous manner. As for philosophy, it is, in the course of making use of these expressions, made well aware of the position, namely, that only one word is used in the face of a variety of concepts. Yet, being unable to discover special expressions which would indicate this properly, it finds itself compelled to have recourse to expressions of such nicety

---

[11] See Kant's footnote on p. 71. [Editors]

that later on it proves impossible to reach any agreement, because one has been unable to signify the difference directly though any expression appropriate to convey it.[12]

The German language has the great good fortune of having at its disposal expressions which prevent this difference from being overlooked. In the place of what in Latin is denoted by a single word, *bonum*, it has two very different concepts, and, at the same time, two expressions just as different. For *bonum* it has *das Gute* and *das Wohl*, for *malum* it has *das Böse* and *das Übel*, or *Weh* ["the good", "welfare"; "evil", "calamity", "misery"]. Hence there are two [105] (Ak60) entirely different ways of judging which are in question, according to whether what is taken into account, in respect of an action, is *das Gute* and *das Böse* or the *Wohl und Weh* (*Übel*), in store for us ["the good", "the evil"; "well-being", "calamity", "misery"]. And from this it follows that the truth of the aforementioned psychological saying is, to say the least, most uncertain when it is rendered "*wir begehren nichts also in Rücksicht auf unser* Wohl *oder* Weh" ["we desire nothing except in reference to the *well-being* or *misery* in store for us"]. If, on the other hand, we render "According to the dictates of reason, we desire nothing, except inasmuch as we hold it to be either good or evil", then the statement in question is indubitably certain; and, at the same time, the matter is expressed with perfect clarity.

Well-being and *calamity* never signify anything other than that there is a reference to the state of *pleasantness* or *unpleasantness* (pleasure or pain) in which we find ourselves. And if it is with this in mind that we desire an object, or hold it in detestation, this happens only in so far as the object is referred to our sensibility and to the feeling of pleasure or pain evoked by the object. As regards the *good* and the *evil*, there is always a reference to the *will*, in so far as it is determined through the instrumentality of the *law of reason* to pursue something as an *object*. And so it is never the object, or the representation of the object, which determines the will directly. On the contrary, the will is a faculty making it possible that a rule issuing in

---

[12] Incidentally, the expression "*sub ratione boni*" is likewise ambiguous: it is possible to signify two things. It means either, "We represent something to ourselves as good, if we *desire* (or will) it, and *because* we desire it;" or else it means, "We desire something, because we *represent* it to ourselves as *good*." There are thus two alternatives, *viz.* that the desire is the ground which determines the object as good, or that the concept of the good determines the desire. In the former case, "*sub ratione boni*" would mean, "There is something which we wish to happen, this being the *basis* of our Idea of something as good." In the latter case, it would mean, "We wish something to happen *in consequence of the said Idea*," (which must thus precede the willing, inasmuch as it is the ground determining the willing).

reason should become the motive of an action in virtue of which an object is capable of being brought into being. Therefore, the good and the evil refer, strictly speaking, to actions, and not to the sensuous condition of a particular person. [106] And should there be something which was (or was held to be) absolutely good (that is to say, in every respect, and with no further condition laid down), that which was designated in this manner could never be anything else but the way of acting, the maxim, that is, whereby the will was prompted — in other words, the acting person himself in his character as a good man or an evil one.

We are told of a certain Stoic who, when in violent pain because of an attack of the gout, cried out, "Pain, you may torture me as much as you like, I shall never admit that you are something evil" (κακόν, *malum*). Now, although it is true enough that people made mock of him on account of this, the fact remains that he was in the right. That the pain was something calamitous he did indeed feel, and his outcry gave evidence of it. However, there were no grounds why he should concede that something evil was attached to him because of it. And indeed, the pain did not in the least diminish the worth of his person. It was only the worth of his condition which was diminished. A single lie of which he had been conscious was bound to have the effect of casting him down and discouraging him, whereas the pain merely served as an occasion of feeling himself uplifted, provided only he was conscious that it had not come upon him through any wrongful action as the result of which he had made himself liable to punishment.

(Ak61) If we are to call something good, this requires that, in the judgment of every man endowed with reason, it should be an object of the faculty of desire, while evil is that which, in everybody's eyes, is to be looked upon as an object of abhorrence. What is necessary, therefore, for this type of judgment, over and above sensibility, is the presence of reason. [107] And this is how the case stands with veracity, as distinct from telling lies, with justice, as distinct from arbitrary violence. On the other hand, something might be referred to as a calamity, even in a case where everyone was bound to agree, at the same time, that it partook of the nature of the good, either good as a means to something else, or in certain instances, even of that which was inherently good. He who allows an operation to be performed upon him by a surgeon doubtless feels this to be a calamitous thing, while yet, in virtue of reason, he and everybody else declares it to be something which is good. And again, if someone who finds his pleasure in teasing and disquieting peaceable people comes to grief at long last, and has a sound beating administered to him, this is doubtless something calamitous, while, on the other hand, everybody applauds it and holds it to be good in itself, even though nothing further should result. As a matter of fact, even the man who receives the beating is bound to recognize, through the instrumentality of his reason, that he is getting his desert, on the ground that the right proportion between well-being and conducting oneself well — this being a consideration which reason inevitably holds out before his very eyes — is here carried into effect with perfect exactitude.

It is indeed true enough that the state of well-being and that of being in misery matter a *very great deal*, and that, as regards our nature as sensible beings, everything does, in fact, depend on our enjoying *happiness*, so long, that is, as this happiness is not judged by the standard of transitory sensation, but by the standard of the influence which these contingent features exert in respect of our entire existence and the contentment which we find in it. [108] Still, it is not true to say that *everything* is *altogether* dependent on happiness. Man, in so far as he belongs to the world of sense, is a being governed by his wants — and to this extent, a commission he cannot refuse has been handed on to him by sensibility, namely, that he should look after its interests, and that, in adopting practical maxims, he is to pay regard also to the happiness to be found in his present life, and, if possible, likewise in a future one. But then, there is the fact that man's nature is not wholly animal, to the extent that he is indifferent to everything reason has to say on its own behalf, and that he employs his reason merely as a tool for the satisfaction of the wants pertaining to him in his character as a sensible being. And indeed, the circumstance that he is endowed with reason is, as regards his worth, of no effect at all in raising him above the level of animality, so long as reason serves no other purpose except to accomplish that which, in the case of animals, is brought about by virtue of instinct. If that is how things stood, reason would be nothing more than a particular contrivance employed by nature, with a view to equipping man for the accomplishment of the very same purpose as that for which it had designated the animals, no higher purpose coming into consideration.

(Ak62) The real truth, however, is this. In conformity with the arrangement once having been made by nature on behalf of man, he does indeed stand in need of reason, so as to be able to take into account at all times that which pertains to his well-being or misery. Yet, over and above this, man has had his reason given to him also in the interests of a higher vocation, *viz.* that he is likewise to take into consideration that which is in itself good or evil, this being a matter upon which only pure reason can pronounce judgment, that is to say, reason, inasmuch as it fails to be interested in any way in what pertains to the realm of sensibility. [109] And more than that: man is called upon to differentiate sharply between this way of judging and the other, while, at the same time, it is enjoined upon him that he is to assign to it the status of being the supreme condition laying it down what is be thought of as good or evil.

As for this way of pronouncing judgment upon what is good and evil itself, as distinct from what can be called so only in reference to well-being or calamity, the following points are to be taken into consideration. *The position is either:* that a principle issuing in reason is conceived of as already providing the ground by which the will is determined. No account whatever is taken of any object of the faculty of desire to be rendered possible, the action thus being performed solely in virtue of the legislative form exhibited by the maxim which is adopted. If that happens, the said principle has the character of an *a priori* practical law, the assumption being that pure reason has practical reason by itself. As for the law, then, it determines the will *directly*, an action which is in conformity with such a will being *good in itself*, while a will which, in adopting maxims, is at all times in conformity with the law in question, is one which is *good absolutely* and *in every respect*, and is, at the same time, the *supreme condition of anything* to be thought of as *good. Or else, the position is the following:* A determining ground having its seat in the faculty of desire takes precedence over the maxim adopted by the will, a ground of this sort presupposing an object evoking either pleasure or pain, in other words, presupposing something that *delights* or is found *grievous*. The maxim deriving from reason which lays it down that the former state is to be promoted, the latter avoided — such a maxim, I say, determines the will in reference to our inclinations. In other words, the actions are good only indirectly, paying regard, as they do, to an extraneous end, and being thought of as the means for accomplishing that end. And so maxims of the sort described, while they may be classed as reasonable practical precepts, can in no circumstances be allowed to have the character of laws. As for the end [110] we are aiming at, that is to say, as for the delight we are in search of, it is by itself not something *good*, but something which pertains to *well-being*. It is not a rational concept, but an empirical one directed towards an object of sensation. Still, as regards the means accomplishing that end, i.e. as regards the action, it is none the less called good (on the ground that its performance requires rational deliberation), good, however, not in the absolute sense, but only in reference to our sensibility, that is, in respect of the feeling of pleasure or pain. The will, on the other hand, whose maxim is affected by such a procedure as this, is not pure will: a pure will is one operative solely in those cases in which pure reason exhibits its power of exerting practical efficacy by itself.

This is the proper place for explaining the paradoxical character of the method to be employed in a critical investigation into the nature of practical reason, the paradox having to be looked for in the following circumstance. (Ak63)*What has to be insisted upon here is that there must be no determination of the concept of the good and the evil antecedently to giving an account of the nature of the moral law, but that, on the contrary (as is here done by us), the determination of the said concept should take place only after the nature of the moral law had been determined, the moral law being, in fact, the means of bestowing determinacy upon the concept of the good and the evil (all this notwithstanding the fact that, to all appearances, the latter concept has to be looked upon as being the very foundation of that law).* The reasons why such a procedure has to be adopted may be set out thus. Let us suppose that we actually possessed no knowledge of the fact that the principle of morality was a pure law determining the will in an *a priori* fashion. To exclude the possibility of our having recourse to principles in a perfectly arbitrary manner (*gratis*), we should still be under an obligation to leave as *an open question* — to begin with, at any rate — whether the will has only empirical grounds of determination at its disposal, or whether it may rely also on grounds which are pure and *a priori*. After all, it is contrary to all the fundamental rules of philosophical enquiry that [111] what remains to be decided should, antecedently to this, be treated as having been decided already. Supposing, then, we meant to start out from the concept of the good, with a view to deriving from it the laws governing the will, the said concept of an object (to be looked upon as something good) would, at the same time, signify that the object was the sole ground determining the will. Now, seeing that the concept did not have any *a priori* practical law at its disposal which might serve as its guide, the criterion of the good and the evil could not be assigned to anything else but to the object's being in conformity with our feeling pleasure or pain. And the employment of reason could consist in nothing else than this: on the one hand, it determined the pain and pleasure referred to, placing them within the entire context of all the sensations arising in the course of my existence; on the other hand, it provided me with the means of securing the object of the feelings in question for myself. But then, it is solely by virtue of experience that it can be made out whether or not something is in conformity with the feeling of pleasure, while, on the other hand, the declaration has been made, in the present case, that it is this feeling upon which the practical law is to be founded, and that it is to be thought of as a condition of the law. And so the very possibility of there being *a priori* practical laws would be excluded, on the ground of one's having come to imagine it to be necessary that one should discover an object for the will, the concept of which, as something good, was to play the part of a universal, though empirical, ground of determination for that will. What was really needful was that one should enquire, antecedently to this, whether there did not, after all, exist a ground determining the will in an *a priori* fashion[112] (as it is impossible that such a ground should ever be found in anything else than a pure practical law, to be thought of as prescribing exclusively the legislative form exhibited by the maxims adopted, no reference being made to any object). Since, however, it had already been presupposed that there was such a thing as an object conformable to the concepts of the good and the evil, while, on the other hand, it was only in accordance with empirical concepts that, in the absence of any law preceding it, such an object was capable of being conceived of in thought, this resulted in one's depriving oneself, from the very outset, of any possibility of ever conceiving of a pure practical law. (Ak64) Instead of this, one should, having recourse to an analytical procedure, have investigated, in the first instance, what was the character of a pure practical law, in which case one would have discovered that it was not the concept of the good, as an object, which determined the moral law, but that, on the contrary, it was the moral law which first determined and made possible the concept of that which was to be looked upon as good, in the sense of being unreservedly worthy of that designation.

The above observation, whose sole concern is with the method to be adopted in investigations into the ultimate nature of morality, should be regarded as important. And indeed, what it does is to explain, all at once, the reason accounting for all the various aberrations of which philosophers have been guilty, in seeking to set forth the supreme principle underlying morality. What they did was that they sought for an object of the will which, in respect of a certain law, was to play the part of being its subject matter as well as the ground upon which it rested (this law, accordingly, being supposed not to be a ground by which the will is directly determined, but to become such a ground through the instrumentality of the feeling of pleasure or pain evoked by the presence of the object). [113] What they ought to have done instead is that they should have gone, first of all, in search of a law which would determine the will, directly and in an *a priori* manner, the object being determined only subsequently in accordance with that will. As things stood, however, it made no difference whether the said object of pleasure, which was to play the part of being supreme in deciding what was to be looked upon as good — whether this object, I say, was assigned to happiness, to perfection,[to the moral feeling,][13] or to the will of God. And indeed, seeing that the principle which they adopted in every case exhibited the characteristic of heteronomy, it was inevitable that they should encounter empirical conditions upon which the moral law was supposedly dependent. This could not be otherwise, because the object of which they spoke as being a ground directly determining the will, did not permit of being called good or evil, except in reference to the direct relation in which it stood to feeling, a relation which can never be anything but empirical in character. It is only a formal law, i.e. one which gives no further prescription to reason except that the form of its universal legislation is to be the supreme condition subject to which maxims are adopted — it is only a formal law, I say, which is capable of being an *a priori* determining ground having its origin in practical reason. The ancients, however, gave evidence quite undisguisedly of the error of which we have spoken, this being due to the fact that, in their moral enquiries, they made everything dependent on the determination of the *summum bonum*, of an object, that is, which they intended subsequently to declare to be the determining ground of the will as exhibited in the moral law. The truth, however, is this: that the *summum bonum* is an object which comes up for consideration at a much later stage. The moral law has first to be established by itself, being vindicated as a ground determining the will directly; and it is only then, the will [114] having been determined in respect of its form, and that in an *a priori* fashion, that the *summum bonum* allows of being exhibited as an object towards which the will is directed. To establish the truth of this is a task we shall undertake in the section where we deal with the dialectic of pure practical reason. As for the moderns, with whom the question regarding the nature of the *summum bonum* has gone out of fashion, or at least, would seem to have become a secondary matter, they disguise the error which is here under consideration through their vague

---

[13] Cassirer left untranslated Kant's *im moralischen Gesetze* which Hartenstein (1838-9) changed to *im moralischen Gefühl*. [Editors]

use of words, this being a procedure adopted by them in a good many other cases. (Ak65) Still, it becomes apparent from the systems advocated by them that they do, in fact, commit this error. This is betrayed by their constantly having recourse to a principle implying a heteronomy of practical reason such as can never give rise to a moral law laying down universally binding commands in an *a priori* fashion.

The concepts of the good and the evil, resulting as they do from an *a priori* determination of the will, presuppose, in accordance with this, the presence of a pure practical principle, that is to say, a causal efficacy which has its origin in pure reason. Hence the original reference is not to objects, in which case their function might be, let us say, to determine, with regard to a manifold of given intuitions, what character it must have to exhibit synthetic unity in the one consciousness, this being the task which is actually performed by the pure concepts of the understanding, *viz.* the categories, which are operative within the field of reason's theoretical employment. As against this, objects are, in the case of the concepts we are here considering, presupposed as something given, while on the other hand, the feature these concepts all share is that they are modes of a single category, that of causality, in so far as the ground of the causality in question is to be found in the rational representation of a law which, as a law exhibiting the characteristic of freedom, reason lays down for itself, furnishing proof of the circumstance that it is endowed with a power of exerting *a priori* practical efficacy. [115] However, since actions are, *on the one hand*, subject to a law which is not a law of nature but one issuing in freedom, while, on *the other hand*, these actions are events taking place in the world of sense, and thus appertaining to the realm of appearances, the conclusion to be drawn is the following. The determination arrived at, on the part of reason, purporting to be operative within the field of practice, will be as nothing, unless reference is made to the world of sense, as it is necessary, accordingly, that there should be conformity with the categories of the understanding. Still, it is not the theoretical employment of the understanding which is in view here (in which case the aim would be that the manifold presented in sensible *intuition* was to be brought within the compass of the one *a priori* consciousness). No, what alone matters now is that it should be possible to impose — and that in an *a priori* fashion — unity of consciousness upon the manifoldness of the *desirings*. And it all comes of practical reason (or a pure will) which, in giving rise to the moral law, assumes its role of holding dominion.

These *categories of freedom* — for that is how we propose to designate them, in contradistinction from the theoretical concept, to be looked upon as categories operative within the realm of nature — have one evident advantage over the other kind. The categories of nature are mere forms of thought which, through the instrumentality of universal concepts, designate objects in general in what is but an indeterminate manner. On the other hand, they have application to any type of intuition which we might possess. As against this, the concern of the other kind of category is with the way in which a *free choice* is determined. Now while it is clear that, in the latter case, it is impossible to supply an intuition which would be in complete correspondence with the concepts, there is something here which does not hold good for any concept pertaining to the theoretical employment of our faculty of knowledge, the circumstance, namely, that there is a pure practical law serving as the foundation of the concepts, and doing so in an *a priori* manner. [116] In the place of the form of intuition (i.e. space and time) which does not lie within the domain of reason itself, but has to be taken from somewhere else, i.e. from sensibility, there is something lying within the domain of reason, that is to say, within that of the thinking faculty itself, which the practical concepts have supplied to them, (Ak66) by way of serving as a foundation: namely, the *form of a pure will*. And so it comes about that, since all precepts having their origin in pure practical reason are concerned solely with the *determination of the will*, not with conditions pertaining to nature (i.e. the practical faculty required for the *execution of one's design*), this has the following result. Practical *a priori* concepts, related as they are to the supreme principle of freedom, acquire at once the status of cognitions, and do not have to wait for intuitions for the purpose of acquiring significance. This occurs for the strange reason that they themselves produce the reality of that to which they refer. And this is by no means the sort of thing which holds good for concepts operative within the field of theory. On the other hand, it is essential to keep in mind that the sole concern of these categories is with practical reason in general, and consequently, as regards the order exhibited by them, they proceed from that which, morally speaking, is as yet indeterminate, and subject to sensible conditions, to that which is not subject to any sensible conditions but is determined solely by virtue of the moral law.

[117] *Table of the Categories of Freedom in reference to the concepts of the good and the evil.*

1 – Quantity

Subjective: in conformity with maxims (*Opinions* deriving from the *will* of the individual)
Objective: in conformity with principles (*precepts*)
A priori: objective as well as subjective principles of freedom (*laws*)

2 – Quality	3 – Relation
Practical rules of *doing*	to *personality*
(*PRÆCEPTIVÆ*)	to the *state* of the person
Practical rules of *leaving undone*	*Reciprocally*: of one person
(*PROHIBITIVÆ*)	to the state of the others
Practical rules of *making exceptions*	
(*EXCEPTIVÆ*)	

4 – Modality

The *permitted* and the *forbidden*
Duty and *contrary to duty*
Perfect and *imperfect duty*

[118] (Ak67) On examining the above table, one will soon come to realize that freedom is here looked upon as a species of causal efficacy not subject to empirical grounds of determination, the reference made being to actions to be thought of as appearances and as taking place in the world of sense, yet rendered possible in virtue of freedom. As regards the reference to the categories, therefore, it is natural possibility which is here in question, while yet each category is taken in so general a sense as to leave open the possibility of presuming that the ground determining the causal efficacy here considered lies somewhere outside the confines of the world of sense, and that it is to be assigned to freedom, thought of as the property of a being which belongs to the realm of intelligences. The position remains the same until the categories of modality are reached, where a transition is made from practical principles in general to principles of morality. It is, however, in a merely *problematic* sense that these are introduced, while it is only subsequently, reference being made to the moral law, that they permit of being exhibited in a *dogmatic* fashion.

There is nothing further I wish to say by way of explaining the present table, seeing that it is intelligible enough by itself. A classification in accordance with principles, such as has here been supplied, has the most salutary effect in the case of any science, because it tends to promote both thoroughness and intelligibility. For example, from the above table — more particularly from the first number of it — one may gather what one's starting point has to be when one comes to deliberate upon problems of practice. One has to begin with maxims, such as each man adopts on the basis of his own inclinations, going on to precepts, which are valid for rational beings of a certain kind (by virtue of the fact that, in respect of some of their inclinations, they are in agreement with one another), until one finally arrives at that law which has validity for everyone, irrespective of their inclinations. [119] One thereby comes to have a survey of the entire scheme, laying down what is to be accomplished, and one even becomes conversant with all the questions requiring to be answered in practical philosophy, while knowing, at the same time, what is the order to be followed in dealing with them.

THE METHOD OF TYPOLOGY
AS EMPLOYED BY THE FACULTY
OF PURE PRACTICAL JUDGMENT

It is the concepts of the good and the evil by which the will finds itself, for the first time, provided with an object. But these concepts themselves are subject to a rule issuing in reason which, when it is pure reason that is in question, determines the will in an *a priori* manner in respect of the object to be pursued by it. Now if what we have to decide is whether an action we have the power of performing, within the realm of sensibility, does or does not come under the said rule, it is required that the faculty of practical judgment should become operative, through whose instrumentality that which was expressed by the rule in general terms (*in abstracto*) is applied to an action *in concreto*. On the other hand, there is, *first of all*, the fact that a *practical rule* deriving from pure reason concerns the existence of an object, by virtue of its being practical, and *secondly*, inasmuch as it is a *practical rule* deriving from pure reason, carries necessity with it, so far as the existence of the action is concerned. In other words, the rule is a practical law, being, however, not a law of nature (Ak68) resting on empirical grounds, but a law of freedom, according to which the will is supposed to be determined independently of anything empirical (merely by virtue of the general representation of a law and of the [120] form exhibited by that law). But then, as regards any instance of possible actions which permit of being encountered by us, they are never anything but empirical in character, that is to say, they appertain to the realm of experience and of nature. It would seem absurd, therefore, to expect to come across, within the world of sense, an instance which, while entirely subject to the law of nature, in the sense specified, should yet permit that a law of freedom was to be applied to it, in which case the position would be that the supersensible Idea of the morally good, intended to be exhibited *in concreto*, permitted of being applied to the instance under consideration.

The conclusion to be drawn from what has been pointed out is that, in matters of pure practical reason, the faculty of judgment is liable to encounter the same difficulties as arose when it dealt with matters pertaining to pure theoretical reason. Still, in the latter case, the faculty of judgment had, notwithstanding all this, a means of escaping from its difficulties, and that by virtue of the following cir-cumstance. What was required, as regards the theoretical employ-ment of the mind, was that there should be intuitions to which the pure concepts of the understanding could be applied. And it turned out that it was possible, after all, to supply such intuitions in an *a priori* manner (although, on the other hand, this held good only in reference to the objects of the senses), and accordingly, to supply them in such a way that (as regards the connectedness exhibited by the manifold to be met with in these intuitions), it is in conformity with the pure *a priori* concepts of the understanding (the said proce-dure being that of employing *schemata*). As against this, the morally good is something supersensible, in respect of the character which it bears as an object, with the result that nothing corresponding to it can be found anywhere within the field of sensible intuition. Thus the faculty of judgment, as subject to laws issuing from pure practi-cal reason, is liable to special difficulties which are attributable to the circumstance that a law of freedom is supposed to have application to actions which, [121] being events occurring within the world of sense, must, as regards this feature of theirs, be assigned to the realm of nature.

Still, there is, on the other side, the fact that there opens up here a favourable prospect for the faculty of pure practical judgment. If what we are called to do is to carry out the subsumption, under a *pure practical law*, of an *action* which it is possible for us to perform within the world of sense, it is not the possibility of the action, thought of as an event taking place in the world of sense, which comes up for consideration. And indeed, as regards pronouncing judgment upon this matter, it appertains to reason in its theoretical employment, in accordance with the law of causality, which derives from a pure con-cept of the understanding, a concept regarding which reason has at its disposal a *schema* which is to be assigned to the realm of sensible intuition. As for physical causality, or the condition subject to which it occurs, it has its place among the concepts pertaining to nature, and the schema operative here is sketched out by the power of transcendental imagination. However, what concerns us at present is not a schema of a particular instance as being in conformity with laws, but the schema (if such an expression is suitable here) to be supplied for a law itself. And the reason why the two cases have to be distinguished from one another is this: that, if the *determination of the will* takes place solely by virtue of the law, in the absence of any other ground of determination, (Ak69) (as distinct from an action thought of in reference to what it accomplishes), the effect is that the concept of causality comes to be bound up with conditions wholly different from those which constitute natural connectedness.

The law of nature, being one to which the objects of sensible intuition [122] are subject, in that they are such objects, requires that a schema should correspond to it, that is to say, a general procedure having its source in the imagination, the task to be performed being that the pure concept of the understanding marked out by the law should be exhibited to the senses in an *a priori* manner. On the other hand, as regards the law pertaining to freedom, which has to be looked upon as a causal efficacy not dependent on any sensible conditions, and thus also as regards the concept of the unconditionally good, there is no way of having recourse to any intuition upon which it might be based; in other words, there can be no schema to be employed for the purpose of its being applied *in concreto*. The moral law can thus rely on no other faculty of knowledge playing the part of the intermediary, and giving it application to objects of nature, except only the understanding — not the imagination. And what the understanding is capable of accomplishing, for the purpose of doing service on behalf of the faculty of judgment, is that it supplies, as the foundation of an Idea of reason, not a schema pertaining to sensibility but a law — a law, however, which allows of being exhibited as such *in concreto*, in reference to the objects of the senses, and which thus has the character of a law of nature, while, on the other hand, it is only its form as a law which is here taken into consideration. And accordingly, we may be permitted to speak of the law in question as serving as the *type* of the law of morality.

The rule holding good for the faculty of judgment, inasmuch as it is at the service of laws which originate in pure practical reason, may be formulated as follows. Ask yourself whether the action you propose to perform (provided it was to occur in conformity with a law governing a realm of nature of which you yourself were a part) was such that you could look upon it as something to be brought into being by virtue of your will. Now it is, in fact, the said rule in conformity with which everybody judges actions, when what is to be decided upon is whether they are morally good or evil; and the matter is, accordingly, stated in terms such as these. Let us suppose *everyone* [123] thought himself justified in committing fraud, whenever it was to his own advantage that he should do so; that everyone thought he had the right to shorten his life the moment he was affected by a feeling of utter distaste for it; that someone looked upon other men's distress with complete indifference. And let it be supposed further that this was an order of things to which you yourself belonged as a member. Now the truth of the matter is that, if a man permits himself secretly to resort to committing fraud, he invariably knows perfectly well that it does not follow from this that, on that account, everybody else will act in the same way. Or, to take a different case, if a man acts in an unloving manner, he knows well enough that this will not have the immediate consequence that everyone will behave like this towards him. And so it is that, although the instituting of such a comparison between, on the one hand, the maxim underlying one's actions, and, on the other, a universal law, is not the ground which determines the will, it is true none the less that the said law serves as a *type* in matters of pronouncing judgment upon actions in accordance with moral principles. If the maxim prompting the action is not such as to pass the test, when measured by the standard that it is to exhibit the form pertaining to a natural law in general, then it is impossible, morally speaking. (Ak70) This is the way in which the position is judged even by a man equipped with the most ordinary power of understanding. And indeed, the notion of a *natural law* invariably underlies the most commonplace judgments men make, even those drawn from experience. The ordinary man, therefore, has it at all times at his disposal, with this difference, that in those cases in which it is causality due to freedom upon which judgment is to be pronounced, he makes the *law of nature* serve merely as the type of a *law of freedom*. And he proceeds in this way because, unless he had at his disposal something to which, in cases of experience, he might refer as providing an example, it would be impossible for him to put the law of pure practical reason to its proper use, and give it an application in practice.

[124] In view of what has been said, it is permissible likewise to use the *nature* of the *world of sense* in such a way as to make it serve *as the type* of a *nature* to be assigned to the *intelligible* realm. There is

this proviso, however, that we must not transfer to the latter intuitions or anything dependent on these, the reference here being exclusively to one feature: namely, that it exhibits in general terms the *form* of being in *accordance with law*. Now this notion is to be met with, even where reason is employed in the most ordinary way; while, on the other hand, it is only when the practical employment of pure reason is in view that it can give rise to determinate knowledge in an *a priori* manner. And indeed, as regards laws considered as such, they are of one and the same kind, simply by virtue of being laws, no matter what are the determining grounds from which they derive.

Moreover, the following facts have to be taken into account. As regards the intelligible realm, nothing whatever pertaining to it is known to us apart from freedom (through the instrumentality of the moral law), freedom being known to us, only inasmuch as it is a presupposition of the moral law and inseparably bound up with it. As for any other intelligible objects towards which reason might lead us, under the direction of that law, they, in their turn, have no other reality for us except on behalf of the same law and the employment of pure practical reason, while, on the other hand, pure practical reason gives us the right, and indeed compels us, to make the realm of nature (in respect of its pure form, as an object of the understanding) do service as playing the part of a "type" for the purpose of the faculty of judgment. And so the purpose of the present observation is to prevent that which appertains merely to the *typology* of concepts from being classed among the concepts themselves. This typology, then, which has its source in the faculty of judgment, guards against the adoption of a principle of *empiricism* in matters of practical reason, [125] a procedure which assigns the practical concepts of the good and the evil solely to the consequences accomplished in the course of experience. (It has to be admitted, however, that the said happiness, as well as the countless advantageous consequences resulting from a will actuated by self-reliance, would, on condition that this will assigned to itself, at the same time, the role of a universal law of nature, serve tolerably well as a "type" representing the morally good, while yet not identical with it.) Besides, the very same typology guards against the adoption of a principle of *mysticism* in matters of practical reason, a way of proceeding which would transform into a *schema* that which once played the part merely of a *symbol*, placing reliance upon (Ak71) the application of moral concepts to real, yet non-sensible, intuitions (appertaining to an invisible kingdom of God), and thus wandering off into the sphere of the transcendent. What alone is suited to the employment of moral concepts is that the faculty of judgment should resort to *rationalism*, which borrows from the realm of sensible nature nothing except what pure reason is also, of its own accord, able to conceive of in thought, i.e. the notion of conformity to law, while, on the other hand, introducing nothing into the realm of supersensible nature except what, under the guidance of a formal rule, laying down the general character of a law of nature, permits of being actually exhibited in reference to actions taking place in the world of sense. Still, as regards placing reliance upon *empiricism* in the field of practical reason, the warning against this is of much greater importance and advisability, seeing that *mysticism* is, after all, still compatible with the purity and sublimity characterizing the moral law. Further, if the course taken stretches one's imagination, with a view to obtaining intuitions of a supersensible kind, [126] such a procedure is indeed neither natural nor is it well-suited to the ordinary way of thinking. As against this, there is the effect which empiricism has upon morality, where the dispositions of the mind are concerned (and it is, after all, in these, and not in actions, that there consists that exalted worth which man can, and in fact ought to, procure from himself), the said effect being this: that it cuts off the very roots of morality, substituting for it an empirical interest, by virtue of which the various inclinations hold commerce with one another. And what happens further — and the same holds good for all inclinations, no matter in what garb they are dressed up — is that, once they are raised to the dignity of playing the part of the supreme practical principle, they result in a degradation of humanity. Seeing that, notwithstanding all this, everyone's disposition is such as to give these inclinations a favourable reception, it follows that empiricism constitutes, for this very reason, a much greater danger than can ever be the case with enthusiastic exaltation, the latter being something which is wholly incapable of featuring as a permanent condition commending itself to large numbers of human beings.

CHAPTER III

THE MOTIVE FORCES
AT THE DISPOSAL
OF PURE PRACTICAL REASON.

The very essence of the moral worth to be assigned to an action is that the *moral law* should *determine the will directly*. If the determination of the will, notwithstanding its being *in conformity* with the moral law, yet takes place only through the instrumentality of a feeling, [127] no matter of what kind, a feeling which has to be presupposed, in order that the said law should become a sufficient determining ground of the will; if, in other words, it is not *for the sake of the law* that such determination takes place, the result will be this: that the action, although exhibiting *legality*, will fail to exhibit *morality*. (Ak72) Provided, then, what is signified by the term "motive force" (*elater animi*) is that it is to play the part of the subjective determining ground of the will, operative in a being whose reason is not necessarily in accordance with the objective law, in virtue of the very nature possessed by the said being, the conclusions to be drawn from this state of affairs will be the following. As regards the divine will, there is no way at all of supposing that it operates by means of motive forces, while, on the other hand, the moving force by which the human will is prompted can never be anything else but the moral law itself, the same holding good for the will of every created rational being. In other words, what is necessary is this: that the objective ground of determination should — at all times, and wholly by itself — be, at the same time, the subjectively sufficient ground of the action, a feature in the absence of which the action will be one which fulfils the *letter* of the law, while yet failing to embody its *spirit*.[14]

If, therefore, the question be, what is to be done on behalf of the moral law so as to procure for it an influence over the will, it is essential that one should not look for any motive force derived from somewhere else, being under the impression that the moral law could be

---

[14] We may say of any action which, while in accordance with the law, has yet not been done for the sake of the law, that it is morally good merely according to the *letter*, but not according to the *spirit* (i.e. as regards the disposition of the mind from which it results).

dispensed with in what one set out to do. [128] Indeed, if one adopted a procedure such as this, nothing could result but a showy pretence, devoid of any stability. In fact, even if we go no further than to permit, *alongside* the moral law, the co-operation of some other motive forces — let us say, that of gaining a personal advantage — the enterprise we are embarking on is a *dubious* one. And so there is only one alternative left to us. We must do no more than determine with accuracy what is the manner in which the moral law becomes a motive force, and what happens, as the result of the said circumstance, to the human faculty of desire, as regards the effect exerted upon it by the determining ground under consideration. On the other hand, the question how a law can, by itself and directly, be a ground determining the will (its being of the very essence of morality that such should be the case) — as regards this question, I say, it is unanswerable to human reason. In fact, it is the same as asking how a free will is possible. What we are thus called upon to demonstrate in an *a priori* fashion is not the reason why the moral law comes to play the part of a motive force, independently of anything else, but what is the effect the moral law exerts (or rather, is bound to exert) upon the mind, inasmuch as it becomes such a force.

Whenever a determination of the will through the moral law is to occur, it is essential that the will should be determined as a free will, that is to say, not merely without the co-operation of any sensible impulses, but to the point of rejecting all these, all inclinations being kept in check, in so far as there is any possibility of their being contrary to the said law. To this extent, then, the effect of the moral law is merely negative in character, and as such allows of being known to us in an *a priori* manner, for the following reasons. Feeling is the foundation of all inclinations [129] and of every sensible impulse, and the negative effect exerted upon feeling, (Ak73) due to the fact that the inclinations find themselves kept in check, is itself a feeling. Consequently, we are in a position to comprehend in an *a priori* manner that the moral law which determines the will, by way of imposing restrictions upon all our inclinations, is bound to evoke a feeling which may be declared to partake of the character of something painful. What has occurred, then, is that we have come across here the first, and perhaps the only, case in which, placing reliance upon *a priori* concepts, we were in a position to determine the relation in which a cognition (in the present instance it is one arising from pure practical reason) stands to the feeling of pleasure and pain. All inclinations, taken in their entirety (and it is quite possible to reduce these inclinations tolerably well to a system, in which we speak of their satisfaction as coming under the general title of private happiness) constitute what is called *self-regard (solipsismus)*. And as for this self-regard, it signifies either a condition of being *favourably disposed* towards oneself (*philautia*), to an extent exceeding all else, or, alternatively, it signifies a condition of finding *satisfaction* in oneself (*arrogantia*). The first is more particularly called *love of oneself,* the second *self-conceit*. Where pure practical reason is concerned, it merely imposes a *check* upon this love one has of oneself, declaring it to be something natural, which is active in us even before the moral law is, the only condition laid down being that there should be agreement with the said law, the condition prevailing in this case being described as *rational self-love*. As for self-conceit, on the other hand, pure practical reason simply *strikes* it *down* to the ground, this being due to the circumstance that any claim to self-esteem made [130] before there is agreement with the moral law is futile and without warrant. In point of fact, as we shall soon explain more clearly, the assurance of having a disposition of the mind which is in agreement with the said law is the very first condition upon which all the worth of the personality depends. And all pretensions, prior to this state having been reached, are false and contrary to law. But then, propensity to self-esteem is to be classed with those inclinations which the moral law keeps in check, proceeding in this way on the ground that the said propensity rests upon sensibility and nothing else. And so it comes about that the moral law strikes down self-conceit. However, since the law is, after all, something positive (exhibiting, as it does, the form of an intellectual causal efficacy, *viz.* that deriving from freedom), it happens that, in being contrasted with its subjective counterpart, that is to say, the inclinations to be met with in us, self-conceit is *weakened* by the moral law which, at the same time, becomes an object of *respect*. Moreover, since it has the effect even of *striking down*, i.e. of humiliating, self-conceit altogether, it comes to be the object of the very highest *respect*. In this way, then, it happens that the law is likewise the ground of a positive feeling which is not of empirical origin and of which we have *a priori* knowledge, the conclusions to be drawn from what has been said being the following. Respect for the moral law is a feeling evoked through the instrumentality of an intellectual ground, and moreover it is the only feeling capable of becoming known to us in a wholly *a priori* manner, while at the same time we are able to comprehend its necessity.

(Ak74) We have seen in the preceding chapter that, if anything offers itself as an object of the will, *prior to* the moral law having been given admittance, its being claimed that, among the grounds deter-

mining the will, it should have assigned to it the title of the unconditionally good, [131] the very possibility of such a claim being granted
is excluded by the moral law, the latter having to be thought of as the
condition which stands supreme, so far as practical reason is concerned. And we have seen further that it is the mere form exhibited
by actions in the field of practice, consisting as it does in the suitability of maxims to be embodied in a universal legislation, which first
determines what is to be looked upon as being, in itself and absolutely, good, and which serves as the foundation of that maxim which
proceeds from a pure will, such a will being that which alone is good
in every respect. But then we find our nature, in so far as we are
beings which belong to the world of sense, is so constituted, that that
which stands for the element of matter, as regards our faculty of desire (i.e. the objects of inclination, evoking either hope or fear), is
what obtrudes itself first of all. Indeed, that aspect of our selfhood
which allows itself to be determined by influences deriving from a
pathological source, announces its claims before anything else does,
just as if it made up the whole of our selfhood. And it proceeds in
this manner, notwithstanding the fact that the maxims to which it
gives rise are wholly unsuited to form part of a universal legislation,
while, at the same time, it makes every endeavour to have these claims
acknowledged as coming first and being fundamental. We may give
the name of *self-love* to this propensity in which we have to take for
our standard what are, in fact, subjective grounds for determining
choice, while making out, at the same time, that it is we ourselves
who are to be thought of as the objective grounds determining all
willing in general. And this self-love, when it invests itself with a
legislative character, assigning to itself the role of laying down an
unconditional practical law, may be given the name of *self-conceit*.
But then, the moral law which alone is truly objective (i.e. objective
in any respect whatsoever) exhibits this feature, that it totally excludes any influence self-love may wish to exert over the supreme
practical principle. And so self-conceit, whose nature it is to prescribe as laws what are, in truth, the subjective conditions underlying self-love, finds itself checked to an unlimited extent. But then
that which, in our [132] judgment, imposes a check upon our self-
conceit has the effect of making us suffer humiliation. The moral law,
therefore, inevitably humiliates all human beings in so far as they institute a comparison between it and the sensible propensity of its own
nature. On the other hand, that whose representation, as a *ground determining our will*, humiliates us, in the consciousness we have of ourselves,
arouses, at the same time, *respect* for itself, inasmuch as it is positive and

plays the part of a determining ground. Accordingly, it happens that the moral law, on its subjective side, provides a ground for evoking respect. Now since anything encountered as a constituent of self-love partakes of the nature of inclination, while all inclination rests upon feelings, it follows that that which imposes a check upon all inclinations, comprehended as they are under a principle of self-love, must, for this very reason, have an influence over feeling. And it is thus that we come to understand in an *a priori* manner how the moral law succeeds in having an effect upon feeling, the result being achieved in the following manner. In the first place, the moral law excludes the inclinations from any co-operation with the supreme legislation; and secondly, it excludes our propensity to assign to these inclinations the status of being the supreme condition in matters of practice. In other words, it repudiates self-love. The effect this has is, in one sense, purely *negative* in character, while, on the other hand, seeing that the ground by which the restrictions are imposed (Ak75) is a ground deriving from pure practical reason, it has its *positive* side as well. However, we are by no means entitled to presuppose, in this connection, the existence of a special kind of feeling, to be designated as a practical or moral feeling, while imagining, at the same time, that the said feeling takes priority over the moral law and serves as its foundation.

[133] The negative effect upon feeling, i.e. the feeling of unpleasantness, is to be looked upon as *pathological* in character, as is the case with any influence exerted upon feeling, and with any feeling in general. On the other hand, it is consciousness of the moral law which is responsible for the effect thought of here, the reference being, accordingly, to a cause that is intelligible in character, namely, the subject as having at its disposal a power of pure practical reason which plays the part of the supreme legislator. In view of this, the said feeling arising in a subject — which, on the one hand, is rational, and on the other, is affected by inclinations — this feeling, I say, may be described as one of suffering humiliation, or being exposed to intellectual disdain. However, there is a positive ground for such humiliation, *viz.* the law; and if that is what is being taken into account, there arises at the same time respect for the law. There is indeed no such thing as just having a feeling for the law, and the truth is that, as it is the nature of the law to clear resistance out of the way, the removal of an obstacle is being looked upon, in the judgment of reason, as making a positive contribution in furtherance of its causal efficacy. That is the reason why the said feeling allows of being spo-

ken of as one of respect for the moral law, and, for both reasons taken together, can be called a *moral feeling*.

The moral law, then, while it is, through the instrumentality of practical pure reason, the formal determining ground of the action, and on the other hand is the material, though purely objective, ground of the objects of the actions — to be designated by the names of the good and the evil — likewise plays the part of the subjective determining ground, that is to say, the motive force leading to the action. This is accomplished by virtue of the circumstance that the law exerts an effect on the sensibility of the subject, evoking a feeling which is conducive to the law's coming to have an influence over the will. [134] What happened here is not at all that there *precedes* in the subject a feeling which tends to predispose towards morality, for there is no possibility of such being the case, because all feeling is sensible in character, while it is essential that the motive force leading to a moral disposition of the mind should be exempt from being subject to any sensible condition. Instead, we find the actual position to be as follows. While it is true enough that the sensible feeling, underlying any and every inclination, is the condition of the occurrence of the sensation we call respect, the fact remains that the cause by which the said feeling finds itself determined has to be assigned to pure practical reason. Thus the sentiment under consideration does not, as regards its origin, allow of being thought of as pathological in character. On the contrary, it is to be looked upon as something *carried into effect* by virtue of the principle of *practice*. And indeed, what happens is this. The representation of the moral law, taking away something from the influence exerted by self-love, as well as from the illusion characteristic of self-conceit, brings it about that the obstacle standing in the way of pure practical reason is diminished in force. Moreover, the effect which, in the judgment of reason, is produced in this connection is that there arises here the representation of the pre-eminence of reason's objective *law* over the impulses (Ak76) deriving from sensibility — the representation, that is, of the weight appertaining to that law relatively to sensibility (in respect of a will liable to be affected by the latter), the removal of the counterweight being the source of such awareness. And so respect for the law does not have the character of a motive force whereby we are led to morality, but instead should be looked upon as morality, subjectively considered, inasmuch as it operates as a motive force, the correct account of the matter being this: that pure practical reason, disdaining all the claims made by self-love, by way of contrasting itself with that self-love, provides authority for the law, which is now the sole source of influence. However, it must be observed here that respect, having the nature of an effect [135] exerted upon feeling, or in other words, an effect exerted upon the sensible element found in a rational being, presupposes the presence of this sensibility, i.e. it presupposes the finitude of beings such as have respect imposed upon them by the moral law. Thus respect for the *law* cannot be attributed to a supreme being, or even to one wholly divorced from sensibility, seeing that, in such a case, there is no possibility that sensibility should play the part of an obstacle opposed to practical reason.

This feeling, then, which goes by the name of a moral feeling, is carried into effect solely through the instrumentality of reason. It does not serve by way of pronouncing judgment upon actions, and still less does it serve as something upon which the objective law of morality is to be founded. But instead it plays the part merely of providing a motive force, the intention being that a man should resolve within himself to adopt the moral law as the maxim by which he is guided. And indeed, how could there be a more appropriate name than "moral feeling", to signify this remarkable feeling which it is impossible to compare with any feeling deriving from a pathological source? The truth of the matter is that it is of so peculiar a character as to be at the disposal of reason alone, or to put it more particularly, of practical pure reason.

Respect is invariably directed towards persons, and never towards things. As for the latter, they can be objects of *inclination*, or if it is animals that are in question — for example, dogs or horses — they can even be objects of *love*. Or else, something can be an object of *fear*, as is the case with the sea, a volcanic mountain, or a wild animal. But none of these can ever arouse *respect. Admiration* is something that comes closer to the feeling under consideration, and when it bears the character of an affection, in which case it is referred to by the name of amazement, [136] it may be directed also towards things, e.g. towering mountains, the magnitude, number and distance of the heavenly bodies, the strength and speed of certain animals, etc. As for man, he may be to me an object of love, of fear, or of admiration — even to the point of astonishment. Yet he need not on that account be an object of respect. His playful mood, his courage, his strength, the power he possesses, by reason of the position he occupies among men: all these are capable of filling us with sentiments of the kind described. Yet, as regards inner respect for him, it may still be missing. Fontenelle says, "I bow down my head to a nobleman, but my spirit does not bow down to him." I may add the following remark. (Ak77) If there be a man of merely humble station, one whose position is that of an ordinary citizen, while yet I recognize that, to a certain degree, he is endowed with a probity of character which surpasses anything I am conscious of in myself, then *my spirit bows* down to him, no matter whether or not I desire this to happen, and however high I may carry my head so as to make it impossible for him to be unmindful of the superiority of my position. Why should that be so? Because the example he is setting places before me a law which, if I use it as a standard to measure my own conduct by, has the effect of casting down my self-conceit, while, as regards the question whether obedience can be rendered to the said law, in other words, whether it has *practicability*, that is something of which I have received proof, before my very eyes, through what has been accomplished in deed. On the other hand, the feeling of respect persists, even in the event of my being conscious that I am endowed with the same degree of probity. Indeed, seeing that with human beings everything good found in them still remains defective, the circumstance that, [137] by an example being offered, the law has been presented to me as something visible, as it were, has had the effect of lowering my pride. And the standard referred to is the other man whom I have before my very eyes, and whom I see in a purer light, because his lack of integrity, which may still be found in him, is not as well known to me as is my own. *Respect* is a *tribute* we cannot refuse to pay to merit, no matter whether or not we desire to do so. In certain cases we may refrain from giving outward expression to it; but we are still unable to avoid feeling it inwardly.

Respect partakes so *little* of a feeling of *pleasure* that it is only with reluctance that we give way to it, where man is concerned. What we do instead is seek to discover something which might have the effect of lightening the burden which is being imposed upon us, to discover something worthy of blame, our purpose being that we should find ourselves compensated for the humiliation inflicted upon us by such an example. Even the dead are not in all cases immune to a criticism of this sort, especially when the example set by them appears to be something that does not permit of being imitated. And indeed, the moral law itself, in its *solemn majesty*, is not exempt from the said endeavour by which we are led on to offer resistance to our holding it in respect. Or is it to be supposed that there could be any other reason for our readiness to degrade the moral law to the level of our inclinations, with which we are so intimately acquainted? Could there be any other reason, I say, for such an effort being made, on everybody's part, to make out the moral law to be a precept operating in our favour, its concern being to secure our personal advantage rightly understood, except this very circumstance, that we wish to rid ourselves of the deterrent effect exerted upon us [138] by the respect so unrelentingly demanded of us, while yet it places our own unworthiness before our very eyes? However, notwithstanding all this, the truth of the matter is that what we encounter here partakes, on the other hand, *so little* of the nature of *pain* that, once we have divested ourselves of self-conceit, allowing practical influences to the said feeling of respect, the effect is that we can never feast our eyes enough on contemplating the law in all its magnificence, the soul believing itself to be uplifted, according to the extent to which it becomes aware of the superiority of the holy law over itself and its own fragile nature. (Ak78) On the other hand, it is quite true that great talents, and an activity proportionate to them, are likewise capable of evoking respect, or a feeling analogous to it. Moreover, it is quite proper to bestow such a feeling upon them; and so it seems as though admiration and the sentiment here spoken of were one and the same thing. However, on examining the matter more closely, we find that, since, where a skill is concerned, it must always remain a matter of uncertainty what part has been played by innate talent, and what part by the cultivation of that talent and one's own industry, the actual position turns out to be this. When the skill in question is represented to us by reason as something presumably due to cultivation, that is to say, as something meritorious, this has the effect that our self-conceit finds itself markedly diminished, reason either reproaching us, regarding this matter, or else imposing upon us the task that we are to follow such an example in the manner appropriate to us. Therefore, the respect we tender to such a man (strictly speaking, to the law which sets him before us as an example to be followed), is something more than simply admiration. And the truth of this is confirmed by the following considerations. The common run of mere amateurs, [139] once they believe they have ascertained the badness of such a man's character (let us say, of Voltaire), cease having any respect for him. As for the true scholar, on the other hand, he persists in feeling respect, at least inasmuch as the man's talents have to be taken into account. And he adopts this attitude because the business and the calling in which he is implicated is of the kind that, to act in imitation of a man such as this, is something prescribed to him as a law, as it were.

Respect for the moral law is thus the sole motive force operative in moral matters, its being indubitably certain, at the same time, that this is so. And it is true likewise that, whenever anything is made the object of this feeling of respect, it is invariably the law in question which serves as the foundation. What happens first is that, conformably to the judgment laid down by reason, the will is determined, objectively and directly, by the moral law. As for freedom, on the other hand, the causal efficacy of which allows of being determined by virtue of the law, and in no other way, its nature consists precisely in this: that there is a certain limiting condition to which it subjects all inclinations — and with them the esteem in which a person is to be held — namely, that obedience should be rendered to the pure law which has its source in reason. Now this limitation exerts a certain effect upon feeling, bringing with it the sensation of pain of which we have spoken, and that is a circumstance which allows (simply by way of appealing to the nature of the moral law) of being known in an *a priori* manner. But then, the aforesaid effect is, to this extent, merely *negative* in character, taking its rise, as it does, in the influence exerted by pure practical reason, with this principal result: that the activity of the subject (inasmuch as inclinations are the ground determining the choice made) has a check imposed upon it, a check being imposed, along with this, upon the opinion held by that subject regarding its personal worth (this worth, in the absence of agreement with the moral law, being reduced to nothing at all). [140] Thus the effect of this law upon feeling has the nature of a humiliation. Still, this tells us nothing about the power possessed by practical reason as a motive force, but only about the resistance it sets up against the motive forces deriving from sensibility. (Ak79) But then, this very law is, after all, something objective, that is, something which, as regards the way in which the matter is represented by pure reason, is thought of as a ground determining the will directly. Seeing, therefore, that it is only relatively to the purity of the law that there occurs the humiliation of which we have spoken, it follows that the check imposed upon the claims made in defence of our personal esteem (i.e. the humiliation on the side of sensibility) amounts, at the same time, on the intellectual side, to an elevation of the moral, i.e. the practical, esteem in which the law is held. In other words, respect for the moral law is a feeling which, in view of its arising from an intellectual source, is likewise positive in character (a feeling, moreover, which is known to us in an *a priori* manner). And this is so on the ground that any lessening of the obstacles standing in the way of an activity amounts to a furtherance of the activity itself.

Now, as regards the acknowledgement given to the moral law, what it amounts to is consciousness of an activity which takes its rise in practical reason and which rests on objective grounds. Moreover, when it fails to express itself, by way of certain actions being carried into effect, that is solely because there are certain subjective causes, i.e. causes which derive from a pathological source, which stand in the way. Respect for the law, then, has to be looked upon likewise as a positive, though indirect, effect which that law exerts upon feeling, inasmuch as, by way of exposing self-conceit to humiliation, it weakens the influence of the inclinations which oppose themselves as obstacles. In other words, the feeling of respect has to be thought of as the subjective ground of the activity, [141] that is to say, as the *motive force* prompting obedience to the moral law, and providing the ground for adopting maxims such as bring into being a way of life which is in conformity with the law. Now out of the concept of a motive force there arises the concept of a *concern*, this being a property which cannot be attributed to any being except to one endowed with reason, while what is signified is a *force moving* the will, inasmuch as such a force is represented through the instrumentality of reason. But then, since, so far as a morally good will is concerned, it must be the law itself which operates as a moving force, *moral concern* must signify one which is divorced from sensibility and the sole source of which is to be found in practical reason. Now the concept of a *maxim* is likewise based upon this concept of a concern, the consequence of this being that a maxim is morally genuine only in the event that its sole concern is about rendering obedience to the law. As for the nature of the three concepts spoken of here, that of a *motive force*, that of a *concern*, and that of a *maxim*, it has to be observed that all three have application only to beings which are finite. Indeed, they all presuppose a being subject to limitations, a being that is, in which the subjective condition determining choice does not, of its own accord, agree with the objective law, its being required, therefore, that it should be impelled towards activity, by some means or other, because there is an inner obstacle opposing itself to that activity. As for the divine will, therefore, it is impossible that the aforementioned concepts should have any application to it.

There is indeed something striking about the boundless esteem [142] in which we hold the moral law (wholly apart from any advantage it may bring) as practical reason represents it to us, (Ak80) to the intent that we should render obedience to that law, reason's voice ringing out so clearly that even the most audacious among evil-doers is made to tremble and has to hide himself away from its sight. And in consideration of all this, it is small wonder indeed that, as regards the said influence exerted upon feeling by a purely intellectual Idea, it remains to speculative reason an impenetrable mystery, and we must rest content with being able to comprehend at least this much in an *a priori* manner, that, in every finite rational being, the representation of the moral law is invariably bound up with such a feeling. True enough, if this feeling were one derived from what constitutes the pathological element in our nature — if, in other words, it were a feeling of pleasure founded on inner *sense* — it would be entirely in vain to seek to discover, in an *a priori* manner, the connection subsisting between, on the one hand, a certain Idea, and, on the other, the feeling which is here being considered. But then, the feeling in question is one the sole concern of which is with the purposes of practice, the truth of the matter being that, if it attaches itself to a law, it does so solely in respect of the form exhibited by that law, and not on account of any object towards which the law is directed. Therefore, it is impossible to think of having to class this feeling as one of pleasure or pain, while yet it is true that it gives rise to a *concern*, namely, that obedience should be rendered to the moral law, this property to be designated as *moral concern*. And accordingly, the capacity for being concerned about the law in this manner (or, to put it in a different way, the respect in which the law itself is held) is to be termed *moral feeling* strictly speaking.

Consciousness of a *free* submission of the will to the law, attended, however, with an [143] inevitable constraint imposed upon all the inclinations (although, on the other hand, it is our own reason which is the source of such constraint), is what is signified by respect for the law. The law which demands, and, at the same time, infuses, the feeling of respect is, as is easily seen, the moral law, there being no law except this which excludes all inclinations from having an immediate influence over the will. The action which takes place in conformity with the said law, to the exclusion of all determining grounds deriving from inclination, is called an action done from *duty* which, precisely because the said exclusion is bound up with its very concept, carries with it the character of a *constraint*, i.e. that of a determination to perform actions, no matter how *reluctantly* they may be done. The feeling arising from the consciousness of the said constraint is not pathological in character, such as would be the case if it were an object of the senses which brought it into being. On the contrary, it is the one and only feeling pertinent to the requirements of practice, in that it is possible only through priority being allowed to an objective determination of the will and to the causal efficacy residing in reason. Seeing, then, that it is *submission* to a law which is demanded by the feeling in question, the part it plays being that of a command proclaiming that a constraint is to be imposed upon the subject, in so far as it is affected by sensibility, what is involved is not pleasure taken in the action but displeasure. On the other hand, seeing that, if there is a constraint, it is wholly due to the legislation which originates in our *own* reason, the idea of being *uplifted* likewise plays a part here, while, as for the subjective effect exerted upon feeling, there can be no more appropriate name for it than *self-approval*, inasmuch as it is (Ak81) pure practical reason which is the sole cause of everything, and that it is this circumstance which is here taken into account. [144] And indeed, what happens is that, without any other concern of ours intervening, we recognize ourselves as being determined wholly through the law, and that we are thus made conscious of something subjectively engendered, i.e. a concern of a quite different kind, one occupied solely with the interests of practice, and which operates in a *free* manner. Now, to have a concern about a dutiful action is not something which some inclination or other suggests to us as an advisable course to take. On the contrary, it is reason which, through the instrumentality of the practical law, inexorably demands of us that we should have such a concern, and which, moreover, actually brings it into being. And that is why it has affixed to it a name of a quite special kind — the name of respect.

What the concept of duty requires, then, so far as an action is concerned, is that *objectively* it should be in conformity with the law, and as for the maxim underlying it, it requires that, *subjectively*, it should spring from respect for the law, as determination of the law is that through which alone the will is determined. It is upon this that there rests the distinction between being conscious of having acted *in conformity with duty*, and being conscious of having acted *from duty*, that is to say, out of respect for the law. In the former case — that of legality — it is possible that inclinations should have been the sole grounds determining the will, while, as for the latter case — that of *morality* — it is necessary that moral worth should be assigned exclusively to the circumstance that the action was done from duty, i.e. that it was done for the sake of the law and for no other reason.[15]

---

[15] In bestowing careful deliberation upon the concept of respect for persons, as expounded in the above, we are made aware that the said respect rests in every case upon the consciousness of a duty having been done, presented by way of our having an example set before us, and that, accordingly, there can be no other ground for it except a moral one. And indeed, even in the event of one's purpose being psychological, it is a very good thing, and one conducive to one's coming to gain knowledge of human nature, that, whenever one comes across a case of this expression being used, one should pay due regard to the way in which man, in coming to judge things, takes the moral law into consideration, as this way of looking at things, however mysterious and wondrous in character it may be, is yet resorted to on frequent occasions.

[145] Whenever judgments made in the field of morals are to be dealt with, it is of the utmost importance that, in the case of every maxim, one should attend, with the greatest possible punctiliousness, to the subjective principle which is in operation, as it is insisted upon, as a matter of necessity, that all morality assignable to actions must have its *source in duty* and respect for the law, as distinct from feeling love and affection for that which the actions are to bring into being. For man, and indeed for every created rational being, moral necessity exhibits in their case the characteristic of a constraint, that is to say, of an obligation; and every action having such a foundation is to be represented as a duty, not as a mode of procedure for which we already have a liking by ourselves, or else, are capable of developing such a liking. Indeed, the adoption of the latter point of view would be tantamount to supposing that, as regards respect for the law (a condition attended with a fear, or at least a certain anxiety, (Ak82) about our making ourselves guilty of transgression) we might, in the end, reach the point where the said respect could be dispensed with, the possibility being left open that, at one time, we might gain possession of a *holiness* of will. And this would come about by virtue of the fact that, after the fashion of the deity, which is exalted over any and every kind of dependence, there was to be met with in us a coincidence of the will with the pure law of morality, this coincidence having come into being of its own accord, as it were, through its having become second nature to us, while, at the same time, there was no longer any possibility of its being shaken. [146] In the end, then, morality might cease to have the nature of a command for us, seeing that it was no longer conceivable that we should be unfaithful to it.

The truth of the matter, however, is this. The moral law is, for the will of a being endowed with all perfection, a law of *holiness*, while, as regards the will of every finite rational being, it is a law of *duty* and of moral constraint, the determination of the actions performed by such a being arising out of *respect* for the law and reverence for one's duty. The assumption that some other subjective principle should play the part of a motive force is inadmissible, since, in such a case, although the action which results may indeed turn out to be what the law prescribes, it remains true none the less that, as the action, although in conformity with duty, is yet not being done from duty, this has the effect that the attitude of mind by which it is prompted fails to be moral. And this is the very point on which everything hinges, as regards the legislation we are here considering.

It is a fine thing indeed to do good to men out of the love one bears them or because of a feeling of sympathetic benevolence to-

wards them. And the same holds good for acting justly by reason of
the love one has for having things proceed in an orderly manner.
Still, the maxim guiding our conduct here is not as yet the genuinely
moral one, i.e. that which is appropriate to the place which, *as men*,
we occupy among rational beings, seeing that the view we take of
things here allows of being summed up thus. While assuming the
role of men offering voluntary service, as it were, and adopting an
attitude of proud conceit, we dismiss the idea of duty from our minds,
as if we were not subject to any command, and we then set out to
accomplish, solely by virtue of our own good pleasure, the very thing
regarding which — so we say — no commandment is [147] necessary for us. The truth of the matter, however, is this: we are subject to
a *discipline* having its source in reason, and, in respect of all the maxims we adopt, we must never lose sight of this subjection or seek to
diminish it in any way. Moreover, we must never detract from the
authority of the law through any self-seeking illusion, on our part, to
the effect that the ground determining the will, although in conformity with the law, is yet to be assigned to something other than the
law and the respect in which we hold it. Duty and obligation are the
only designations we must affix to the relation in which we stand to
the moral law. We are indeed legislative members of a realm of morals to be rendered possible in virtue of freedom, a realm represented
to us by practical reason as an object of respect. Yet it is true none the
less that we are, at the same time, subjects of that realm and not its
head. And if we misconceive the humble place we occupy as created
beings, our self-conceit leading us on to act in a defiant manner against
the authority of the holy law, this already amounts to an apostasy
(Ak83) from it, as far as its spirit is concerned, even though it may be
fulfilled in the letter.

   We are told *"Love God above everything, and your neighbour as
you love yourself"*.[16] Now the possibility of there being a command
such as this agrees quite well with what has been said. And indeed,
[148] the demand being made here, in the form of a commandment,
is, after all, that respect should be paid to a law which *commands love*;
and it is not left to arbitrary choice whether that love is adopted as a
principle. But then, love of God thought of as an inclination, i.e. as
something deriving from a pathological source, is an impossibility,
seeing that God is not an object of the senses. To bear love to men,

---

[16] There is a strange contrast between this law and the principle of private
happiness, which certain people would wish to declare to be the supreme principle
of morality, the principle of private happiness allowing of being summed up thus:
"Love yourself above everything, and love God and your neighbour for your own sake".

on the other hand, is indeed possible but it cannot be commanded, since it is not within anybody's power to love someone, simply because he has been told to do so. From this it follows that the love in question in this, the most fundamental of laws, is exclusively *practical love*: loving God, as it is understood here, means one *gladly* follows his commandments, and loving one's neighbour means one *gladly* performs all one's duties towards him. On the other hand, the commandment which lays it down that this is to be adopted as one's rule cannot mean that one is commanded to *have* this disposition, as regards one's dutiful actions, but only that one is to *strive* after having it. For the truth of the matter is this. A commandment that we are to do something gladly is self-contradictory, seeing that, if it is already known to us what is obligatory upon us, while, over and above this, we are conscious that we do it gladly, any commandment given would be wholly unnecessary. On the other hand, if we do it, not indeed gladly but out of respect for the law, then a commandment laying it down that this respect is to be the motive force prompting the maxim [149] would have the effect of directly counteracting the disposition of the mind which has been the subject of the command. What this law of all laws does, therefore, — and at the same time holds good for every moral precept to be found in the Gospel — is that it exhibits the moral disposition of mind in all its perfectness, exhibiting it as an ideal of holiness which, while incapable of ever being attained to by any created being, yet serves as an archetype, the obligation imposed upon us being that we are to strive to get ever closer to it and become like it, all this coming about by way of an advance which, although interrupted, yet proceeds *ad infinitum*. And indeed, this is how things stand: were it ever possible for a created rational being to reach a state where it followed all moral laws *gladly* and with no reluctance, that would simply amount to excluding the very possibility of there ever being a desire by which it might be provoked to deviate from them; for the overcoming of such a desire is invariably at the cost of some sacrifice, on the part of the subject, and it thus requires self-constraint, that is to say, an inner compulsion to do what one is not quite glad to do. (Ak84) However, it is never possible for any created being to attain to a moral disposition reaching the degree of moral perfection which has been spoken of — and that for the following reason. Since it is a created being, and since it thus finds itself in a state of dependence, as regards what it requires so as to be wholly content with its condition, it is impossible that it should ever be entirely free from desires and inclinations, seeing that these, resting as they do on physical causes, are not of themselves in agreement with the moral law which derives from quite different sources. And the inevitable consequence of these desires and inclinations intervening is this: that the disposition of the mind, by virtue of which one's maxims are adopted, should at all times be founded upon moral constraint, not upon readily offered devotion — in other words, it should be founded on respect, which *demands* that the law should be obeyed, [150] however unwillingly this may be done, as distinct from being founded upon love, no anxiety being present, in this latter case, lest there be an inner rejection on the part of the will. However, as regards the pure love of the law (the attainment of which would result in the law's ceasing to have the character of a *commandment*, while morality, on its subjective side, was transformed into holiness, ceasing to be *virtue*) we are none the less called upon to set this love before ourselves as the permanent, yet never fully attainable goal of our endeavours. And indeed, what happens, if there be a thing which we hold in high esteem, while yet we are in awe of it, because we are conscious of our weakness, is that, by its becoming easier and easier for us to satisfy the demand made, reverend awe is transformed into affection and respect into love. At any rate, this is what would be signified by a disposition of the mind devoting itself to the law and having been brought to perfection, provided, that is, that it were ever possible for a created being to attain to such a state.

What I have had in mind here, in putting these reflections before the reader, has not been so much to bestow greater distinctness upon the evangelical command quoted above, my aim being to prevent a spirit of *enthusiastic exaltation* coming to prevail in the field of *religion*, as regards the correct view to be taken of the love of God. What I set out to do, instead, was to provide an accurate determination of moral disposition, inasmuch as this has an immediate bearing upon the character belonging to the duties we have towards men, my aim being to combat and, if possible, to prevent the arising, solely within the field of *morals*, of a spirit of *enthusiastic exaltation*, a way of thinking whereby the minds of large numbers of persons tend to be infected. The moral status found by man to be assignable to him (and so far as our insight reaches, the same holds good for every created rational being) is that he should hold the moral law in respect. As for the disposition of mind, which it is obligatory upon him to have, it is that he should obey it from duty, [151] not as the result of an affection spontaneously felt, or of an endeavour which he gladly takes upon himself, and concerning which he has perhaps received no commandment at all. The moral condition which alone is attainable to him at any time is that of *virtue*, that is to say, that of moral

disposition engaged in a *struggle*, not one of *holiness*, as it is pretended that he enjoys *possession of* complete *purity*, concerning the
dispositions of the will. It is simply the result of one's finding oneself
in a state of moral exaltation, and of one's self-conceit having been
carried to extremes, if one sets about exhorting men's minds, by way
of describing to them certain actions as having the quality of nobility
about them, and as being sublime and magnanimous. And indeed,
what one achieves in this way is simply that men fall victim to a
delusion, (Ak85) to the effect that what constitutes the ground determining their actions is not duty, i.e. respect for the law which puts a
yoke upon them which they are *compelled* to bear, whether they like it
or not (although, on the other hand, it is a yoke lightly borne, seeing
that it is our own reason by which it is imposed upon us). Thus,
when human beings follow the law, i.e. *render obedience* to it, this
invariably has the effect that they find themselves humbled. Here,
however, the pretence is that the aforementioned actions are not to
proceed from duty but instead are expected to result from merit pure
and simple. And so, should an imitation of the actions of the sort
described come about, and should it be a principle such as this which
was adopted, the effect would be that the spirit of the law would not
have been satisfied in any manner whatsoever, this spirit consisting
in a submission to the law, on the part of the disposition of the mind,
not in conformity to law, on the part of the action (no matter what
principle is at work). Moreover, seeing that the motive force prompting the action is here *pathological* in character, i.e. based on a feeling
of sympathy, or perhaps even on self-love, as distinct from being
moral, i.e. based on the law, the effect such a way of proceeding has
is to produce a disposition of the mind, unsubstantial, high-flying,
[152] and in pursuit of mere fancies, men flattering themselves that
they are imbued with a spontaneous kindheartedness reaching such
a degree as to stand in no need of any commandment, and not to
require either spur or bridle. And the result of all this is that men
come to be unmindful of their obligation, this being what they ought
to be thinking of rather than of merit. To bestow praise upon other
men's actions performed — and that merely for duty's sake — at the
cost of great sacrifice, and to refer to these by the name of *noble-
minded* and *sublime* deeds, is indeed a permissible procedure. But even
that can be done, only in so far as we are led by all the evidence there is to
suppose that they have been done solely out of respect for duty, and that
it is not stirrings of the heart which are their source. If, on the other
hand, one's purpose is to set such actions before someone as models to be
followed, then it is emphatically necessarily that respect for the law —

the only feeling which is genuinely moral — should be referred to as playing the part of the motive force, the solemn and sacred precept at work here being one that leaves no freedom to our vainglorious self-love to play dalliance with certain impulses of ours which are pathological in character (inasmuch as these have something analogous to morality about them), the precept in question being, moreover, that in virtue of which we are debarred from ever crediting ourselves with possessing *meritorious* worth. And indeed, as regards actions worthy of commendation, we shall invariably find, if only we look hard enough, that there is a law which lays down a *commandment* and which does not leave things at the discretion of our particular propensity to find something to our liking. This is the only way of representing the matter which provides moral cultivation for the soul, because it alone is capable of being founded upon solid and accurately defined principles.

[153] If what is signified by *exaltation*, taken in its most general sense, is the overstepping of the limits set by human reason, in obedience to certain principles, *moral exaltation* is an overstepping of the limits set by practical pure reason. What the latter disallows is that the (Ak86) subjective determining ground of dutiful actions, i.e. the moral motives, should ever be looked for anywhere else but in the law, or that the disposition of the mind thus introduced into the maxims which are adopted should ever be looked for anywhere but in the respect in which the law is held. In other words, what is commanded is that the thought of duty (which strikes down to the ground all *arrogance* as well as the vaingloriousness deriving from *love of self*) is to be made the supreme *principle of life*, as regards any morality to be found in human actions.

Such being the position, it can be seen that the policy of introducing *moral exaltation*, in place of a sober, yet, at the same time, prudent, discipline of morals, is resorted to not only by the writers of novels or by sentimental educationalists (no matter how vigorously that may declaim against sentimentalism) but at times also by philosophers, in fact, even the most rigorous among them, *viz.* the Stoics, although it is true, on the other hand, that the type of exaltation prevalent among the Stoics tended to be of the heroic mould, while the exaltation characteristic of the other men was distinguished rather for its shallow and melting quality. And in consequence of what has been said, one may assert in all truth, without making oneself guilty of hypocrisy, that, as regards the moral teaching propounded in the Gospel, it was there that the moral principle was first exhibited in all its purity. And since it was insisted upon, at the same time, that the

principle was to be made consonant with [154] the limitations holding good for finite beings, the Gospel teaching subjected all good
conduct to be found in men to the discipline of duty set before men's
very eyes, men thus being disallowed to wander about in the midst
of dreamed-of moral perfections. And so it came about that self-
conceit and self-love, which are both so apt to misconceive the limits
set to them, had erected before them barriers founded on humility,
that is to say, in self-knowledge.

Duty, bearer of a name truly great and sublime, you, whose very
nature is averse to seeking favours or to doing anything by way of
seeking to ingratiate yourself, demanding, on the contrary, that you
are to be submitted to, while yet, in seeking to set the will in motion,
you refrain, at the same time, from threatening anything which could
evoke natural aversion in the mind, or else terrify it; but instead of
proceeding in this manner, you restrict yourself to propounding a
law which, of its own accord, finds entry into the mind, and which
procures for itself, however much this may be going against the grain,
a feeling of veneration (although indeed not invariably obedience), a
law before which all the inclinations, even in the event of their secretly operating in opposition to it, are reduced to silence. What is
the fount of your worthy origin, and where do we find the root of
your noble descent which proudly disdains any kinship with the inclinations, that root from which to have sprung is the indispensable
condition of there coming into being that worth which is the only
one which human beings can, through their own efforts, provide for
themselves?

It can be nothing less than that by which man, as part of the
world of sense, find himself raised above himself, that circumstance
in virtue of which he is tied to an order of things capable of being
conceived of by the understanding alone. And as for this order, it is
true, [155] at the same time, that the entire world of sense, and
along with it, man's empirically determinable existence in time, (Ak87)
is something that is subordinated to it, the same holding good for
the system comprising the totality of ends (that system alone having
appropriateness to practical laws of an unconditional character, such
as the moral law). What manifests itself here is nothing other than
personality, that is to say, freedom from, and independence of, the
mechanism governing all nature, as this personality is thought of, at
the same time, as the power possessed by a being subject to specific
laws, namely, pure practical laws, supplied to it by its own reason;
and so the position is that the person, as belonging to the world of
sense, is subjected to its own personality, in so far as it belongs, at the

same time, to the intelligible world. Small wonder, then, if man, belonging as he does to both worlds, when taking into consideration his supreme destiny spoken of second, finds it impossible to contemplate his own nature without a feeling of reverence, and is bound to hold the laws governing that destiny in the highest respect.

A number of expressions which designate the worth of objects in conformity with moral Ideas are attributable to this origin. The moral law is *holy*, i.e. inviolable. As for man, he is indeed far from holy, while yet *humanity*, in his own person, must be holy to him. In the whole of creation anything and everything over which one has power may be used also *as a mere means*. Only man, and with him every rational creature, is an [156] *end in himself*. For he is the subject of the moral law, which is holy, and is so by virtue of the autonomy arising from his freedom. And indeed, it is for the sake of this autonomy that every will, in fact, even every person's own will, directed towards the person himself, is made subject to a condition: namely, that it should be in agreement with the *autonomy* appertaining to a rational being. What is being laid down is that the rational being must not be subjected to any purpose, with regard to which it would be impossible for it to come into existence in conformity with a law arising from the passive subject's own will. In other words, it is never to be used as a mere means but always, at the same time, as an end in itself. Moreover, the aforesaid condition is rightly attached even to the divine will, as regards the way in which it deals with the rational beings in the world, inasmuch as they are its creations; for it rests upon the circumstance that they have a *personality*, and it is by virtue of this alone that they are ends in themselves.

This Idea of personality, which arouses a feeling of respect in us, places before our very eyes the sublimity of our nature, as regards the destiny we are marked out for, while, at the same time, through our being made aware that, in our conduct, there is a lack of accordance with the said Idea, the effect produced is that it strikes down our self-conceit. And indeed, this is something natural and readily discernible to human reason, even to one operating on the most ordinary level. Is it not a fact that any man, even one endowed with an honesty no more than average, has found, on occasions, that he has refrained from telling an otherwise harmless lie which would have had the effect of extricating him (Ak88) from a troublesome situation, or perhaps would even have been of advantage to a well-deserving [157] friend whom he holds dear — and that he acted in the way he did solely to prevent his being under the necessity of having a secret contempt for himself in his own eyes? Can it be denied that an honest man, finding himself in the greatest distress that life can bring, a distress he could have escaped from, if only he had set duty at naught, is sustained by the consciousness that he has, in spite of it all, preserved the dignity of humanity in his own person, that there is no reason why he should be ashamed of himself, or why he should stand in dread of facing the inward glance of self-examination? This consolation is not happiness, not even in the smallest degree; for there is no one who would wish to be in that position, perhaps not even anyone who would desire to be alive in such circumstances. But he continues living, and what he cannot endure is that, in his own eyes, he should be unworthy of life. This condition of being inwardly set at rest is thus purely negative in character, as regards anything capable of making life pleasant, for what it amounts to is the averting of the danger of one's personal worth sinking in a situation where the worth of one's outward condition has already been given up as entirely lost. What is operative, as regards this state of being set at peace, is the effect of a respect entertained for something quite other than life, something by comparison with which, and in contrast with which, life, with all its pleasantness, is devoid of any worth whatsoever. If the man goes on living, that is solely for duty's sake, and not because he finds the least satisfaction in life.

[158] Here, then, we have the one authentic motive force operative within the domain of pure practical reason, and this is the character exhibited by it. It is nothing else but the pure moral law itself, in so far as it stirs up in us a feeling for the sublimity appertaining to our supersensible existence, and in so far as, along with this, it engenders, on its subjective side, a feeling of respect for their higher destiny, on the part of human beings who are, at the same time, conscious of their sensible existence and of their consequent dependence on their nature as being, to a very considerable extent, affected by influences deriving from a pathological source. Now it is indeed perfectly possible to combine with the aforesaid motive force so many attractive and pleasant features of life that, for the sake of these alone, it would be the wisest choice, on the part of a follower of Epicurus distinguished for good sense, if, on reflecting on the question where the greatest possible well-being was to be found, the decision he came to was in favour of good conduct. Moreover, it might be an advisable course even that, as regards this supreme moving cause which is competent by itself to determine what ought to be done, one should set out to combine it with the prospect of a cheerful enjoyment of life. Still, if such a policy is adopted, this should be solely by way of providing a counterpoise against the blandishments which vice does not

fail to offer on the opposite side. On the other hand, when it is duty which is in question, it is essential that the power which, properly speaking, sets us in motion should not be assigned to this circumstance. And indeed, the suggestion that such was the case would amount to one's intending to contaminate the moral disposition at its very source. (Ak89) The essential dignity appertaining to duty has nothing to do with enjoyment of life. It has its own peculiar law and its own peculiar tribunal. And indeed, even though one should set about shaking the two together, using one's strength to the utmost, while offering them, [159] mixed up with one another, as a medicine, as it were, to be administered to the ailing soul, the effect will only be that, in no time at all, they will, of their own accord, part company. And if that does not happen, there can be only one result, namely, that the moral ingredient will fail to be of any effect at all, while, even though physical life might gain some strength in the process, moral life would vanish away altogether, with no possibility whatever of its being rescued.

CRITICAL ELUCIDATION
OF THE ANALYTIC
OF PURE PRACTICAL REASON.

By a critical elucidation of a science, or of the branch of a science which by itself constitutes a system, I understand an enquiry, offered by way of vindication, into the question why it should have to exhibit a certain systematic form and no other, a comparison being instituted between it and a different system based on a cognitive faculty of a similar nature. Now practical and speculative reason are based upon the same cognitive faculty to this extent, that it is *pure reason* which is operative in both cases. The difference between them, in respect of their systematic form, will, therefore, have to be accurately determined, by way of comparing them with one another; and the ground why there should be such a difference will have to be specified.

The Analytic which formed a part of the enquiry into pure theoretical reason was concerned with objects [160] which were of such a kind as to permit it that they should be presented to the understanding by way of their being given. It was necessary, therefore, that one should start out from *intuition*; or, in other words, seeing that intuition can never be anything but sensible in character, from sensibility; that it was to be, subsequently to this, that one came to concern oneself with concepts (relating to the objects of that intuition), and ending up with *principles* of the understanding only after intuition and concepts had been dealt with. Practical reason, on the other hand, is not directed towards objects, with a view to gaining knowledge of them, but with its own faculty of *making* objects *real* (in accordance with the knowledge of these objects at its disposal). In other words, it is concerned with a *will*, the nature of the will being that of a causal efficacy, inasmuch as it is reason which provides the ground determining it. It is, therefore, not an object of intuition which is to be set forth, but instead, reason, in its character as practical reason, has *only* one task to perform, namely, *to set forth a law* (the concept of causality invariably involving a law which determines the existence of the constituents of a manifold, in respect of the relation in which they stand to one another).

And so it is that a Critique of reason embarked upon in the present Analytic, has (inasmuch as it is practical reason which is operative here, this being the very problem to be solved) to start out by enquiring into the *possibility* of (Ak90) there being *a priori practical* principles. It was only after having done so that the Analytic was in a position to proceed to an examination of the *concepts* pertaining to practical reason — i.e. the concepts of the absolutely good and the absolutely evil — with a view to exhibiting them in conformity with the aforesaid principles, there being no possibility that any cognitive faculty should, antecedently to these principles, supply concepts as having reference to that which was looked upon as good or evil. And it was only after all that had been done that the section could be concluded in the last chapter, [161] which dealt with the relation subsisting between pure practical reason and sensibility and with the necessary and *a priori* knowable influence exerted by pure practical reason over sensibility, that is to say, which dealt with *moral feeling*. The Analytic of practical pure reason thus proceeded in a manner entirely analogous to what was done in the Analytic which concerned itself with questions of theory, and had this in common with it: it examined, in their entirety, all the conditions subject to which reason was to be used, with this difference, however, that the order was reversed. The Analytic of pure reason, in the theoretical field, was divided into Transcendental Aesthetic and Transcendental Logic, that of practical reason, conversely, into Logic and Aesthetic of pure practical reason (if I may be permitted, merely for the sake of analogy, to employ these expressions here which, in other respects, are quite unsuitable). The Logic, in its turn, was there divided into an Analytic of concepts and one of principles; here into one of principles and of concepts. As for the Aesthetic, it was there sub-divided into two further parts, by reason of the fact that sensible intuition exhibited itself in two forms, while here sensibility is not thought of as a capacity for intuiting at all, but merely as a feeling capable of operating as a subjective ground of desire. And in consideration of this, the investigation into pure practical reason allows of no further sub-divisions.

The reason is likewise easily comprehended why the division into two parts, along with their sub-divisions, has actually not been adopted here (although, to begin with, one might well have been induced to make such an attempt, led on by the example set by the first Critique). [162] Since it is *pure reason*, in its practical employment, which is here being examined, and since, accordingly, one sets out not from empirical grounds of determination but from *a priori* principles, the division of the Analytic of pure practical reason will have to take a form resembling that of a syllogism. What happens is this. Starting out from the universal which is contained in the *major*, that is to say, from the moral principle, one then proceeds, in the *minor*, to carry out the task of subsuming under the major certain possible actions that are to be looked upon as either good or evil; and next one goes on to the *conclusion*, i.e. to the subjective determination of the will (which here is a concern about the good to be rendered possible in virtue of practical action, and about the maxim founded on this circumstance). (Ak91) Those who have been able to convince themselves of the truth of the propositions set forth in the Analytic will derive pleasure from comparisons such as these; for they will rightly arouse the expectation in them that one day they may be successful in gaining insight into the unity appertaining to the entire pure employment of reason, on its theoretical as well as on its practical side, and that they will be in a position to derive everything from the one principle. And indeed, the ability to do so is an inescapable requirement on the part of human reason which can never find itself fully satisfied except in achieving complete systematic unity of its cognitions.

If, then, we take into consideration likewise the content of the knowledge which it is possible for us to have of pure practical reason, and by means of it (as that knowledge is set forth in the Analytic dealing with the said faculty), we find that, while there is a remarkable analogy between this Analytic and the one dealing with questions of theory, [163] there are at the same time differences just as remarkable. As regards the theoretical Analytic, the existence of a *faculty* which provides *rational knowledge* of a *pure* and *a priori* character could be established quite easily and in a manner carrying conviction, by way of referring to examples taken from the sciences. And indeed, seeing that the principles operative in the sciences are, by the methodical use to which they are put, tested in so many different ways, there is less danger, than is the case with knowledge of the ordinary sort, of there being a secret admixture of grounds of knowledge derived from empirical sources. On the other hand, as regards the circumstance that pure reason has of itself the power of exerting practical efficacy, with no admixture of any determining grounds derived from experience, it must be possible, I say, to demonstrate this by referring to the manner in which *reason* is *used in the most ordinary* circumstances, in the field of *practice*, the credential which is provided for the supreme practical principle being this: that the natural reason of every human being acknowledges it — in a manner wholly *a priori* and independent of all sensible data — as the supreme principle by which the will of man is governed. What was necessary, first of all, was to provide confirmation and justification of the principle, by showing that purity of origin was assigned to it, even in the *judgment of the said ordinary reason*. And it was only after this task had been performed that the principle could be taken in hand by science, with a view to making use of it. The principle had thus to be looked upon as a fact, as it were, taking precedence, and excluding every possibility of engaging in sophisticated reasonings concerning its possibility and the inferences to be drawn from it. On the other hand, that this should be the true state of the case can be explained by reference to something pointed out a short way back. Practical pure reason is under the necessity of beginning with principles; and from this it follows that any scientific enquiry undertaken in this field must occupy itself with these principles as the first [164] data upon which everything else is to be founded, the possibility thus being precluded that it should be science which first gave rise to the principles. However, this justification of moral principles — to be thought of as principles derived from pure reason — merely by way of appealing to the judgment laid down by man's ordinary understanding, is quite feasible and a sufficiently safe procedure to adopt, for the following reason. Anything of an empirical nature, seeking to play the part of a ground determining the will and being (Ak92) desirous to introduce itself by stealth into our maxims, at once *makes itself known* for what it is, by virtue of the feeling of pleasure or pain necessarily attaching to it, inasmuch as it has its source in desire, while pure practical reason proceeds right away to *offer resistance* to it, and to forbid it to have entry into its principle as a condition upon which it was to be made dependent. The heterogeneity of the determining grounds — the empirical, as distinct from the rational — is signified by this antagonism on the part of reason (which plays the part of legislator in the field of practice) to any inclination seeking to intervene, this taking place by virtue of a specific kind of *sentiment*, which, however, does not precede the legislation, but, on the contrary, owes its existence to it alone, the nature of the sentiment in question being that of a constraint. It is a feeling exhibiting respect which is here in operation, a feeling such as no man has for inclinations, of whatever kind they may be. Yet men *do* feel respect for the law, the difference between the two cases being so clearly marked and of so striking a character that no man, not even one equipped with but the most ordinary capacity for understanding, could fail to become aware in an instant, on the occasion of having an example presented to him, of this circumstance: that while empirical [165] grounds of willing might indeed suggest to him that he should follow the attractions they offer, only one thing could take it upon itself to demand that he should *render obedience* to it, namely, the pure practical law which owes its origin to reason.

There, then, is that distinction between the *doctrine of happiness*, on the one hand, and, on the other, the *doctrine of morals*, the former being based entirely upon empirical principles, whereas in the case of the latter, they fail to play any part whatsoever. And to bring out the contrast between them is the first and foremost task incumbent upon the Analytic of pure practical reason, in the performance of which it must proceed as *scrupulously*, or one might say, *painstakingly*, as any geometrician has to do in pursuit of his business. As for the philosopher, however, there are greater difficulties he has to contend with here (the same being true of any rational knowledge which advances on the strength of mere concepts, no construction of concepts being in question); this is attributable to the circumstance that, his present concern being with a reality which is purely noumenal in character, he is unable to place reliance upon any intuition as forming the foundation of the concepts he is dealing with. Still, the philosopher has this advantage: proceeding in almost the same way as a chemist does, he is at all times in a position to carry out an experiment, the object of this experiment being the power of practical reason to be met with in every human being, and its purpose is to discriminate between the moral, i.e. the pure, ground of determination and, on the other hand, a ground deriving from an empirical source. This would be the procedure taken if, for example, he referred to the empirically affected will (let us say, that of a man wishing to tell a lie, because he could gain an advantage by this) and placed the moral law, as a ground determining action, side by side with the will as affected by a motive deriving from an empirical source. Things would then be very much as they were are when a man versed in chemical analysis adds alkali to a solution of lime in hydrochloric acid, the acid at once separating from the lime, and combining [166] with the alkali, while the lime is precipitated. Correspondingly to this, let us suppose that an honest man (or else, one who does no more than put himself, on this occasion, in the place of an honest man) (Ak93) has the moral law presented to him by virtue of which he is made to realize the worthlessness of a man who is a liar. The immediate result will be that the man's practical reason, as to the judgment it makes about what ought to be done by him, separates itself from the advantage to be gained, and unites itself with that which preserves the respect in which he holds his own personality, that is to say, with truthfulness. But then, as for the advantage having had all admixture of anything pertaining to reason removed and cleared away from it, it is now being pondered over by everyone finding himself in these circumstances, the rule being laid down that, though it may very well be the case that the advantage should enter into combination with reason in different circumstances, it must never do so where there is the possibility that it is contrary to the moral law, from which reason never separates itself. On the contrary, it must remain united to it in the most intimate manner conceivable.

The *distinction* between the principle of happiness and that of morality does not, however, immediately imply that they are *incompatible* with one another. What is demanded by pure practical reason is not that the claims to happiness should be renounced, but only that they should be *left out of account altogether*, when it is duty which is in question. Indeed, in certain respects it can even be our duty to provide for our happiness, partly because this may involve the presence of certain means requisite for the performance of our duty (the possession of a skill, of good health, of riches — in that order), and partly because want of happiness, due, [167] for example, to poverty, may involve temptations for transgressing one's duty. Only one thing is out of the question, namely, that promotion of one's happiness should ever be the immediate source of duty; still less is it possible that it should be the principle underlying all duty. Seeing, then, that all grounds determining the will, with the sole exception of the pure practical law issuing in reason, i.e. of the moral law, are invariably empirical in character, and seeing further that, by virtue of this very circumstance, they come under the principle of happiness, it is essential that one should separate them off, one and all, from the supreme principle of morality, never embodying them in it as a condition upon which it is to be made dependent. And indeed, if that were done, the effect would be that all moral worth was brought to nought altogether, in the same way as, in the case of geometrical principles, the admixture of anything deriving from empirical sources brings to nought all mathematical evidence — a fact about mathematics which, in the judgment of Plato, is its most excellent attribute, and which is indeed a feature taking precedence over any utility it may have.

On the other hand, there was no way of establishing the supreme principle deriving from pure practical reason by way of supplying a deduction of it, that is to say, by offering an explanation accounting for the possibility of there being an *a priori* cognition of this sort. And all we could do instead was draw attention to the circumstance that, provided we were capable of comprehending the possibility of there being an efficient cause operative through the instrumentality of freedom, we should likewise be in a position to comprehend not merely the possibility, but the necessity, that the moral law must be declared to be the supreme practical law for rational beings such as are to be thought of as endowed with freedom, as regards the causal efficacy exerted by their will. And the reason why this is the true account of the matter is that the two concepts are so inseparably bound up with one another that practical freedom could be legitimately defined as (Ak94) independence of the will of anything except only the moral law. [168] Yet the supposition that an efficient cause should be brought into operation through the instrumentality of freedom is something the possibility of which we are wholly incapable of comprehending, particularly when it is to be thought of as taking place within the world of sense. Indeed, we are fortunate enough, if we have sufficient guarantee that no proof establishing the impossibility of freedom is capable of being brought forward, and if, by virtue of the moral law, which postulates freedom, we find ourselves obliged, and, for this very reason, also entitled, to presuppose the existence of freedom. However, in spite of all that, there are, after all, a good many people who still hold on to the belief that freedom allows of being explained on empirical principles, like every other power nature has endowed us with, looking upon freedom as a *psychological* attribute, the explanation of which requires nothing more than an investigation into the *nature of the soul* and into the motive force prompting the will, in contradistinction from freedom thought of as a *transcendental* predicate pertaining to the causal efficacy exerted by a being which belongs to the world of sense (this being the point which alone is pertinent here). These men forfeit the glorious disclosure pure practical reason has vouchsafed to us through the instrumentality of the moral law — the disclosure, that is, of an intelligible world which has reality bestowed upon it by virtue of the concept of freedom which, in every other way, is something transcending our knowledge. Moreover, the procedure adopted by these men results in bringing to naught the moral law itself which, by its very nature, can never grant admittance to any determining ground which derives from an empirical source. In view of all this, then, it is essential that we should here add a number of observations, by way of protesting against such a system of delusions and against the way in which things are represented by *empiricism* in all its threadbare superficiality.

[169] The concept of causality thought of as partaking of *natural necessity* (as distinct from causality taking place by virtue of *freedom*) pertains only to the existence of things, in so far as it is *determinable in*

time, that is to say, pertains to them only in respect of the character which is assignable to them as appearances, as distinct from the causal efficacy exerted by them, inasmuch as they are things-in-themselves. Now if the properties displayed by things, in respect of the existence they have in time, are taken to be properties attaching to them as things-in-themselves (which is the ordinary way of representing the matter), this results in there being no way at all of reconciling necessity, in respect of causal relatedness, with freedom, but that the two are instead contradictorily opposed to one another. And indeed, what is implied by the former conception is that every event and, accordingly, likewise every action occurring at a certain point in time, is necessarily determined by what has happened in time past. But then, since that past time is something over which I have no longer any power, it follows that every action I perform must be rendered necessary by virtue of determining grounds which are *not within my power* — in other words, that I am never free at the point of time when I am acting. And indeed, the truth of the matter is that, even though I were to suppose that my whole existence had to be looked upon as independent of any cause other than myself, independent, for example, of God, and that none of the (Ak95) grounds determining my existence were external to myself, such a state of affairs would not in the least have the effect of transforming the said natural necessity into freedom; for it would still remain true that I was, at any point of time, subject to the necessity of being determined to [170] action by what was *not within my power*. That is, in obedience to an order of things already predetermined, it would merely continue the series of events, infinite in respect of what had gone before, this series thus being one which never in any circumstance began of itself, while the causal efficacy exerted by me would invariably exhibit the characteristic of a natural chain steadily continued, and never that of freedom.

If, therefore, one proposes to assign the property of freedom to a being whose existence is determined in time, one cannot (at least, not in the sense specified) exempt it from the law of natural necessity, as regards all the events pertaining to its existence, and, consequently also, as regards its actions; for that would amount to leaving it at the mercy of mere chance. Now since the law in question inevitably applies to whatever causal efficacy things exhibit, in so far as their *existence* is determinable *in time*, it would follow that, if it was in this manner likewise that the existence of things had to be represented in the character pertaining to them as *things-in-themselves*, freedom would have to be rejected as a futile concept involving an impossibility. And thus, if one still desires to salvage freedom, there is only one way left, namely, that the existence of a thing as determinable in time — and accordingly, likewise the causal efficacy which it exerts in obedience to the law of *natural necessity* — should be assigned to it, *merely*, inasmuch as its character is that of an *appearance*, while *freedom* is assigned *to the very same being, in so far as it is a thing-in-itself.* To adopt such a procedure is indeed inevitable, if one wishes to maintain, at one and the same time, these two concepts which are so antagonistic to one another. Still, great difficulties arise when one comes to apply them, combining them in reference to one and the same action, [171] while setting out to render such a combination intelligible. And so it seems as though the attempt to combine them with one another was not really feasible.

If I assert, with regard to a man who has committed theft, that his deed is in conformity with the law of natural causality, the necessary consequence of certain determining grounds which belong to the time preceding his action, this means that it was impossible that it should have been left undone. In what way, then, should judging things by the standard set by the moral law make any difference to this, presupposing that the deed could, after all, have been left undone, because what the law proclaims is that it ought to have been left undone? In other words, how is it possible that, with regard to one and the same action, a man should be declared to be wholly free at the same point in time — and in precisely the same respect — at which he is subject to an inescapable necessity of nature? (Ak96) There are those who would seek to escape from the dilemma by dwelling upon the *kind* of determining ground at work in the causal efficacy exerted by man in accordance with the law of nature, while seeking to accommodate it to a concept of *comparative* freedom. In conformity with this, a free effect is sometimes spoken of where the natural ground determining a thing resides *inwardly* in the thing which acts. For example, we speak in this way of what happens when a projectile is in free motion, the word freedom being used here, on the ground that, while the thing is in motion, it is not propelled by anything external to it. Or else, the movement made by a watch is called a free movement, because it is the watch which sets the hands in motion, [172] there being no need that they should be pushed by anything external. In the same way, the actions of men (notwithstanding that they are necessary by virtue of their determining grounds antecedent to them in time) are yet called free, because what is at work is, after all, inner representations produced by our own powers — desires being engendered by these, as occasion serves — and because, in consequence, what results are actions carried into effect by ourselves and at our own discretion. However, as regards all this, it is, in fact, nothing more than a miserable makeshift, while it is true enough, on the other hand, that certain people still let themselves be fobbed off with this sort of thing, coming to imagine that, by engaging in petty juggling about words, they have arrived at a solution of this difficult problem, so difficult indeed that men have, for thousands of years, been labouring in vain to solve it. Accordingly, it is scarcely probable that its solution should be found to lie so entirely on the surface. And indeed, if the question concerns that freedom upon which all moral laws, as well as the responsibility consequent upon these, are to be founded, it does not matter whether the causality, determined in conformity with a law of nature, acquires its necessary character through determining grounds residing *within* the subject or *outside* it, and if the former be the case, whether the causality in question acquires its necessary character through the operation of instinct or through determining grounds conceived of by reason. If, as is indeed admitted by these men themselves, the determining representations here in question have the grounds of their existence, after all, in something existing in time, namely, in the *preceding state* — this state, in turn, depending on one by which it is preceded — it is of no account whatever whether these determinations are inner ones, exhibiting psychological, as distinct from mechanical, causality, [173] whether, that is, they produce action by virtue of representation or by virtue of bodily movement. And indeed, no matter how much they may differ from one another in this respect, it remains true none the less that the said *determining grounds* refer to a species of causality which pertains to a being, in so far as the existence of that being is one determined in time. In other words, if they impose necessity, they do so by way of having reference to conditions which belong to past time, i.e. to conditions which are *no longer within the subject's power* at the moment when it is called upon to act. Hence the determining grounds at work, while allowing psychological freedom (if one wishes to use this term to signify a purely internal concatenation of representations arising in the soul), carry with them a necessity which appertains to nature. In other words, they leave no room for (Ak97) *transcendental freedom*, which must be conceived of as a state of independence of everything empirical, and thus of nature in general, no matter whether it is considered as an object of inner sense, located in time only, or whether it is considered as an object likewise of the external senses, located in both space and time. But then, in the absence of such freedom (taken in its proper signification to which we have just drawn attention), its being that species of freedom which alone has *a priori* efficacy in the field of practice — in the absence of that freedom, I say, there can be no moral law, nor can there be any imputation in conformity with it. And it is for this very reason that all necessity pertaining to things in time, in accordance with the law of natural causality, may be given the name of a *mechanism* of nature, notwithstanding the fact that the things so designated do not have to be actual *machines* in the material sense. What is being taken into consideration here is merely the necessity pertaining to the connection of events in a temporal series, as it unfolds itself in accordance with the law of nature; [174] and it is of no significance whether the subject with which this process occurs is to be entitled an *automaton materiale* (in which case it is matter that provides the impelling force for the entity which partakes of the nature of a machine) or whether, with Leibniz, we entitle it an *automaton spirituale*, where the propelling force is provided by representations. If the freedom of the will is nothing but the one spoken of last (let us call it psychological, or comparative, freedom, as distinct from transcendental, and thus absolute, freedom), it would be the freedom enjoyed by a turnspit, a contrivance which likewise, once it has been wound up, performs its movements of itself.

There is the case at present occupying our attention, namely, the apparent incompatibility between natural mechanism and freedom as applied to one and the same action. Now what one has to do to be able to show up the falsity of the supposition in question is to remind oneself of the assertions made in the Critique of pure reason as well as of the conclusions to be drawn from these. It was pointed out there that the said natural necessity, which did not allow of being made consistent with the possession of freedom, on the part of the subject, had application exclusively to the properties manifested by that thing which was subject to conditions pertaining to time, thus attaching to the acting subject only in its character as an appearance. It is to this extent only that the grounds determining each and every action of that subject resided in that which belongs to past time, and which, accordingly, is *no longer within the subject's power* (there having to be included in this the deeds already done by the subject, as well as the character attributable to it, by virtue of these, a character which, in the subject's own eyes, has the status of a phenomenon it finds itself presented with). However, [175] the very same subject, being likewise conscious of itself as having the character of a thing-in-itself, considers its existence, also *in so far as conditions pertaining to time have no authority over it*; and it looks upon itself as determinable by no laws except such as it lays down for itself under the guidance of its own reason. Now as regards this aspect of its existence, it takes the view that there is nothing antecedent to the determination of the will. On the contrary, any action, indeed any determination of its existence at all (undergoing variation in accordance with the condition by which inner sense finds itself affected), (Ak98) in point of fact, the whole series of its existence, in so far as it belongs to the world of sense, is looked upon, in the consciousness it has of its intelligible existence, as a consequence of the causal efficacy appertaining to it, inasmuch as it has the character of a *noumenon*, and never as a ground upon which the said causal efficacy is dependent. Viewing the matter in this light, the rational being can rightly say, with regard to every unlawful action it performs, that it could have been left undone — and this notwithstanding the fact that the said action, *quâ* an appearance, is sufficiently determined by what has happened in past time, and that, in this sense, it is due to an inescapable necessity. And indeed, the view here taken of things amounts to this. The action in question, and along with it, the entire past conditioning it, is thought of as constituting a single phenomenon, that of the character of the rational being, supplied by itself, without aid from any other source, and it is in conformity with this character that it imputes to itself, as a cause wholly independent of sensibility, the causality governing the appearances in question.

The judicial pronouncements delivered by conscience — that wondrous faculty to be met with in ourselves — are in perfect agreement with what we have pointed out. [176] In remembering an unlawful deed, a man may use as much artifice as he pleases, seeking to picture that deed to himself as the result of an unintentional error, as due to mere carelessness which can never be wholly avoided — in other words, as a thing regarding which he has been carried away by the stream of natural necessity. Still, what he discovers is that the advocate speaking in his favour has by no means the power of reducing to silence the accuser within himself, provided only he is conscious that, at the time when he did the deed, he was in his senses, that is to say, in possession of his freedom. He might none the less *offer an explanation* of his transgression, arguing that it was due to a certain bad habit he had contracted through a gradual failure to pay proper attention to himself, this reaching such a degree that he was entitled to look upon what he had done as being the natural consequence of that bad habit. Still, the man finds that none of this is effective in securing him against self-reproach and the reprimand which he administers to himself. As for the state of feeling repentance over a deed committed in time long past, at every remembrance of that deed, it is one which rests on the same foundation, its nature being that of a painful sentiment engendered by a moral disposition of the mind. Still, it is a feeling which, as regards the purposes of practice, is devoid of significance, seeing that it cannot serve to undo what has been done. And indeed, if that were the intention, it would be absurd. (The view that repentance is, in fact, absurd is one taken by Priestley who, in advocating it, assumed the part of the *fatalist* reasoning in a consistent manner. And surely, in connection of his sincerity, he is deserving of higher commendation that are the men who, while, in actual fact, hold that it is mechanism which governs the will, [177] proclaim freedom of the will with their words, wishing it to be understood that they propose to embody the said repentance within their syncretistic system, (Ak99) while yet they are not in a position to render an imputation of this sort comprehensible.) On the other hand, if repentance, thought of as a feeling of pain, has validity conceded to it, such a procedure is perfectly appropriate, in consideration of the following circumstance: that, when what is in question is the law governing our intelligible existence (i.e. the moral law), reason acknowledges no distinctions concerning the time at which something occurred, the only thing it enquires into being whether a certain act is attributable to me as my deed. And if it is, it is one and the same sentiment which becomes invariably associated with it, no matter whether the deed is happening now or whether it happened in time long past. Indeed, the position may be summed up thus. When considered in reference to the *intelligible* consciousness, that is to say, in reference to freedom, the life *pertaining to sensibility* exhibits the absolute unity of but a single phenomenon which (seeing that it contains mere appearances deriving from the disposition of the mind which is the concern of the moral law, that is to say, deriving from the character) must be judged not by the standard of natural necessity appertaining to it, inasmuch as it is an appearance, but by the standard of the absolute spontaneity of freedom.

One, therefore, may concede — provided we had the power of gaining so thorough an insight into a man's way of thinking, as it manifests itself in his actions, internal as well as external, that every motive force prompting him, even the least significant, became known to us, and that all external occasions having an effect upon these became known to us at the same time — that we could calculate the man's future conduct with the same degree of certitude as we can calculate the eclipse of the moon or the sun. Yet we should still be entitled [178] to assert that man was a being endowed with freedom. And indeed, if an additional insight into the nature of things were within our power, that of having at our disposal an intellectual intuition of the same subject (a faculty which, however, has by no means been granted to us, our being compelled instead to place sole reliance upon the concept with which reason supplies us,) then we should be made aware, after all, of the circumstance that this whole chain of appearances was, as regards what could be of any concern from the point of view of the moral law, dependent on the spontaneity exerted by the subject, inasmuch as it is a thing-in-itself, a spontaneity exhibiting a characteristic which does not allow of any physical explanation. Now, in default of such a power of intuition, it is the moral law which assures us of the legitimacy of the distinction to be drawn between, on the one hand, the relationship subsisting when actions are, in their character as appearances, looked upon as pertaining to us, inasmuch as we partake of the nature of sensible beings, and, on the other hand, that relationship by virtue of which this sensible being is itself brought into relation with the supersensible substrate to be met with in us.

This view of the matter, which is natural to our reason, though, at the same time, it is incapable of offering any explanation of it, may serve to justify certain judgments which, although passed with complete scrupulousness, yet seem, at first sight, to be contrary to all fairness. There are cases of men who, from childhood onwards, notwithstanding their receiving an education which proved profitable when others received it at the same time, display, so early in their lives a malicious disposition, advancing ever further on their course as they reach manhood, that one considers them to be born villains and looks upon them, so far as their conduct is concerned, as entirely incorrigible. Yet, in spite of it all, [179] (Ak100) one passes judgment upon them because of what they do or leave undone, and reprimands their criminal acts as the result of their own guilt. And in fact, they — the children — themselves believe these reprimands to be perfectly justified, just as though, notwithstanding the hopelessness of their natural disposition attributed to them, they remained just as responsible as every other human being. This could not happen unless it is presupposed that everything arising from a person's choice (as is doubtless the case with every action intentionally performed) is founded upon a causal efficacy having its source in freedom, which expresses its character, from earliest youth, in the appearances to which it gives rise, that is to say, in the actions performed, which, by virtue of the uniformity displayed by them, as regards the way a person conducts himself, give evidence of a natural connectedness. It is not, however, this latter circumstance which renders necessary the lamentable condition of the will. On the contrary, the condition of the will is the consequence of certain evil principles, showing no variation, which have been voluntarily adopted, a circumstance which makes the man in question all the more despicable and worthy of punishment.

However, there is still one difficulty to be faced by freedom, in so far as it is to be combined with natural mechanism in a being that belongs to the world of sense, a difficulty which, even though everything said so far was to be conceded, would still have the effect of threatening freedom with complete annihilation. And yet, notwithstanding that danger, there is, at the same time, one circumstance arousing the hope that there might, after all, be a happy outcome for the assertion of freedom: [180] namely, that the same difficulty presses much more heavily (and, in fact, as we shall soon see, exclusively) upon the system whereby the existence of things as determinable in space and time is taken to be the existence pertaining to them as things-in-themselves. This being the position, there will indeed be no need for us to abandon our fundamental presupposition concerning the ideality of time as a mere form of sensible intuition, and as being no more than a mode of representation which attaches to the subject, inasmuch as it belongs to the world of sense. And all that will be necessary is to reconcile the view we take of the nature of sensible existence with the Idea of freedom.

The difficulty we have in mind may be stated thus. Let the possibility be conceded to us that, in respect of an action coming up for consideration, the intelligible subject should remain free, notwithstanding the fact that, as a subject belonging to the world of sense, it is mechanically conditioned in respect of the very same action. Now let us assume further that *God*, to be thought of as the all-embracing original being, must likewise be the *cause* responsible for the *existence of substance*. (And the assertion that such is his nature can never be abandoned, without this having the effect of our likewise doing away with the concept of God as the being of all beings, and along with this, with his all-sufficiency, an attribute of his on which everything centres in theology.) But then, if that is the correct view, it seems as though another thing had to be conceded, *viz.* that the actions of man had their determining (Ak101) ground in something *wholly beyond man's control*, namely, in a causal efficacy deriving from a supreme being, distinct from man, as man's existence is completely dependent on that being, the same thing holding good, in its entirety, for the causal efficacy which he exerts. [181] And indeed, but for the fact that the actions of man which appertain to him, as that which determines his existence in time, are determinations of him merely as an appearance and not as a thing-in-itself, there would be no way of coming to the rescue of freedom. Man would be like a puppet, like one of the automatic contrivances which Vaucanson designed, put together and wound up by the master who stands supreme in producing articles of art. As for the consciousness man had of himself, it is true that it would make a thinking automaton of him. Still, if the consciousness of spontaneity present in such a being were taken to be freedom, this would simply be a delusion, because it would deserve that name only in a comparative sense, seeing that, although the proximate determining causes of motion, as well as a long series of these, up to those which, in their turn, determined that series, would all be internal, it would still remain true that the one encountered last, and standing supreme, was found to be entirely in the hands of another. As for those, then, who still adhere to the view that space and time are to be looked upon as properties pertaining to the existence of things as they are in themselves — as for those men, I say, I, for my part, find it impossible to divine how, in the case at present under consideration, they think that they can escape the conclusion that actions are ruled by fatality. Or else, if (as was done by Mendelssohn, otherwise a man of great acuteness) they are prepared to argue, with no hesitation at all, that, while space and time pertain necessarily to the existence of finite and derivative beings, they do not apply to the infinite original being — if, I say, that is the view being advocated, I fail to comprehend how they propose to justify such a procedure, or from what source they think they can derive the right to make such a distinction. As a matter of fact, there is no way of comprehending how these men can suppose that they will even be successful in making their escape from the [182] contradiction into which they fall by virtue of their looking upon existence in time as a property attaching to things in respect of what they are in themselves. And indeed, on their view, things would turn out as follows. Since God is supposed to be the cause of the existence in question, while yet it is impossible that he should be the cause of time itself, or of space (seeing that, on this hypothesis, time must be presupposed to take precedence over the existence of things, the part being played by time being that of a necessary *a priori* condition of this existence), only one conclusion in possible: that God's causality (in respect of the existence of these things taken to be things-in-themselves) is one which, so far as the aspect of time is concerned, has to be thought of as being conditioned in character. And so all sorts of features, incompatible with the concept of God's infinity and independence, here make their appearance. As for the position taken up by ourselves, on the other hand, it is quite easy for us to determine the divine existence as independent of all conditions pertaining to time, in contradistinction from a being belonging to the world of sense, conceiving of the former as the *existence of a being in itself*, as distinct from a *thing* having its place in the realm of *appearance*. If, therefore, one refuses to accept the view advocating the ideality of space and time, only one expedient is left: namely, that one should embrace the doctrine of Spinoza (Ak102) which takes space and time to be properties essentially appertaining to the original being itself, while the things dependent on it (ourselves included) are declared not to be substances but mere accidents inhering in that being. What accounts for this view being defended is that, if these things exist *in time*, and are nothing more than effects produced by the original being, while time, for its part, is thought of as the condition of the existence they have as things-in-themselves, the correct conclusion would be that the actions of these beings were, in actual fact, simply the actions of the original being, performed by it in some place or other and at some time or other. And so [183] the doctrine of Spinoza, notwithstanding the absurd character of the fundamental idea upon which it rests, does, in fact, draw its conclusions with much greater cogency than anything which can be accomplished by a creationist theory such as supposes *beings to exist in time* as what they are in themselves, and to partake of the nature of substances, and, on the other hand, declares the beings in question to be effects proceeding from a supreme cause, while yet refusing to acknowledge that they form part of the supreme being and of the activity exerted by it, but looking upon them instead as having the character of self-subsistent substances.

The aforesaid difficulty is resolved easily and convincingly in the following manner. If existence *in time* pertains to a merely sensible mode of representation, on the part of the thinking beings in the world, and if, accordingly, it does not concern them, in so far as they are things-in-themselves, it follows that the creation of these beings is a creation of them as things-in-themselves. This cannot be otherwise, seeing that the concept of creation has no bearing upon the sensible mode of representation or upon causality, noumena being, in fact, the only entities to which it is capable of being applied. So if I assert that beings who are dwellers in the world of sense have been created, they are, to this extent, being looked upon as noumena. Now, as there would be a contradiction in saying that God was the creator of appearances, so is there a contradiction in saying that God, as a creator, is the cause of the actions which take place in the world of sense, that is to say, take place as appearances, although he is indeed the creator of the acting beings in their character as noumena. Now if (provided only that we assume that existence in time pertains solely to appearances and not to things-in-themselves) there is the possibility of presupposing the reality of freedom, notwithstanding [184] the mechanism of nature governing things, inasmuch as they are appearances, then the circumstance that the acting beings owe their origin to creation cannot make the least difference to this, because creation concerns only their intelligible, as distinct from their sensible, existence. And accordingly, it is incapable of being looked upon as the ground by virtue of which their existence as appearances is determined. On the other hand, the position would be quite different if the existence which the beings in the world have *in time*, were one appertaining to them as things-in-themselves, because, in that case, he who created the substance would likewise be the author of the whole machinery of mechanical processes associated with that substance.

This goes to make plain the great importance of the task undertaken in the Critique of pure speculative reason: (Ak103) namely, the severance of time (and of space as well) from the manner in which things exist as things-in-themselves.

Still, as regards the solution of the difficulty which is here being advocated, the objection will be made that there is a good deal of complication about it, and that it scarcely allows of being set forth with any degree of lucidity. But is there any other solution which has been attempted, or might be attempted, which is easier or more readily comprehensible? On the contrary, one would be fully entitled to make this assertion, that those teaching metaphysics in the dogmatic style had supplied evidence of being endowed with ingenious cunning rather than with any degree of sincerity, by the way in which they moved this difficult point out of sight, in the expectation that, if they never mentioned it, the probability of its ever occurring to anyone else was remote indeed. The correct procedure, however is this. What one is called upon to do, if one's purpose is really to be of service to a science, is to *lay open* all the difficulties, and even to *search out* [185] those which might still stand in the way, without this being apparent; for each of these difficulties calls forth a remedy, the discovery of which cannot but have the effect that the science makes a gain in respect of either scope or precision. And so it comes about that the very obstacles become means for promoting the thoroughness of the science. If, on the other hand, the difficulties are intentionally covered up or else, one seeks to remove them by having recourse to mere palliatives, they are bound sooner or later to break out in incurable evils, with the result that the science succumbs to complete scepticism and is brought to ruin.

Since, strictly speaking, it is the concept of freedom which alone, among all the Ideas arising from pure speculative reason, provides so extended a range in the field of the supersensible, although only in respect of practical knowledge, I should wish to raise this question: *How does it come about that such productiveness has been apportioned exclusively to this concept*, while the other concepts issuing from reason, although signifying the empty place to be taken up by purely intelligible entities (allowed to be conceivable in thought), have no means at their disposal of bestowing determinacy upon the entities referred to in the various concepts? I soon perceive that, since, in the absence of a category, nothing allows of being conceived of in thought at all, the first thing I have to do is look out for the category to be met with in reason's Idea of freedom which is at present occupying my attention, the category in question being that of *causality*. Further, I note that, while, in the case of *reason's concept* of freedom, [186] there is (seeing that the reference here is to something transcending experience) no possibility that there should be a corresponding intuition serving as a foundation of the concept, on the other hand, there is the circumstance that the *concept of the understanding*, that of causality (its being in respect of the synthesis present in this concept that the unconditioned is demanded by the concept of reason) must, first of all, have a sensible intuition at its disposal, this being the way in which objective reality is, for the first time, secured for it. (Ak104) Now the categories are divided in such a way that each one of them comes under one of two classes. There are the *mathematical* categories, the sole concern of which is with the unity of synthesis encounterable in the representation of objects; and there are the *dynamical* categories concerned with the representation of objects as existing.

The former kind of category (the categories concerning magnitude and quality) invariably contains a synthesis of that which is *homogeneous*. Now as regards that which, in respect of such a synthesis, is to play the part of the unconditioned, to be set over and against what, within the field of sensible intuition, is given in time and space as something conditioned — as regards this type of unconditioned, I say, there is no possibility at all that it can be encountered within the context of such a synthesis, since, in such a case, it would itself belong to time and space. Accordingly, it is out of the question that it should be anything but conditioned in character. And so it was found (in the section dealing with the dialectic emerging within the field of pure theoretical reason) that the two opposite methods resorted to, with a view to discovering the unconditioned and reaching up to the totality of conditions, in respect of the said synthesis — that both these methods, I say, were based upon error.

The categories of the second group, on the other hand, that of causality and that of the necessity of a thing, did not by any means require such homogeneity, as regards the way in which they performed the synthesis between the conditioned and its condition, seeing that what was to be represented here was not an intuition (as composed of a multiplicity of constituents present in that intuition) but merely the manner in which the existence of the conditioned object, corresponding to such an intuition, comes to be combined with the existence of the condition, [187] (the understanding looking upon it as connected with it). This being the position, it was permissible that, by way of contrast with that which, as belonging to the world of sense, was wholly conditioned (in respect of both causality and the contingent character pertaining to the existence of things) we should assign the unconditioned to the intelligible world — the matter being left entirely indeterminate in every other respect — , the result of the said procedure being that the synthesis was made to transcend the boundaries of the sensible world. And so it was that, in the section dealing with the dialectic emerging in the field of pure speculative reason, it was found that no contradiction was involved in the two opposite methods resorted to, with a view to finding the unconditioned, to be set over and against that which was conditioned in character. For example, as regards the synthesis pertaining to causality, there is nothing contradictory about conceiving in thought (over and against the conditioned to be met with in the series of causes and effects occurring in the world of sense) that species of causality which is no longer sensibly conditioned. In other words, the view here taken amounts to this: that the same action which, as belonging to the world of sense, is sensibly conditioned, that is to say, mechanically necessary, has yet for its foundation a causality which is not dependent on sensible conditions, one that pertains to the acting being, in so far as that being belongs to the intelligible world. And the conclusion to be drawn from all this is that there is the possibility that this being should be conceived of as endowed with freedom.

There was only one thing which mattered now, i.e. that this *possibility* should be transformed into a *reality*, that is to say, that, by reference to an actual case, we should be in a position to furnish proof — by virtue of a fact, as it were — that certain actions presupposed such a causality (i.e. the intellectual one, which is not dependent on sensible conditions), its making no difference to the truth of such a view where the said actions were actually existent or were merely commanded, that is to say, objectively necessary in a practical sense. [188] (Ak105) As for actions actually given in experience, seeing that these have to be thought of as events taking place in the world of sense, there was no hope of our encountering such a connection in them, on the ground that it is only outside the world of sense, in the intelligible realm, that causality by means of freedom can ever be looked for. Consequently, the only alternative remaining was the discovery of an irrefutable, and thus objective, causal principle such as excluded all sensible conditions from having a determining effect upon the said causality. In other words, a principle was to be found of which it was true to say that reason no longer made an appeal to *anything else* as playing the part of a determining ground in the matter of causality, but already contained, by virtue of the said principle, the causality within itself, the position then being that, as *pure reason*, it exerts practical efficacy by itself. Now the principle here under consideration requires no searching after; neither is there any need to have recourse to invention. It has long since been present to the reason of all men and is embodied in their very nature, being, in fact, no other than the principle of *morality*. As regards that unconditioned causality, then, and the power by virtue of which it is exercised, that of freedom, and further, as regards the circumstance that a certain being (I, myself), while belonging to the sensible world, belongs likewise to the intelligible one — as regards all this, I say, it is not merely conceived of in *thought* in an indeterminate and problematic manner (this being something which could already be ascertained by speculative reason), but is, on the contrary — and that *by virtue of the law* pertaining to that causality operative through the instrumentality of freedom — something which is *known* to us in a *determinate* and assertoric manner. And so, as regards the question of the actuality of the intelligible world, this is a piece of knowledge about which we have received definite information, so far as the field of practice is concerned, [189] with the result that an assertion which, if employed for the purposes of theory, would be *transcendent* (exceeding its proper bounds), is *immanent* when it is employed in the interests of practice. Yet as regards the second dynamical Idea, that of a *necessary being*, we were unable to take a step of this sort. Apart from such intervention as the first dynamical Idea might be ready to offer, there was no possibility that, moving away from the sensible world, we should be in a position to reach up to such a being. Indeed, if we proposed to make such an attempt, that would amount to our venturing to make a leap away from everything given to us, mounting up to something regarding which we have likewise nothing given to us, which could serve by way of mediating the connection subsisting between such an intelligible being and the world of sense. (This would be so on the ground of its having to be supposed that the necessary being should become known to us as something which is *outside ourselves*.) If, however, it is *our own* subject which is under consideration, inasmuch as, *on the one hand*, it recognizes itself as determined by the moral law, and thus, by virtue of freedom, having the character of an intelligible being, and recognizes itself, *on the other hand*, as being, by virtue of the said capacity, active in the world of sense, it is by now perfectly evident that such a state of affairs is quite conceivable. It is solely in the case of the concept of freedom that we do not require to go outside ourselves to come upon the unconditioned, over and against that which is conditioned, to find the intelligible, over and against that which is sensible. And this is so because it is our own reason itself which by virtue of the character of (Ak106) the supreme and unconditioned practical law, as well as that of the being which is conscious of the said law (i.e. our own personality) recognizes itself as belonging to a purely intelligible world, to the extent even [190] of being able to determine the manner in which it is capable of being active in such a capacity. It is in this way, then, that it becomes comprehensible to us why, within the entire range of the exercise of reason, it can be *only* that which belongs to the field of *practice* which helps us pass beyond the world of sense, supplying us with cognitions pertaining to an order and a connection that is supersensible, while, on the other hand, the said cognitions can, for this very reason, only be extended to the point where they are required for purely practical purposes.

There is only one more thing to which I may be permitted to draw attention on the present occasion. When one comes to deal with matters pertaining to pure reason — and this holds good even in the field of practice, where no regard is paid to subtle speculation — one discovers that each step one takes is, of its own accord, in the strictest possible conformity with all the various aspects of the Critique of theoretical reason. And this happens, just as though every one of these steps had been thought out, of set purpose, with the intention of securing such confirmation. The justice of this observation will have to be acknowledged by any man, if only he is prepared to carry moral enquiries up to their ultimate principles. And indeed, as regards the circumstance that there should be so thorough a correspondence — not sought after in any way but being found to come about spontaneously — between, on the one hand, the principal propositions emanating from practical reason, and on the other, the reflections which the Critique of speculative reason has to offer, reflections which often have the appearance of being unduly subtle and somewhat uncalled for; as regards all this, I say, it is bound to occasion surprise, and indeed, astonishment. On the other hand, what finds confirmation here is the maxim, already acknowledged and recommended by others, that, in every scientific enquiry, one should pursue one's course undisturbed, with all possible thoroughness and straightforwardness, [191] paying no attention to the question whether or not what one has to say is agreeable to something asserted in a different context, but pursuing one's investigation by itself, to the utmost of one's power, in a spirit aiming at truthfulness and completeness. When engaged in an enterprise of this sort, it has frequently happened to me that, when my task was but half performed, certain features manifested themselves which, in consideration of doctrines propounded elsewhere, appeared to be most dubious in character. Yet, provided only I left such doubts out of account, for the time being, my sole concern being with the business at hand until it was completed, I have invariably observed, once my task was brought to a close, that in the end, contrary to expectation, everything was found to be in perfect agreement with what had been discovered entirely separately, without the least regard for these doctrines, and with no partiality or predilection in their favour. And as for those whose business it is to be authors, they would spare themselves many errors and much labour lost (by reason of its resting on an illusory foundation) if only they could bring themselves to proceed in the performance of their task with a somewhat higher degree of straightforwardness.

DIALECTIC OF PURE PRACTICAL REASON

CHAPTER I

THE GENERAL NATURE
OF A DIALECTIC SUCH AS EMERGES
WITHIN THE FIELD
OF PURE PRACTICAL REASON.

P ure reason invariably gives rise to a dialectic, whether it is considered in its speculative or in its practical employment. What
it demands is the absolute totality of conditions, in respect of a
given conditioned, while, on the other hand, it is absolutely impossible that such totality should be encounterable anywhere except in
things-in-themselves. Now all concepts about things are under the
necessity of being referred to intuitions, which, with us men, can
never be anything but sensible in character, and which, in consequence of this, do not provide us with knowledge of objects, in so far
as these are things-in-themselves, but only in so far as they are appearances. And thus there is no possibility whatever that the unconditioned should be encounterable within the series of appearances
which comprises the conditioned as well as the conditions bringing
it into being. [193] When, therefore, reason's idea concerning the
totality of conditions, that is to say, concerning the unconditioned,
is being applied to appearances, as though they were things-in-themselves (and that is what they are invariably taken for, in default of a
Critique which warns against such a supposition being made), this
cannot but give rise to an inescapable illusion. And indeed, there
would be no possibility of the deception ever being discovered, were
it not for the fact that it betrays itself through the circumstance that
a *conflict* arises within reason itself, on the occasion of its coming to
apply to appearances its principle of presupposing the existence of
something unconditioned, to be set over and against everything which
is conditioned. However, by virtue of there being such a conflict,
reason finds itself compelled to trace the said illusion back to its
source, enquiring where it may derive from, and in what way it may

be possible to bring it to nought, this task being incapable of accomplishment except by way of undertaking an exhaustive critical examination of the power of pure reason, its entire range being enquired into. As for the antinomy of pure reason, then, which becomes manifest by way of reason's getting implicated in a dialectic, there is, in fact, no more beneficent error into which reason could have fallen, seeing that it is this antinomy which, in the end, impels us to search for the key which will provide us with the means of making our escape from such a labyrinth. And that key, having once been found, opens up to us something else which we were not searching for, although we did indeed stand in need of it: namely, the prospect of our making our entry into a higher and immutable order of things, of which even now we are a part, there thus arising the possibility of our being enjoined, in virtue of definite (Ak108) precepts, to continue our existence in pursuit of our supreme destiny to which reason calls us.

[194] As regards the speculative employment of reason, the question as to how one resolves this natural dialectic, and how one is to guard against an error springing from an illusion which admittedly comes about in a perfectly natural manner — as regards all this, I say, it has been dealt with at length in the course of the investigation examining the character of the faculty operative in this matter. Still, reason fares no better in the field where it is employed for the purposes of practice. As pure practical reason, it likewise looks out for the unconditioned, to be set over and against that which is conditioned in the practical sense, i.e. it rests upon inclinations and natural wants. And it takes such a course, not in the sense that it looks upon the unconditioned as a ground determining the will, but in the sense that, even after it has been supplied with such a ground as residing in the moral law, it searches for the unconditioned totality of the *object* towards which pure practical reason is directed, affixing to that object the title of *summum bonum*.

There is a task to be performed, namely, to determine this Idea of the *summum bonum*, so that it becomes relevant to the purpose of practice, that is to say, in a manner adequate to make it play the part of a maxim prompting man's rational conduct. This task is undertaken by the *doctrine of wisdom* which, in turn, when it is pursued as a *science*, is entitled *philosophy*, in the sense in which that word was understood by the ancients, with whom it meant the directing of the mind towards the concept signifying that to which the *summum bonum* was to be assigned, and towards that conduct by means of which the *summum bonum* was capable of being obtained. It would

be a good thing if we retained the word "philosophy" in its old signification, that of a *doctrine about the summum bonum*, in so far as
reason endeavours that, in this matter, it should attain to the status
of a *science*. Such a course would be advisable because the restrictive
condition here attached to the word would be suited to the Greek
use of the term (love of *wisdom* being what is signified to the Greeks)
while yet adequate to the purpose of comprising [195] love of *science*
under that name — love, that is, of all speculative knowledge deriving from reason, in so far as that knowledge is serviceable, as regards
both the concept here under consideration and the supreme ground
determining man in the field of practice. And yet philosophy's principal purpose (in consideration of which alone it deserves to be called
a doctrine of wisdom) would never be lost sight of. Besides, provided
our intention was to have something at our disposal which might act
as a deterrent against self-conceit coming to hold dominion over a
man who ventured to claim the title of a philosopher for himself, it
would be no bad thing if, by virtue of our very definition, we put
before his eyes a standard by which his self-esteem was to be measured, such as would have the effect of markedly reducing the claims
he makes. And indeed, holding the place of a *teacher of wisdom* would,
after all, appear to mean something more than being a pupil who, in
the sure expectation of attaining to so high an aim, is not sufficiently
advanced as to be competent to serve as his own guide, let alone be
competent to serve as guide to another. It would signify a man who
was a *master in the knowledge of wisdom*, something more being expressed by this than what anyone equipped with proper modesty will
wish to arrogate to himself. (Ak109) As for philosophy, or wisdom
itself, it would still retain its character, playing the part of an ideal,
the complete representation of which, on its objective side, was not
to be found anywhere but in reason alone, while, on its subjective
side, it would be for the particular individual only the object of an
unceasing striving after it. And should someone claim to be in possession of it, by way of taking the name of a philosopher upon himself, the truth of the matter is that a man is entitled to put forward
such a claim only on condition that he can show that philosophy has
had a never-varying effect upon him, [196] and that he has the right
to point to his own person as setting an example (evidence of this
being provided by the way he has gained mastery over himself, and
by the concern for others of which he has given indubitable proof,
chiefly in promoting the general good. And indeed, the setting of
such an example was what the ancients demanded of a man who was to
be thought worthy of that honourable title).

As regards the dialectic of pure practical reason, there is one pre-liminary observation I have to make, by way of a reminder, the pertinent point being that of a correct determination of the concept of the *summum bonum*. (In the event of successfully resolving this dialectic, this should rightly arouse the expectation of a most beneficial result, just as happened in the case of the dialectic emerging in the theoretical field, inasmuch as the contradictions arising within the domain which is the concern of pure practical reason have the effect — when stated frankly and with no concealment — of compelling us to undertake a thoroughgoing critical investigation into the faculty belonging particularly to practical reason.)

This, then, is what we wish to say here. The moral law is the sole ground determining the pure will. Now, since this law is entirely formal in character, that is to say, since the demand it makes is that it should be solely the form of the maxim which is to play to part of being universally legislative, it abstracts, as regards anything to be thought of as operating as a determining ground, from everything which, in respect of the willing, stands for the element of "matter", that is to say, from everything that is the object of the willing. Consequently, true though it be that the *summum bonum* is to be looked upon as the *object* of pure practical reason, taken in its completeness, it is not on that account to be regarded as the *determining ground* of the will. On the contrary, it is the moral law which exclusively provides the ground why the realization and furtherance of the *summum bonum* is chosen as an object to be sought after. [197]A reminder such as this is of considerable significance in a delicate case, like the present one, where one's concern is with a correct determination of moral principles, and where even the slightest misrepresentation has the effect of debasing the disposition governing men's minds. And indeed, it will have been gathered from what was said in the Analytic that if, in antecedence to the moral law, any object is supposed (while having the name of something good affixed to it) to be the ground which determines the will, the supreme practical principle being subsequently derived from that object, the inevitable result must be the emergence of a heteronomous principle and the supplanting of the principle of morality.

On the other hand, there is this self-evident circumstance: if the moral law has already been included in the concept of the *summum bonum*, then the *summum bonum* is something more than merely the objective of the pure will, as it is true, on the contrary, that the concept of the *summum bonum* and the representation of its existence as something to be rendered possible through the instrumentality of practical reason, apart from its being an *object* of the pure will, is, over and above this, a *ground* by which that will finds itself to be *determined*. (Ak110) This must be so, because it would, in fact, be the moral law — already having been included in the concept of the *summum bonum* and being thought alongside it —, and not any other object, which determined the will, in obedience to the principle of autonomy. That this is the proper order pertaining to the concepts under consideration is a circumstance which must never be lost sight of, for otherwise we inevitably come to misunderstand ourselves, and are under the impression that self-contradiction is present in a case where, in actual fact, everything is in complete harmony.

THE DIALECTIC TO WHICH PURE REASON GIVES RISE AS IT SETS OUT TO DETERMINE THE CONCEPT OF THE HIGHEST GOOD.

If there be a concept referring to something as occupying the *highest* place, this already involves the presence of an ambiguity which, when left unattended, may become the source of unnecessary disputes. The "highest" may either mean that which stands supreme (*supremum*), or else it may mean that which exhibits completeness (*consummatum*). The former stands for a condition which is itself unconditioned, i.e. not subordinate to any further condition (*originarium*); the latter stands for a whole, which is such as not to form part of a still more comprehensive whole of the same kind as itself (*perfectissimum*). It has been shown in the Analytic that *virtue* (thought of as worthiness to be happy) is the *supreme condition*, in respect of anything which may appear to us as desirable, i.e. in respect of all our quest for happiness, and that, accordingly, it is virtue which is the *supreme* good. Yet virtue is not on that account the entire and complete good, when it plays the role of being an object of the desiring faculty on the part of finite rational beings. And indeed, the presence of *happiness* is likewise required for anything which is to have the character of such a good, and that not only [199] from the partial point of view of a particular person making of himself an object the interests of which have to be pursued, but even in the judgment of an impartial reason, which looks upon each and every person as having the nature of being an end in himself. For this is how the case really stands. As regards the condition of finding oneself in need of happiness, being worthy of it, at the same time, and yet not partaking of it, that is a state of affairs wholly inconsistent with the perfect willing of a rational being such as is, over and above this, possessed of all power, if, for the sake of experiment, we entertain the thought of such a being. It is virtue and happiness jointly which constitute the possession of the *summum bonum* in one person, and it is presupposed, at the same time, that happiness is distributed in exact proportion to morality (this state of affairs being looked upon as constituting the value of the person and his worthiness to be happy). Such is the nature of the *summum bonum*, the reference being to a world to be rendered possible. And accordingly, it is a totality which is signified in the *summum bonum*, i.e. the good made complete, the case in point being that virtue (inasmuch as it is a condition having no other condition which is subject over it) (Ak111) always remains the supreme good, while happiness, although always pleasant to him who possesses it, is of itself not absolutely, and, in every respect, good, the position being, on the contrary, that it invariably presupposes, as its condition, a line of conduct rendering obedience to the law of morality.

If two predicates come under one concept in such a way as to be *necessarily* combined with one another, they must be connected as ground and consequent, either in the sense that the *unity* in question is *analytic* (logical connection), or in the sense that it is *synthetic* (real connection), the former to be looked upon as coming about in virtue of the law of [200] identity, the latter in virtue of the law of causality. As for the connection subsisting between virtue and happiness, it can be understood as signifying this: that the endeavour to be virtuous, on the one hand, and the rational quest after happiness, on the other, are not to be looked upon as two distinctive activities, but instead should be thought of as wholly identical, in which case there would be no need for the maxim serving as the foundation of virtue to be other than the one which forms the foundation of making oneself happy. Or else, the connection in question is understood in the sense that virtue produces happiness, as something quite distinct from consciousness of virtue, in the same way as a cause produces an effect.

Among the schools of philosophy in ancient Greece it was, strictly speaking, only two which, in setting out to strive at a proper determination of the *summum bonum*, employed one and the same method, in that they would not allow virtue and happiness to be two distinct elements in the *summum bonum*. In other words, in their search for a unity of principle, they followed the rule of identity. Still, they parted company in the choice which they made as to which of the two was to be thought of as the fundamental idea. The followers of Epicurus asserted that what constituted virtue was being conscious of the fact that the maxim adopted was one which led to happiness. The Stoics asserted that what constituted happiness was being conscious of the fact that one was virtuous. To the former being *prudent* was one and the same thing as being moral; to the latter, by whom a more exalted title was assigned to virtue, it was *morality* which alone constituted true wisdom.

[201] One may rightly admire these men who, in such early times attempted every conceivable way of making philosophical conquests. At the same time, however, it must be a matter of regret that their acuteness of mind should have been so greatly misapplied when they set out to excogitate with so much labour an identity between concepts as heterogeneous in character as happiness and virtue. Still, that they should have adopted such a procedure was in keeping with the dialectical spirit of the time during which they lived. And indeed, even at present it occasionally happens that men distinguished for their subtlety yield to the temptation of attempting to remove differences in respect of principles (such as are, in actual fact, essential differences incapable of ever being reconciled with one another), by alleging that these differences have their source in merely verbal disputes. In this way, then, men set about painstakingly to excogitate an apparent unity in a case in which, in fact, nothing has been done except to give things names other than the customary ones. (Ak112) This is a procedure most commonly resorted to where the point at which heterogeneous principles allow of entering into combination with one another is placed so high or so low; or else, the position is that so thoroughgoing a transformation would be required with regard to principles accepted elsewhere, within the philosophical system, that men show a reluctance to concern themselves too deeply with the real difference, and prefer to treat the discrepancy as one having merely formal significance.

While both schools of philosophy made painstaking attempts, with regard to the practical principles of virtue and of happiness, to excogitate the uniformity of their character, they were not on that account in agreement as to the means to be employed to extract the alleged identity. On the contrary, as far as this matter was concerned, they were separated from each other by a gulf, truly infinite in nature, one party placing its principle on the aesthetic, the other on the logical, side, one attributing the principle, which it embraced, to the consciousness of a want appertaining to sensibility, the other to the independence of a practical reason of all [202] sensible grounds of determination. The concept of virtue is, according to the followers of Epicurus, already contained in the maxim laying it down that one is to promote one's own happiness, while, according to the Stoics, consciousness of virtue already contained happiness. But then, if there be something contained in another concept, it is identical with part of that which contains it, but it is not on that account identical with the whole of it — and besides, two wholes, although made up of the same constituents, may yet, apart from this, be specifically different from one another, that being the position if the parts of which they consist are combined into a whole in totally different ways. The Stoics maintained that virtue was the *summum bonum* in its *entirety*, with happiness, having to be thought of as something appertaining to the condition of the subject, being nothing more than consciousness of the possession of virtue. The followers of Epicurus maintained that happiness was the *summum bonum* in its *entirety*, with virtue as nothing more than the form exhibited by the maxim adopted with a view to attaining happiness, and consisting in the rational employment of the means appropriate to accomplishing happiness.

Now it is evident from what has been said in the Analytic that maxims embraced for the purpose of producing virtue, and on the other hand, those embraced for the purpose of securing one's own happiness, are wholly different from one another, as regards the supreme practical principle serving as their foundation. And far from being of one and the same kind, they impose, when present in the one subject, severe limitations upon one another, operating to each other's *detriment* — and this notwithstanding the fact that they are part of the one *summum bonum*, being conditions of its very possibility. [203] The question remaining to be answered, therefore, is this: *How is the summum bonum* to be rendered *possible*, as something to become operative in the field of *practice?* This problem remains unsolved to this day, in spite of all the *attempts* which have so far been made to reach a *compromise.* Now it is, in fact, a point which has been dealt with in the Analytic which may serve to explain why it is so difficult to provide a solution to this problem. As happiness and morality are *elements* in the *summum bonum* which are wholly and specifically *distinct* from one another, it is *inconceivable* that knowledge of the connection subsisting between them should be obtainable by way of *analysis* (in the sense that he (Ak113) who pursues his happiness should, as regards this conduct of his, discover, merely by analyzing the concepts guiding him, that he was virtuous; or else, that he who is in pursuit of virtue should, in the consciousness of such conduct, find himself *ipso facto* happy). What is here required instead is a *synthesis* of the concepts under consideration. Now since the connection enquired into at present has to be thought of as an *a priori* one, i.e. one which is necessary, in respect of practice, and since, accordingly, knowledge of it cannot be something derived from experience (the possibility of establishing the reality of the *summum bonum* on empirical principles thus being excluded), it follows that the *deduction* of the said concept will have to be *transcendental* in character. It is *a priori* necessary (morally speaking) that the *summum bonum* should be *brought into being through the instrumentality of the freedom of the will.* The condition establishing its priority, therefore, must be accounted for solely in reference to *a priori* sources of knowledge.

I.

[204] THE ANTINOMY
TO WHICH PRACTICAL REASON GIVES RISE.

In the *summum bonum* which is supposed to determine our practice, that is to say, which is to be brought into being through the instrumentality of our will, virtue and happiness are conceived of as being necessarily connected with one another. Accordingly, the position is that practical reason finds it impossible to presuppose one of them as belonging to the *summum bonum* without it being presumed that this likewise applies to the other. Now this connection between virtue and happiness must be either *analytic* or *synthetic* in character (this holding good for any and every connection. But then, seeing that it is impossible that the connection here in question should be analytic (as has just been demonstrated), it has to be looked upon as synthetic — to be more precise, as having the character of a nexus between a cause and an effect. This is because it concerns a good which is to be pertinent to practice, i.e. one to be rendered possible in virtue of action. Accordingly, the position must be either that the desire for happiness is the cause moving us to adopt maxims pertaining to virtue, or else, that virtue has the nature of an efficient cause resulting in happiness. The first is *absolutely* impossible, seeing that (proof of this having been given in the Analytic) the truth is that maxims such as make the determining ground of the will reside in the agent's desire for happiness are not moral maxims at all, and accordingly, are incapable of serving as a foundation of virtue. But the second is *also impossible*, because any connection subsisting between causes and effects, in the field of practice, being encounterable in the world and having to be thought of as resulting from the [205] determination of the will, in no way depends on moral dispositions of the mind. On the contrary, everything here turns on the knowledge of the natural laws which one has at one's disposal and on one's physical powers to make use of these laws for one's own purposes. And from this it follows that a necessary connection between happiness and virtue such as would meet the requirements of the *summum bonum* cannot in this world be expected even from the most scrupulous observance of moral laws. (Ak114) Now since the furtherance of the *summum bonum* (the very concept of which implies the said connection) is an object of our will, pertaining to that will necessarily and in an *a priori* manner, and since, moreover, it is an object inseparably bound up with the moral law, the impossibility of there being a *summum bonum* cannot but furnish proof of the spurious character of the moral law. In other words, since it is impossible that the *summum bonum* should be brought into being, by way of acting in conformity with practical rules, the moral law which commands that the *summum bonum* is to be promoted must be one which is in pursuit of fantasies and of vain and imaginary purposes — being, in fact, a law which has an inherently spurious character.

II.

CRITICAL RESOLUTION OF THE ANTINOMY GIVEN RISE TO BY PRACTICAL REASON.

As for the antinomy, which arose in the field of pure speculative reason, a similar conflict made its appearance, that between natural necessity and freedom, in respect of the causal efficacy exhibited by the events in the world. It was resolved by demonstrating that it was not a true conflict, [206] provided only that one was prepared (as, in fact, one ought to be) to regard these events — and indeed, the world within which they occur — as having the character of appearances merely, the true state of the case being the following. While the agent exhibits a causal efficacy, within the world of sense, which is invariably in conformity with the principle of natural mechanism — this being so, inasmuch as that agent is to be thought of *as having the status of an appearance*, even with regard to what his inner sense confronts him with — it still remains possible that, in reference to the same event, the acting person should, in looking upon himself as a *noumenon*, i.e. as a pure intelligence (in respect of that aspect of his existence which does not permit of being determined by what is temporal), contain a ground which determines the said causality (i.e. the one governed in obedience to natural laws), the ground in question being one which itself is not subject to any natural law.

As regards the antinomy which concerns us at present, that taking its rise in pure practical reason, the position is the same. The first of the two propositions, that asserting that striving after happiness is a ground producing virtuous disposition, is *absolutely false*. The second proposition, on the other hand, the one asserting that virtuous disposition necessarily produces happiness, is *not absolutely* false, but only if virtue be taken to exhibit the species of causality which governs what occurs in the world of sense — in other words, only if existence in the world of sense is presupposed to be the sole kind of existence appertaining to a rational being. The proposition under consideration, therefore, is false only in a *conditional* sense. But then, as for my conceiving of myself as existing also as a noumenon, that is something more than a merely legitimate assumption. On the contrary, in being provided with the moral law, I have at my disposal a ground (Ak115) which is purely intellectual in character, a ground determining the causal efficacy exerted by me in the sensible [207] world. Hence it is not impossible that there should be a necessary connection (although indeed not immediately, but mediately, i.e. through the instrumentality of an author of nature belonging to the intelligible realm) between morality of disposition as the cause, and happiness as the effect produced by it in the world of sense — a combination which in a natural realm, i.e. one which was nothing more than an object of the senses, could never be anything but fortuitous in character, while, at the same time, failing to come up to what is required for the purposes of the *summum bonum*.

It follows from what has been said that, notwithstanding the apparent self-contradiction in which practical reason gets implicated, the *summum bonum* is the necessary and supreme end aimed at by a will which finds itself under the direction of morality. And indeed, seeing that the *summum bonum* permits of being brought into being through what happens in the field of practice, it is a true object of that will. Moreover, as regards maxims proceeding from that will which are directed towards the *summum bonum* as their subject matter, they have to be thought of as having objective reality. Initially, this seemed to be ruled out, because of the antinomy which arose when it was supposed that virtue and happiness were connected with one another, in conformity with a universal law binding them together. However, it was in fact mere conception which gave rise to the conflict, the true cause of which was that what held good of the way in which appearances are related to one another was taken to be applicable likewise to the relationship subsisting between things-in-themselves and these appearances.

In seeking to account for the possibility of there being a *summum bonum* — the nature of which is that of an ultimate goal of moral desirings which all rational beings set before themselves through the instrumentality of their reason — we found ourselves obliged to place the said *summum bonum* at so great a distance, as to derive its character from the connection in which it stood with an intelligible world. So [208] it cannot but seem strange that, notwithstanding this being the true state of the case, philosophers have let themselves be persuaded, in both ancient and modern times, that a combination of virtue, on the one hand, and, on the other, happiness, in an entirely acceptable proportion to the former, was something already encounterable in *this life*, i.e. in the world of sense; or else, they supposed that they were conscious in themselves of the said combination. And indeed, both Epicurus and the Stoics extolled happiness to be found in this life, forthcoming as the result of one's consciousness of leading a virtuous life, as a condition surpassing everything else. With Epicurus, the disposition of his mind, as is plain from the precepts he laid down, was by no means as ignoble as one might be led to conclude from the principles underlying the theory he propounded, the purpose of which was to explain and not to call for action; or else, one might come to infer, from the way this theory was misinterpreted by many who allowed themselves to be misled by Epicurus' use of the expression "lust", as being an equivalent of contentment. On the other hand, he looked upon the most disinterested exercise of goodness as one of the ways of coming to enjoy the most intense delight. Moreover, as regards self-sufficiency and the subduing of the inclinations — reaching as high a degree as might be demanded by the most rigid among moral philosophers — , these were part of his scheme of pleasure. (What he understood by this was the ever cheerful heart.) He differed from the Stoics chiefly in that he assigned to such pleasure the ground moving to action, a thing which the Stoics rightly refused to do. The reason why he took the line he did was that Epicurus, the man of virtue (and this is true, even in the present day, with regard to many men who, while (Ak116) morally well-disposed, fail to reflect upon their principles with sufficient profundity) — that Epicurus, I say, fell into the error of presupposing the presence of a virtuous *disposition* of the mind, when what he really meant to do [209] was to give, first of all, an account of the motive force whereby men are led to action. (And it is indeed true enough that the man who is upright finds it impossible to feel happy, unless he be first of all conscious of his uprightness; and this is so because, the disposition of his mind being what it is, the reproaches which, in the event of his being guilty of transgressions, he was compelled to make against himself by virtue of his own way of thinking — and the moral condemnation consequent upon this — would have the effect of depriving him of all enjoyment of pleasantness which his condition might call for in other respects.) However, what is really in question is this. How is it possible, in the first instance, that such a disposition of the mind and such a way of thinking should become operative in assessing the worth of one's existence, seeing that, prior to this stage having been reached, no feeling for moral worth would be encounterable in the subject at all? It is indeed undeniable that a virtuous man will come to no proper enjoyment of his life unless he is conscious of the presence of uprightness with regard to every action which he performs, no matter how greatly fortune may favour him, where the physical side of his existence is concerned. But if what one is called upon to do is that one should, first of all, make him virtuous — in other words, when one is dealing with him at a time when moral worth is not as yet held in such high esteem — is there any sense in extolling to him the calmness of soul which would result from his being conscious of his uprightness, in consideration of the fact that such uprightness is a condition to which he is at present not susceptible?

Still, as regards the matter here under consideration, the fact remains that it does, after all, provide the occasion for men becoming guilty of committing a certain fault, that of scoring a point in a surreptitious manner (*vitium subreptionis*), it all being due to what is an optical illusion, as it were, an illusion from which even those most versed in these matters cannot wholly escape. The point on which everything turns here is that of having consciousness of oneself as *doing* something, as distinct from *having a feeling* about something. [210] The moral disposition of the mind is inextricably bound up with a consciousness of the fact that the will finds itself to be *directly determined by the law*. Now to be conscious of there being such a determination of the will invariably provides the ground, on the part of the faculty of desire, for taking a delight in the resulting action. Yet this pleasure, this delight, which the agent takes in himself, is not the ground whereby the said determination of the action is produced. On the contrary, it is the determination of the will, directly and solely by means of reason, which is the ground of the feeling of pleasure; and as for the pleasure here in question, it accordingly remains a determination of the will which is purely practical in character as distinct from being aesthetic. On the other hand, since this determination of the will exerts, inasmuch as it plays the part of a force impelling towards activity, exactly the same effect as would have been the case with a feeling of pleasantness, it easily happens that what is, in fact, the result of our own doing is taken for something which we merely feel (Ak117) in a purely passive manner, the motive force grounded in morality being mistaken for a sensible impulse. (The position here is the same as it invariably is with an illusion of the senses so-called, inner sense being what is in question in the present case.) There is something truly sublime about human nature, as directly determined towards action by means of a law which is purely rational in character; and this holds good even for the illusion, as the result of which the subjective aspect of this intellectual determinability of the will is taken for something aesthetic and for the effect of a particular sensible feeling (for an intellectual feeling would be a contradiction in terms). [211] Moreover, it is of great importance to draw attention to this aspect of our personality, and to cultivate as much as possible the effect reason exerts upon that feeling. However, in concerning ourselves with this moral determining ground as playing the part of a motive force, we must be careful, at the same time, to refrain from resorting to spurious panegyrics in its favour, seeking to make out that it is based upon special feelings of joy to be conceived of as grounds of actions (whereas the truth is that they are merely the result of these). And indeed, the effect of our having recourse to such a procedure is this: that we come to degrade and disfigure what is, in truth, the proper and genuine motive force, the law itself which is here, through the way we deal with it, placed within the setting of a counterfeit foil. As for the object of our investigation, then, which is respect (not pleasure or enjoyment of happiness), its nature cannot be that of a feeling lying at the root of reason and *antecedent* to it, since a feeling of this sort could never be anything but aesthetic and pathological in character. And indeed, consciousness of the fact that the will finds itself, by virtue of the law, subject to an immediate compulsion is scarcely an analogue of the feeling of pleasure, seeing that though the effect produced in relation to the faculty of desire is exactly the same, it has to be assigned to different sources. It is only if the matter is presented in the way we have described that one can accomplish what one desires, namely, that actions should not merely be in conformity with law, while resulting from feelings of pleasantness, but that they should be done from duty, this being the true end of all moral cultivation.

But do we not have an expression which, while not referring to an enjoyment, as happiness does, yet signifies a delight one takes in one's existence, an analogue of happiness, [212] necessarily present, whenever a man is conscious of his virtuous state? Indeed, there is such an expression, *viz. contentment with oneself*, which, when properly understood, never refers to anything else but a negative delight which one takes in one's existence; and what this signifies is that one is conscious of not standing in need of anything. As for freedom, and what goes with it, i.e. consciousness of it as being the power of obeying the moral law, by virtue of a disposition of the mind prevailing over everything else — as for such freedom, I say, it signifies *independence of the inclinations*, at least in the sense that we are independent of them as grounds determining us in respect of what we consider desirable, although not in the sense that they are grounds failing to *affect* us. Moreover, in so far as, in acting in obedience to our moral maxims, we are conscious of freedom, that freedom is the sole source of a contentment necessarily associated with it, a contentment which does not rest on any special feeling and which is not susceptible to change, (Ak118) being a condition rightly thought of as intellectual in character. Aesthetic contentment, on the other hand (the name "contentment" not being properly applicable in this case), which rests on the satisfaction of the inclinations, never comes up to what one supposes it to be, no matter what ingenuity may be brought to bear upon devising a satisfactory scheme. Indeed, the truth of the matter is that the inclinations suffer alteration, so that the more indulgently they are treated the more they increase, always leaving a greater gap than that which one intended to fill. This is why a rational being invariably looks upon them as *troublesome*, and that although it is not in a position to divest itself of them, they exact of it a desire to be rid of them. Even an inclination towards that which is in conformity with duty (e.g. the exercise of benevolence), although it may make it very much easier to carry *moral* [213] maxims into effect, is yet incapable of producing any. And indeed, so far as a moral maxim is concerned, everything turns upon the circumstance that it should be the representation of the law which operates as the determining ground, this being of the very essence if the action is to contain not merely *legality* but *morality* as well. Inclination is blind and servile, no matter whether or not it is good-natured; and as for reason, it must, where morality is at stake, not confine itself to the role of acting as a guardian over the inclinations, but leave them out of account altogether, while its sole concern, as pure practical reason, must be with pursuing its own interest. Even the feeling of pity and soft-hearted sympathy, provided it precedes deliberation as to what duty requires, playing the part of a ground determining action, is looked upon by right-thinking people as burdensome in their own judgment and throws their well-considered maxims into confusion, evoking in them a desire to be quit of sentiments such as these, and to be subject to law-giving reason alone.

What has been said may serve to explain how it is that when consciousness arises, on the part of pure practical reason, it is possessed of such power (the deeds performed, those having their source in virtue, being the grounds of that realization), that this produces in the agent a consciousness of having gained mastery over his inclinations, of being independent of them, and of thus being independent also of the feeling of dissatisfaction with which these inclinations are invariably attended. In other words, what is engendered is a negative delight taken in one's condition, i.e. a *contentment*, which is primarily one concerning one's own personality. As for freedom itself, it becomes in the way described (i.e. indirectly) capable of being attended with an enjoyment, [214] a condition which cannot be characterized as one of happiness, because it is not dependent on any positive co-operation of a feeling, while, on the other hand, it is not, strictly speaking, a state of *blessedness*, seeing that it does not imply an entire independence of inclinations and needs. Still, it bears some resemblance to blessedness, in so far as at least this much is accomplished here, that the determination of the will is kept free from the influence of inclinations and needs. And accordingly, the said state has, at least in respect of its origin, something analogous to that of self-sufficiency, which, for its part, can strictly be attributed only to the supreme being.

(Ak119) The conclusion to be drawn for the solution of the antinomy of practical pure reason advocated here is the following. As to the question whether there is encounterable, in the field of practical principles, a natural and necessary connection between consciousness of morality, on the one hand, and on the other, the expectation of a state of happiness, proportionate to morality and consequent upon it — as regards all these things, I say, they must be allowed to be at least possible (although it is true enough that none of this allows of being understood or comprehended properly). As against this, there is no possibility whatever of the principles concerned with acquiring happiness producing morality. The inference to be drawn from this is that it is morality which is the *supreme* good, and that it must be looked upon as the condition which comes first, as far as the *summum bonum* is concerned. Happiness, on the other hand, although standing for the second element in the *summum bonum*, occupies this position merely as a consequent conditioned by morality, although, at the same time, it is to be thought of as a consequence necessarily following from it. It is only by way of things being subordinated to each other in the manner described that the *summum bonum* is allowed to play the role of being the entire object of pure practical reason, reason, for its part, being under the necessity of representing the *summum bonum* to itself as something that is possible; and this is due to the circumstance that there is an injunction, which likewise has its source in reason, laying it down that everything possible ought to be done so as to make the *summum bonum* a reality. [215] But then, if the question be to account for the possibility of such a connection subsisting between the conditioned and what conditions it, everything here appertains to the manner in which things are related to one another in the supersensible realm, and there is no way at all of making anything intelligible through having recourse to laws governing the world of sense — and this is so notwithstanding the fact that the practical consequences of the Idea under consideration, i.e. the actions which are directed towards the realization of the *summum bonum*, belong to the world of sense. In consideration of this, we shall make the attempt to exhibit the grounds establishing the possibility of there being a *summum bonum* by relying, first of all, upon that which is in our power, and placing reliance, secondly, upon what our reason presents us with, by way of our supplementing our incapacity, the purpose of it all being this: that the *summum bonum* (looked upon by practical principles as something which is necessary) is to have its possibility established.

III.

WHEN PURE PRACTICAL AND SPECULATIVE REASON ARE BROUGHT INTO CONNECTION WITH ONE ANOTHER IT IS TO THE FORMER THAT THE PRIMACY IS TO BE ASSIGNED.

What I understand by "primacy", in respect of two or more things which are brought into connection with one another, through the instrumentality of reason, is the pre-eminence to be attributed to one of them as being the ground which comes first in determining the connection with all the rest. In its narrower practical sense, it means the pre-eminence attaching to the special concern characteristic of the one thing, inasmuch as the special concern pertaining to the others is subordinate to it, while it cannot itself have second place assigned to it where these are concerned. [216] In the case of every faculty of the mind it is possible to single out a particular concern it has, that is to say, a principle containing the condition subject to which it has the effect of promoting the exercise of the faculty in question. Reason, being the faculty dealing with supreme principles, determines, with respect to all the other powers of the mind, what is the particular concern appertaining to them, (Ak120) while it is reason itself that determines what is to be the nature of the concern peculiar to it. The concern particularly appertaining to reason's speculative employment is that of obtaining *knowledge* of the object up to the highest *a priori* principles, while the concern attaching to reason's practical employment consists in this: that the *will* should be determined in such a way as to be directed towards that end which is to be thought of as standing supreme and embodying completeness. As regards that which is requisite, so that any employment of reason should be possible at all, that is to say, as regards the circumstance that the principles and assertions issuing in reason must not contradict one another, it forms no part of the concern which reason has, but instead should be looked upon as the condition of our having any reason at all. When something is thought of as having the nature of a concern of reason, it is not mere self-consistency which we have in mind but the circumstance that reason finds itself extended in respect of its scope.

If practical reason is not entitled to presuppose, or conceive as given, anything in addition to what *speculative* reason is of itself capable of offering to it, as something resulting from its own insight, then it is speculative reason to which the primacy belongs. If, on the other hand, the position is this, that practical reason is the independent source of a number of original *a priori* principles, inseparably bound up with certain theoretical assumptions which are yet withdrawn from any insight possible to speculative reason (although there is no need that they should be in contradiction with it), then the question is [217] which of the two concerns stands supreme (not which has to give place, seeing that they are not necessarily incompatible with one another). Is speculative reason, ignorant as it is of what practical reason has to offer for its acceptance, to allow entry to the said propositions, although they transcend anything it is itself capable of knowing? Is it obliged to reconcile the aforesaid propositions with the concepts deriving from itself, looking upon the former as a possession from a foreign source which it has had transferred to it? Or is the truth rather that speculative reason is justified in obstinately pursuing its own particular concern, in conformity with the canon laid down by Epicurus, that everything is to be repudiated as having its source in empty sophistry, except that which can provide a credential of its having objective reality, by way of pointing to a manifest instance exhibited in the field of experience? In fact, however closely interwoven the matter in question may be with the special concern pertaining to the practical employment of pure reason, and true though it be that there is nothing here which is incompatible with what the theoretical asserts, there is every appearance that all this ought to be disallowed, simply on the ground that the course recommended actually does seem to be detrimental to the concerns of speculative reason, inasmuch as the limits reason sets itself are here being removed, there thus being the risk that it should be left at the mercy of all sorts of absurd and even insane notions having their source in sheer imagination.

And indeed, if what was supposed to serve as a basis were practical reason, as conditioned by pathological influences, that is to say, as merely ministering to the concerns of the inclinations, under the governance of the principle of happiness, it would be absolutely impossible to approach speculative reason with a view that it should accede to a demand such as this. It would then be things such as Mohammed's paradise, or else, *theosophers* or *mystics* melting into unity with the deity, each man describing things under the direction of his own fancy [218] (Ak121) which imposed their monstrosities upon reason; and it would be just as well to have no reason at all than to allow that, in such a manner, it should be made the victim of dreamlike fantasies of every sort. If, on the other hand, the truth is that pure reason has the capacity for being by itself practically efficacious, and actually exerts this capacity (consciousness of the moral law providing evidence of this circumstance), then the position is, after all, that it is one and the same reason which, having either a theoretical or practical purpose in view, pronounces judgment in conformity with certain *a priori* principles. And so it is made evident that, even though so far as its theoretical purposes are concerned, reason were to lack the power to provide a positive demonstration of the truth of certain propositions (which, however, are not incompatible with what is asserted by reason elsewhere in this field), it is under obligation (as soon as it appears that these propositions are *inseparably* bound up with pure reason's *practical concerns*) to grant admittance to them, looking upon them as something offered to it from a foreign source, as something which, while it has not grown up on its own soil, is yet sufficiently authenticated. Moreover, it is called upon to compare and connect the said propositions with everything that has become known to it in the exercise of the power pertaining to it as speculative reason. On the other hand, while humbly acknowledging that the insights under consideration are not of its own making, speculative reason must come to realize the fact that they serve none the less by way of extending the scope of reason's employment in respect of a purpose other than its own, that of practice. And this is in no way contrary to the concern of which it is itself the guardian, that of imposing a check upon the vicious tendency to engage in idle speculation.

And so it is that, when pure speculative and pure practical reason are brought into connection with one another, as forming the basis of a piece of knowledge, the *primacy* belongs to the latter, provided, that is, that the said connection, far from being a *fortuitous* and [219] arbitrary one, is, on the contrary, an *a priori* one founded upon reason — in other words, that it is a *necessary* connection, the truth of the matter being that the absence of such subordination would be the source of a contradiction arising within reason itself. And indeed, if the relationship subsisting between them were one of simple co-ordination, that would have the effect that speculative reason came to close up its boundary within narrower limits, refusing to accept inside its territory anything appertaining to practical reason, while the latter proceeded to extend its boundary over everything else, making the attempt, whenever its own need required such a course, to comprise the domain of speculative reason within its own. On the other hand, as regards the alternative, namely, that, the position being reversed, practical reason should be sought to be subordinated to the speculative one, it is inconceivable that such a thing could be demanded of speculative reason, seeing that any concern of whatever kind is at bottom something appertaining to the field of practice, and that even the concern which has its basis in speculative reason is merely conditional in character, as it is only by virtue of the practical employment of reason that it is capable of reaching completeness.

IV.

THE IMMORTALITY OF THE SOUL AS SOMETHING POSTULATED BY PURE PRACTICAL REASON.

(Ak122) That the *summum bonum* is to be realized in the world is an object necessarily pursued by a will which is capable of being determined by the moral law. But then, one element encountered in the *summum bonum* is that the disposition of the mind should be such as to be in *complete conformity* with the moral law, as this is the supreme condition of there being a *summum bonum*. Such conformity must thus be possible (just as is the object towards which it is directed), seeing that [220] this is implicit in the very same injunctions as lays it down that the object in question is to be promoted. Now what is signified by complete conformity of the will to the moral law is called *holiness*, this being a state of perfection which cannot be attained by a rational being belonging to the world of sense at any moment of its existence. Since, however, the demand for holiness is none the less made, as something indispensable to the purposes of practice, it follows that holiness is incapable of being met with any-where except in an advance towards the said conformity which *progresses ad infinitum*. And accordingly, it is necessary, in obedience to certain principles deriving from pure practical reason, to presup-pose that such a practical progression is to be thought of as having the status of a real object of our will.

Now such an advance is conceivable only on condition of its being assumed that the *existence* and personality of the rational being are such as to continue into *infinity* (this property being what is called the immortality of the soul). The *summum bonum* is thus possible, practically speaking, only if one is entitled to presuppose the immor-tality of the soul, the supposition of which, as being inseparably bound up with the moral law, has, accordingly, the character of a ***postulate*** deriving from pure practical reason. (What I understand by this expres-sion is a *theoretical* proposition, not demonstrable in a theoretical sense, in so far as it is inseparably connected with a *practical* law which, for its part, is valid in an *a priori* manner and unconditionally.)

As for the declaration made concerning our moral destiny, that it is only by way of an advance progressing into infinity that it is possible for us to attain to complete conformity with the [221] law of morality, the proposition which asserts this to be the case is of the greatest possible use, not merely in respect of the matter concerning us at present (i.e. that it serves by way of supplementing a deficiency pertaining to speculative reason), but also in respect of the interests of religion. And indeed, if this point is left out of account, the effect is either that one allows the moral law to suffer utter degradation, taking its *holiness* away from it, by way of distorting its true nature, the law being looked upon as being *lenient* and indulgent in charac-ter, and the purpose of it all being that it suits our convenience. Or else, the position is this: that as regards men's way of conceiving of their vocation, and the expectation they entertain with respect to it, people come to strive after reaching an unattainable destination, namely, a hoped-for acquisition of a complete holiness of the will, thus losing themselves in fantastic dreams of the *theosophic* sort, (Ak123) which run contrary to all true self-knowledge. In both cases mentioned the sole effect is that obstacles are being put in the way of an incessant *striving* for rendering a punctilious and constant obedi-ence to a commandment grounded in the truth. This command-ment, however stern and inflexible it may be, is none the less not in pursuit of a baseless idea, but on the contrary, of an idea which has its source in truth. The only thing attainable to a being which, while rational in character, is yet finite, is the advance *ad infinitum* from lower to higher degrees of moral perfection. The *infinite* being, to whom no condition pertaining to time means anything, apprehends in this series, unending from our point of view, the sum-total of conformity with the moral law. And as for the holiness inexorably demanded by his commandment, it requires, if it is to be in conformity with his justice, that it should be according to it, that each man has his share in the *summum bonum* apportioned to him, while, at the same time, the said holiness is present to the infinite being in a single intellectual intuition it has of the existence of the rational beings. [222] But then, if the question be, what is the situation of a created being, as regards the hope it may entertain of obtaining such a share, there is nothing it could consist in except the consciousness it had of possessing a character which had stood the test. And the effect of such consciousness would be this. Bearing in mind the progress it had so far made from the worse to the morally better, as well as the circumstance, having become known to it in this way, that its power of resolution was unshakeable, it would come to entertain the hope[17] that it would pursue its course uninterruptedly in the future, no matter how far its existence was extended, and indeed, even beyond this life. [223] And so the position would be this: that such a being was, neither at the present moment nor at any foreseeable time in the future, ever in a state of complete adequacy to the

---

[17] It seems, however, to be impossible that a created being should ever by itself be able to reach a *settled conviction* that, in its advance towards the good, the disposition of the mind was such as to be incapable of ever being shaken. And that is why the teaching propounded by the Christian religion supposes this conviction to be wholly derived from the very same spirit as brings forth sanctification, as brings forth, in other words, so firm a resolve, and along with it, the consciousness of one's perseverance in moral progress. On the other hand, it is natural enough that he who is conscious that for a long period of his life, and indeed, to the very end of it, he has persisted in his progress towards the better, and that from motives genuinely moral, is entitled to the comforting hope — although, admittedly, not to the certainty — that, in the course of an existence continued beyond this life, he will go on adhering to the principles in question. And, although he is in this matter never entitled — in view of a hoped-for increase of his natural perfection, which, on the other hand, goes along with an increase of his duties — to entertain a firm hope at any time, he may still have a prospect into a *blessed* future, as regards this progress towards a goal which, though being placed at an infinite distance, yet is, in the eyes of God, something held in possession. I speak of blessedness, because this is the expression reason employs to signify a condition of *well-being* which has been brought to perfection, one which is independent of all the fortuitous causes by which the world is governed, and which, like *holiness*, [223] has the status of an Idea which is not to be met with anywhere except in an infinite progress and the totality comprised in it, and which, accordingly, is incapable of ever being fully attained by a created being.

will of God, and that, whenever the idea of such adequacy was entertained, (Ak124) the reference was invariably to the infinity of its continuance, surveyable to no one but God in himself. Moreover, there
is no question here of showing indulgence or granting remission, for
this way of proceeding is irreconcilable with the idea of God's dis-
tributing justice.

V.
THE EXISTENCE OF GOD AS SOMETHING POSTULATED
BY PURE PRACTICAL REASON.

The result of the analysis of the moral law, supplied in the fore-
going, was that a certain problem pertinent to practice presented
itself (solely through the instrumentality of pure reason, and with no
motive forces deriving from sensibility playing any part) — the problem of how the requisite completeness was capable of being attained
to, in respect of the first and principal element in the *summum bonum*,
i.e. in respect of *morality*. And since it is only within the compass of
eternity that the said problem allows of finding a complete solution,
this resulted in the emergence of the postulate of *immortality*. Now
the very same law leads up to another necessary demand, namely,
that of establishing the possibility of the second element in the *summum bonum*, that is, the possibility of there being a state of *happiness* proportionate to morality, this problem arising — [224] as happened in the previous case — with no ulterior motives, impartial
reason being its sole source. And so it came about that the way was
led to the presupposition of the existence of a cause adequate to produce the effect under consideration, the presupposition that is, of
the *existence of God* as something necessarily to be postulated, by
reason of its being involved in the very possibility of there being a
summum bonum which, for its part, is to be looked upon as an object
inextricably bound up with the moral legislation which has its source
in reason. In what follows we propose to exhibit, in a manner carrying conviction, the connectedness which is operative here.

Happiness is the condition in which a rational being, placed in
the world, would find itself, provided that, as regards the whole of its
existence, everything was *in conformity with what it willed and desired*, and it thus rests on the circumstance that nature should be in
agreement with the sum-total of the end pursued, this holding good
likewise for the ground which is fundamental to the way its will is
determined. But then, the moral law, as a law of freedom, lays down
its command in virtue of determining grounds which (as motive

forces) are supposed to be wholly independent of nature, and of whatever agreement there may be between nature and our faculty of desire. As for the rational being which acts in the world, on the other hand, it is, after all, a fact that it is not, at the same time, the cause of the world and of nature itself. Hence there is nothing in the moral law which would provide the least reason for supposing that there was a necessary connection between morality, on the one hand, and, on the other, a state of happiness proportionate to it, to be found in a being which — belonging to the world as part of it, and thus dependent on it — is, for this very reason, incapable of being, by virtue of its will, the cause of nature. Accordingly, such a being, in securing its own happiness, is without any means of bringing about, [225] by its own powers, the complete accordance of nature with its practical principles. (Ak125) Yet, as regards the practical task which is set by pure reason, i.e. as regards the necessary working towards the *summum bonum*, such a connection is here postulated as necessary. We *ought* to act in pursuit of the *summum bonum*, which, if that is so, must be something that is possible. From this it follows that what is *postulated* likewise is a cause of the whole of nature, a cause which, being distinct from nature, contains the ground of the connection in question, namely, that there is a complete agreement between happiness and morality. But then, what this supreme cause is supposed to contain is not merely the ground for nature's agreement with a law governing the will of the rational beings, but nature's agreement with the representation of the said law, in so far as it is conceived of by these rational beings as the *supreme ground determining the will*. In other words, the supposed agreement is not merely one with morals under their purely formal aspect, but with the morality of the rational beings as constituting the motive by which they are prompted, that is to say, with the moral disposition of their minds. Accordingly, if there is to be a *summum bonum* in the world, this is possible only on the supposition that there is a supreme cause of nature exerting a causal efficacy which makes things dependent on their according with a moral disposition of the mind. Now a being which has the capacity for performing actions in such a way as to be guided by the representation of laws is what is called an *intelligence* (*viz.* a rational being); and what is present when the causal efficacy of such a being is exerted, as guided by the said representation of laws, is its *will*. The supreme cause of nature, therefore, [226] thought of, inasmuch as it requires to be presupposed for the purpose of the *summum bonum*, has as its character a being which, by virtue of its *understanding* of its *will*, is the cause, and thus the author, of nature. In other words, it is

God who is that being. As for the postulate, therefore, whose concern is with the possibility of there being the *highest derivative good*
(the best world), it is, at the same time, the postulate asserting the
reality of the *highest original good*, that is to say, asserting the existence of God. We have seen that to act in furtherance of the *summum
bonum* is something that for us is a matter of duty. In other words, to
presuppose the possibility of this *summum bonum* is not merely something we are permitted to do; it has the character of a requirement
necessarily bound up with duty. Now since it is only on condition
that God exists that the *summum bonum* is capable of coming about,
the presupposition that he does exist is something inseparably bound
up with duty. In other words, it is morally necessary to assume the
existence of God.

However, we shall do well to take note here of the circumstance
that the said moral necessity is *subjective* in character (i.e. a requirement on the part of the subject), not *objective* (i.e. not itself a duty).
Indeed, there can be no such thing as a duty to assume the existence
of a thing, since this is a matter which pertains solely to the theoretical employment of reason. Moreover, what we have said is not to be
taken as signifying that the assumption of God is necessary, in the
sense that it is to be looked upon as serving as the *universal foundation in respect of all obligation*. And indeed, as to the question of what
this foundation is, sufficient proof has been furnished of the circumstance that, as regards the nature of obligation, it is the autonomy
(Ak126) of reason itself which provides its sole basis. What alone has
a bearing upon duty here is that we are set a task — that of the
production and promotion of the *summum bonum* in the world —
and thus it is legitimate to postulate its possibility. [227] But then,
our reason looks upon this possibility as conceivable in no other way
than on the supposition that there is a supreme intelligence. And
from this it follows that to assume the existence of such an intelligence is a matter connected with the consciousness we have of our
duty. Yet, as regards the assumption itself, it belongs to the domain
of theoretical reason, while, when it is considered solely in reference
to theoretical reason, in respect of the part it plays as a ground of
explanation, the said assumption — that of a supreme being — may
be said to have the character of a *hypothesis*. If, on the other hand,
what we have in view is to make intelligible an object (i.e. the *summum
bonum*) which is set before us through the instrumentality of the moral
law — if, in other words, our concern is with a requirement pertaining
to practice, the attitude which is in operation may be spoken of as having
the nature of a *faith*. To be more precise, it has the nature of a purely

rational faith, since it is pure reason which (in its theoretical as well as practical employment) is the sole source from which it arises.

In view of this *deduction*, we are now in a position to understand why the Greek schools of philosophy were never capable of arriving at a solution of the problem which they set before themselves, that of explaining the practical possibility of the *summum bonum*. The reason was that they placed sole reliance upon the rule to be employed by the will of man in the exercise of his freedom, imagining that this constituted the sole and by itself sufficient ground accounting for the possibility of there being a *summum bonum*, and that, as regards the existence of God, it was something which they did not require for their purpose. These men were indeed wholly in the right in determining the moral principle by itself and independently of the postulate concerning God's existence, taking the line of establishing it solely in reference to the relationship subsisting between reason and the will, and thus assigning to it the role of the *supreme* practical condition of there being a *summum bonum*. Yet the truth of the matter is that it did not on that account constitute the *entire* condition of its possibility.

[228] It is indeed true that the principle *the followers of Epicurus* adopted, as standing supreme in the field of morals, was an entirely spurious one, and that they falsely assigned the character of a law to a maxim which, in actual fact, results from arbitrary choice, being prompted by each man's individual inclination. Still, they proceeded *consistently* enough in this, so that, conformably to the base character of the principle adopted by them, they let their *summum bonum* suffer degradation, not expecting it to yield any greater happiness than what can be obtained by human resourcefulness (temperance and the moderation of the inclinations having to be included in this class). But then, everybody knows such resourcefulness for the wretched thing it is, and that it must vary very greatly according to circumstance, not to mention the fact that there perpetually arose the need for the Epicureans to allow exceptions in the case of their maxims, these being unsuitable, by virtue of this very circumstance, ever to acquire the status of laws. As for *the Stoics*, on the other hand, their supreme practical principle — virtue as the condition of the *summum bonum* — had indeed been quite correctly chosen. Still, by representing the degree of virtue demanded by the law, in all its pureness, as a thing completely (Ak127) attainable in this life, they put a strain upon *man's* moral capacity, affixing to him the title of *"the wise"*, and in so doing they went beyond all limits set to his nature, assuming it to be an actual fact about men, but which in reality is contrary to all the

experience we have of their nature. But not only this: they would
have nothing to do with the second *constituent* of the *summum bonum*,
viz. happiness, being by no means prepared to allow it to be a distinct object of the human faculty of desire. [229] On the contrary, in
their description of the *wise* man, they depicted him as someone
bearing a likeness to a deity, as someone who, in the consciousness of
the excellence of his person, was wholly independent of nature, so
far as his contentment is concerned. Moreover, while exposing him
to the evils of life, they thought of him as not subject to them, at the
same time representing him as free from anything wicked. And so it
came about that they actually discarded the second element in the
summum bonum, i.e. private happiness, making the latter reside in
action merely and in the contentment found in one's own personal
worthiness. In other words, happiness was for them something which
was implicit in the consciousness one had of being endowed with a
moral disposition, this being a supposition which nature's own voice
within them should have been sufficient to refute.

The doctrine of Christianity,[18] even though one were, for the
time being, to leave out of account the fact that it is a religious doctrine, [230] is seen to supply, as regards the point under consider-

---

[18] It is commonly held that the Christian precept holds no advantage, in respect of its purity, over the concept defended by the Stoics. The truth, however, is
that the difference between the two is very clearly marked. What was done by the
system advocated by the Stoics was that consciousness of one's strength of mind
was made the pivot around which all moral dispositions were to revolve. And indeed, even though the adherents of that system spoke of duties, and moreover,
were reasonably skilful in determining their nature, the fact remains that they assigned the force moving the will (as well as the ground which, properly speaking,
determined it) to the circumstance that men's way of thinking was one exalted over
the sordid motive forces deriving from sensibility, infirmity of soul being what
alone gave these latter any power which they might have. Virtue was to the Stoic a
certain kind a heroism, on the part of the *wise* man, who, endowed with self-
sufficiency, lifted himself up above mankind's animal nature, being a man who,
while prescribing duties for others, was yet exalted over them, not being subject to
any [230] temptation which could lead to his transgressing the law. Now the truth
of the matter is this: if the Stoics had — as is the case with the precept set down in
the Gospel — represented the said law to themselves, in all its purity and strictness,
they could, in fact, not have argued on lines such as these. Moreover, there is this
further point. If what is signified by the term "*Idea*" is a state of perfection of such
a kind that nothing adequate to it allows of being given in the field of experience,
this does not bear the implication that moral Ideas are confined to a transcendent
region, as is the case with the Ideas originating in speculative reason which are
such that we are in no position to determine the concepts signifying them with
sufficient accuracy, or else, refer to entities with regard to which we cannot
even be certain whether they have any objects corresponding to them all. As

ation, a concept of the *summum bonum*, (Ak128) that of the Kingdom of God, which alone satisfies in all its strictness the demand insisted upon [231] by practical reason. The moral law is holy, that is to say, uncompromising, and what it demands is holiness in respect of morals, this attitude being taken notwithstanding the fact that no perfection man is capable of attaining to is ever anything more than virtue, i.e. a disposition of the mind which conforms to the law by reason of its being held in *respect*. This implies consciousness of the presence of a constant propensity towards transgressing the law, or at least, of a lack of purity on the part of the motive. In other words, when obedience is being rendered to the law, there is at the same time an awareness of an admixture of many motives which lack genuineness, that is to say, which are non-moral in character. In consequence, the respect in which we hold ourselves is one attended with humbleness. And the conclusion to be drawn from this is that, as regards the holiness demanded by the Christian law, it cannot, when it is a created being which is in question, consist in anything other than in an advance proceeding *ad infinitum*; while, on the other hand, it is precisely for this reason that such a being is entitled to entertain the hope that its existence will continue *ad infinitum*. A disposition of the mind *completely* adequate to the requirements of the moral law is one possessing infinite *worth*, seeing that, as regards any degree of happiness capable of being attained to, it is, in the judgment of a

---

against this, moral Ideas serve as archetypes of practical perfection, and moreover, as a *standard of comparison*. If, then, I consider *Christian morals* from a philosophical point of view, instituting a comparison between them and the Ideas advocated by the Greek schools of philosophy, the position is seen to be this. The Ideas relied upon by the *Cynics*, the *Epicureans*, the *Stoics* and the *Christians*, respectively, are the following: *nature* in her *simplicity*, *prudence*, *wisdom* and *holiness*. As for the means required for attaining to these, the Greek philosophers differed in this, in that the Cynics believed that *man's* ordinary *understanding* was sufficient, while the others held that it could be accomplished only through taking the *pathway of science*. In other words, both parties were of the opinion that the *employment of powers* deriving from mere *nature* was sufficient for the purpose in question. Christian morality, on the other hand, seeing that the precepts it commends are set forth in so pure and uncompromising a manner (this being, in fact, the very thing which ought to happen) — Christian morality, I say, takes away from man all confidence that he will ever succeed, at least where this life is concerned, in conforming wholly to what its precept demands of him. Still, it does, in its turn, raise up such confidence again, by allowing us to entertain the hope that, if we act as well as it is in our *power* to do, that which is not in our power will be supplied to us from a source other than ourselves, no matter whether or not it is known to us in what way this will happen. As for Aristotle and Plato, they differed from one another only in respect of the account they gave of the *origin* of our moral concepts.

wise and all-powerful apportioner, subject to no other restriction than a lack of adequacy, on the part of the rational beings, in the performance of their duties. As against this, the moral law does not of itself hold out any *promise* of happiness, seeing that, when it is concepts laying down the general character of a natural order which are relied upon, there is no thought of any necessary connection between the moral law, on the one hand, and happiness, on the other. As for the Christian doctrine of morality, it does, in its turn, make up for this defect (regarding the second indispensable constituent of the *summum bonum*) by way of positing a realm the members of which devote themselves, heart and soul, to the moral law. [232] This realm is conceived of as a *Kingdom of God*, wherein nature and morals are brought into a condition of being in harmony with one another, a state of affairs foreign to both of them by themselves, and which is being accomplished through the instrumentality of an Author of all things who is endowed with holiness, it being he who renders possible the emergence of the highest good, in the derivative sense of that word. (Ak129) *Holiness* of morals is something which the rational beings have enjoined upon them already in this life, having the character of a canon with which they are to be in conformity; while, as regards a condition of well-being proportionate to the said holiness — as regards the state of *blessedness*, in other words — it is represented as something attainable only in eternity. And if things are arranged in such a way, this is because *holiness* has to serve as an archetype guiding the conduct of these rational beings, no matter what state they may find themselves in, and because progress towards it is possible, and indeed necessary, even within this life. As for *blessedness*, on the other hand, and, for that matter, anything coming under the general title of happiness, there is no way at all of its being attained to in this life by the exercise of any of our powers; and this is why it is declared to be an object of hope merely. Still, the Christian principle of *morals* is not in itself theological, that is, the character pertaining to it is not that of heteronomy. On the contrary, what is being advocated here is the principle of the autonomy of pure practical reason, the principle, that is, of reason operating by itself, as the following consideration will serve to show. The Christian moral doctrine does not suppose that knowledge of God and his will is that in which the laws in question are grounded. It merely supposes that God and his will are grounds for the attainment of the *summum bonum*, while, at the same time, laying down the condition that these laws are to be obeyed. Indeed, even though the question be what is, strictly speaking, the *motive force* prompting obedience, the Christian doctrine does not assign this to the thought of desirable consequences resulting from obedience being rendered to these laws. On the contrary, what it looks upon as the motive force is solely the representation of duty, its being the faithful observation of that duty which alone constitutes the worthiness to acquire a share in the *summum bonum*.

[233] And so it is that the moral law leads the way towards *religion*, this coming about through the instrumentality of the concept of the *summum bonum*, the *summum bonum* having, for its part, to be looked upon as being the object and the ultimate end towards which pure practical reason is directed. And what happens as a result of religion being brought in is that *all duties are recognized as divine commandments*. However, they are indeed *far from being sanctions*, that is to say, *arbitrary and in themselves contingent enactments* having their source in *someone else's will*. On the contrary, the character assignable to them is that of fundamental *laws* to which every free will is subject in virtue of its own nature. Still, they are none the less to be thought of as commandments enjoined by the supreme being, on the ground that all the hope we can have of attaining to the *summum bonum* (as it is the moral law which imposes upon us the duty to make the *summum bonum* the object of our endeavours) rests upon the existence of a moral will embodying perfection, that is to say, of a will which is holy and beneficent, while at the same time being in possession of all power, as our attainment of the *summum bonum* is accomplished by way of our being in conformity with that will. And so, even here, everything remains disinterested and founded solely upon duty: there is no need to suppose that either fear or hope are here operative as forces moving the will, the intervention of the said sentiments, once they acquire the status of principles underlying actions, invariably having the effect of destroying their moral worth altogether. What the moral law enjoins upon us is that the accomplishment of the highest possible good is to be made the ultimate object of all our conduct. But then, there can be no hope of our achieving this in any other way than through our will being in conformity with the will of a holy and beneficent Author of the world. Moreover, as regards the *summum bonum* (which signifies a whole represented [234] as combining, in the most exact proportion conceivable, the greatest happiness, and attended with it, the highest degree of moral perfection (Ak130) attainable to created beings) — as regards the *summum bonum*, I say, it is indeed quite true that *our own happiness* is likewise included in it. Still, what we must take note of here is that what operates as the ground determining the will (while

having it, at the same time, enjoined upon it that the *summum bonum* is to be promoted) is not the aforementioned state of happiness but the moral law, which, for its part, severely limits our boundless desire for happiness to the fulfilment of certain conditions.

It is thus apparent that morality is, strictly speaking, not the doctrine telling us how to *make* ourselves happy, but the doctrine telling us what we must do to be *worthy* of happiness. And it is only when religion is brought in as well, that there arises, over and above this, the hope that, at some future time, we shall be made to partake of happiness, to the extent that we have made it our endeavour not to be unworthy of it.

A man is *worthy* to possess a thing, or to find himself in a certain condition, provided the circumstance that he is in possession of it is something which is in accordance with the *summum bonum*. But then, what we have said should have made it readily comprehensible by now that, if it is worthiness which is in question, everything depends on moral conduct, seeing that, as regards the concept of the *summum bonum*, moral conduct is the condition of everything else, i.e. of everything pertaining to the state in which one finds oneself, one's share in happiness being what is here in question. From this it follows that morality, considered by itself, must never be treated as a *doctrine of happiness*, that is to say, as one giving instruction how we are to become partakers of it, as morality's sole concern is [235] with the condition for there being happiness which is laid down by reason, the *sine qua non* of happiness, and has nothing to do with determining the means to be employed for acquiring it. On the other hand, after a full account of the nature of morality has been given (whose sole business it is to impose duties, as distinct from telling us what measures to adopt for the execution of our self-regarding wishes), it is then, and only then, that the moral wish — based upon a law — to promote the *summum bonum* (to bring the Kingdom of God to us) can make its appearance, the character of the said wish being that there was no possibility that it should arise, at a previous stage, in any soul in pursuit of self-interest. And it is after the step towards religion has been taken, on behalf of that wish, that the doctrine of morals allows likewise of being spoken of as a doctrine about happiness, because it is only by way of having recourse to religion that the *hope* of achieving happiness first arises.

There is yet another conclusion to be drawn from what has been said. In supplying an answer to the question what was the *final end* which *God* pursued in creating the world, we must not name the *happiness* of the rational beings inhabiting it, but the fact that he meant them to gain possession of the *summum bonum*. And as regards the character assignable to the *summum bonum*, it is this: that these beings have a condition insisted upon, over and above the wish for happiness which they have, namely, that they should render themselves worthy of that happiness. In other words, the additional condition is that in these rational beings morality should be present as well, *morality* being that which alone supplies the standard in conformity with which they may entertain the hope that, at the hand of a *wise* Author of things, they will be made to partake of happiness. And indeed, since what is signified by *wisdom*, taken in its theoretical sense, is the presence of *knowledge of the summum bonum*, while wisdom, taken in its practical sense, (Ak131) signifies *appropriateness, on the part of the will to the purpose of obtaining the summum bonum*, it is impossible to presuppose that a wisdom standing supreme and being independent of anything else, in pursuing its end, should place [236] reliance on mere *kindness*. It could not be otherwise, seeing that the operation of such a wisdom, when it comes to apportioning happiness to the rational beings, does not allow of being thought of as having appropriateness, unless it be made subject to a restrictive condition, namely, that it should exhibit a property appertaining to the will of God, that of *holiness*,[19] the latter having to be looked upon as playing the part of the highest original good there is.

And so it is that the men who asserted that the holding of God in honour was the end aimed at in creation might rightly be said to have hit upon the most appropriate expression available (provided, that is, that it is not used anthropomorphically, signifying a desire to

[19] I wish to make here only these further observations, my purpose being to bring out the distinctive character of the concepts relevant in the present context. God has certain properties attributed to him which, as regards the quality exhibited by them, we find to be applicable also to created beings, the sole difference being that, in his case, they are raised to the highest possible degree. For example, there are these: might, knowledge, being present, kindness, etc. And the designations which we employ in connection with these are: infinite might, omniscience, omnipresence, infinite kindness, etc. Still, there are three attributes, all of them moral in character, which are assigned to God alone, and nothing additional about a high degree being reached is predicated in their case, because absence of limitation is something already implicit in these concepts, the attributes in question being these. It is he who *alone* is *holy*, who *alone* is *blessed*, who *alone* is *wise*. And in accordance with this order of concepts he is also the *holy legislator* (as well as the creator), the *kind governor* (as well as the preserver) and the *just judge*. Now as regards these three attributes, there is contained in them everything in virtue of which God becomes an object of religion, the metaphysical perfections appropriate to them adding themselves of their own accord, by virtue of their coming to be contemplated by reason.

be praised). And indeed, there is nothing which honours God more than the thing which is to be most highly esteemed in the world, namely, holding his commandment in respect and observing the holy duty imposed upon us by his law, [237] there being added to this his glorious plan that an order of things, so full of beauty, is to be crowned with a state of happiness proportionate to that order. And if the circumstance mentioned last makes him worthy to be loved — to put the matter in human terms — it is by virtue of the fact mentioned first that he becomes an object of adoration. Indeed, even in the case of men, well-doing may, it is true, procure love by itself alone, while, at the same time, it cannot procure respect, the conclusion to be drawn from this being that even the greatest possible beneficence does honour to them, only inasmuch as it is exercised by the rule of worthiness.

Moreover, what has been said plainly shows the position to be this. As regards that order of things whose concern is with the nature of ends, man (and with him every rational being) is to be thought of as being *an end in himself,* that is to say, he is never to be used by anyone, not even by God himself, as a mere means. On the contrary, he is always to be treated, at the same time, as an end in himself. From this it follows that, as regards our own personality, we are bound to consider the element of *humanity* embodied in it to be something to be held *holy* by ourselves. This is because man occupies, in respect of the *moral law,* the position of being the *subject* of its operation, the subject, that is, of that which is holy in itself. (Ak132) And indeed, nothing whatever allows of being spoken of as holy, unless this be done on behalf of the moral law, and on account of things being in conformity with that law, the position being as we have described it for this reason: that the moral law has its foundation in the will of man, inasmuch as it is a will endowed with freedom. And the very nature of such a will is that, by virtue of the universal laws governing it, it is, if it is to *render submission,* under the necessity of insisting that everything should depend on its finding itself, at the same time, able to be *in agreement* with what has been demanded of it.

VI.

[238] THE GENERAL CHARACTER OF THE POSTULATES ORIGINATING IN PURE PRACTICAL REASON.

The postulates do, one and all, emanate from the principle of morality which itself is not a postulate but a law through the instrumentality of which reason determines the will directly; and it is the very fact that the will finds itself so determined — in other words, the fact that it is a pure will — which leads to the demand that the aforementioned principle should come into operation, the postulates, for their part, having to be looked upon as conditions necessarily implied in the circumstance that obedience is being rendered to what that will prescribes. These postulates, then, are not theoretical tenets but *assumptions* made on the ground that it is required that such a course should be taken, this being so in view of certain considerations which pertain to the field of practice. Thus, although these postulates do indeed fail to supply an extension of speculative knowledge, they yet procure objective reality for the Ideas of reason in a *general* sense, i.e. by virtue of their being brought into relation with the field of practice, reason thus being entitled to resort to concepts regarding which it would otherwise not even be in a position to assert that they referred to anything which was possible.

The postulates in question are these. The postulate of *immortality*; the postulate of *freedom* (freedom being taken in its positive sense, as the causal efficacy pertaining to a being, inasmuch as it belongs to the intelligible world); and the postulate of *the existence of God*. The *first* postulate has its source in a condition being laid down, as something necessary for the purposes of practice, namely, that the duration of the agent's existence should be such as to be adequate to the demand that the moral law is to be completely fulfilled. The *second* postulate has its source in what is a necessary presupposition, namely, that the agent should be in a state of independence of the sensible world, and should have at his disposal a faculty enabling him to determine his will in conformity with [239] the law governing a world which is intelligible in character — in conformity, that is, with the law of freedom. The *third* postulate arises from the circumstance that, provided there is to be an intelligible world capable of playing the part of the *summum bonum*, it is necessary to presuppose the existence of that which constitutes the condition of this being the case, the reality of the highest self-subsistent good, that is to say, in other words, to presuppose the existence of God.

Respect for the moral law inevitably has the consequence that one sets oneself the aim of attaining to the *summum bonum*; and this, in turn, gives rise to the assumption that the *summum bonum* has objective reality. And so it comes about that, by virtue of the postulates originating in practical reason, one's way is led in the direction of certain concepts of the kind that, when speculative reason concerned itself with them, it was indeed able to exhibit them as presenting problems, while, on the other hand, it could do nothing to enable it to arrive at a solution of these problems. (Ak133) The way was led, *first of all*, towards a problem, that of immortality. This was such that, when speculative reason applied itself to its solution, the sole result was that it made itself guilty of committing *paralogisms*; and that happened because the characteristic of permanence was not here available, for the purpose of supplementing the psychological concept of the ultimate subject (a property necessarily assigned to the soul, in that it has consciousness of itself) in such a way as to give rise to the representation of a real substance. Practical reason, on the other hand, accomplishes its task by way of postulating a state of continued existence such as is required for the purpose of there being accordance with the moral law, this accordance being met with in the *summum bonum*, which, for its part, is to be looked upon as embodying the totality of the end pursued by practical reason. *Secondly*, the way is led here towards that field where speculative reason achieved no further result than that it got implicated in an *antinomy*. And in proceeding to offer a solution of the said antinomy, it was able to rely on nothing but a concept which, although thinkable in the problematic sense, yet did not allow of being established by way of proof, or being clearly defined in such a way as to have its objective reality assured to it. The concept pertinent here is the *cosmological* Idea, [240] predicating an intelligible realm of things, and, over and above this, the consciousness we have of our existence in this realm. This matter is dealt with by virtue of the postulate of freedom, while, on the other hand, it is the moral law which discloses the reality of that freedom, and along with this, the nature of that law by which the intelligible world is governed, with speculative reason unable to do anything more about the concept in question other than merely to point to it, without being capable of bestowing any determinacy upon it. *Thirdly*, significance is provided for that which speculative reason was indeed able to conceive of in thought but which yet, as having the status merely of a transcendental *ideal*, it had to leave undetermined, that is to say, for the *theological* concept of the original being, as it is a purpose pertaining to practice which is here in question, i.e. a condition thought of as accountable for something which is an object of the will as determined by the moral law. And the part assigned to the original being is that it is the supreme principle holding sway over the *summum bonum*, and that it occupies its place in the intelligible realm by virtue of the authoritative moral legislation exerted by it in that realm.

Is the position, then, that our knowledge is actually extended in its scope through what is accomplished by pure practical reason, and

that that which had a *transcendent* character, in the domain of speculative reason, has acquired the characteristic of *immanence*, where
practical reason is concerned? No doubt this is so, but *only* in reference to what is required for the *purposes of practice*. And indeed the
truth of the matter is that we do not in this way acquire any knowledge either of the nature of the soul, or of the intelligible realm, or of
the supreme being, in respect of what they may be in themselves. In
fact, all we have done is to have brought the concepts under consideration into connection with the *practical* concept of the *summum
bonum*, the *summum bonum*, for its part, having indeed to be looked
upon as an object towards which our will is directed, and as something arising through pure reason in a wholly *a priori* manner. Still,
this happens only through the instrumentality of the moral law, and
thus also only in reference to it, nothing being in question here except that which the moral law commands us to pursue. [241] On the
other hand, there is nothing here which would serve to make it comprehensible how freedom was even possible, and how such a kind of
causal efficacy was to be conceived of in the theoretical sense; and
what actually occurs is that the existence of the said causal efficacy is
postulated by the moral law and on behalf of it. The same holds good
for the other Ideas, no human understanding ever being in a position to
fathom how they are possible, while yet no amount of sophistry (Ak134)
will ever succeed in taking away, from even the most ordinary of men,
the conviction that they are concepts which represent the truth.

VII.

How is it conceivable that there should be an extension of the scope of pure reason, in respect of practice, without this having the effect that its scope as speculative reason should find itself likewise extended?

To avoid putting the matter in terms unduly abstract, we propose to proceed immediately to give our answer to the above question by applying it to the case at present under consideration. In
order that a piece of pure knowledge should come to be extended in
scope, in a *practical* sense, it is required that there should be supplied
to us an *a priori purpose*, that is to say, an end to be looked upon as an
object of the will, the said object being represented (by virtue of an
imperative determining the will directly, that is to say, by virtue of a
categorical imperative) as something which is to be thought of as

necessary from a practical point of view, with no part played here at all by any theoretical principles. The object in question in the present case is the *summum bonum*. Now there is no possibility of there being a *summum bonum*, unless three theoretical concepts are brought into operation: these concepts, seeing that they pertain solely to pure reason, [242] do not allow any corresponding intuition to be supplied for them. Accordingly, there is no means discoverable for securing their objective reality by reliance upon any theoretical method. The concepts in question are those of freedom, of immortality, and of God. And what happens is that, through the instrumentality of the practical law — which, for its part, demands the existence of the highest conceivable good in the world — there is postulated the possibility of these objects of pure speculative reason, and, along with this, their objective reality which speculative reason was unable to secure for them. In this way, then, the theoretical knowledge of pure reason is indeed augmented, but the said augmentation consists merely in the circumstance that concepts which in every other way, when considered by theoretical reason, have a problematic character, that is to say, are merely thinkable, are now assertorically declared to be concepts such as have objects actually appertaining to them. And this line is taken on the ground that practical reason inescapably requires the existence of the objects in question, for the purpose of establishing the possibility of the *summum bonum*, the latter being something which, from the point of view of practice, is absolutely indispensable. Theoretical reason, then, in consideration of all this, is entitled to presuppose the existence of the aforementioned objects. Nevertheless, this extension of scope does not amount to any extension in the field of speculation, as becomes plain, when one sets out, with a *theoretical purpose* in mind, to make a positive use of what has been learned. And indeed, the matter stands thus. Nothing at all has been achieved by practical reason in its enterprise except that it has been shown that the said concepts are real ones, and that the objects to which they refer are, in fact, possible ones. Still, we are not supplied here with anything which would pertain to the intuition of these objects (the demand that this would happen being plainly one which cannot fairly be made). In consequence, there is no way that the reality of the said objects, which, admittedly, has been conceded, should have the effect of giving rise to any synthetic proposition. Hence [243] the disclosure made to us does not help us in the least, as far as any theoretical purpose is concerned, while yet, in respect of the practical employment, it leads to an extension of that branch of our knowledge.

(Ak135) The three Ideas of speculative reason mentioned above do not by themselves as yet have the character of cognitions, while, on the other hand, they are *thoughts* (referring to something transcendent) which contain nothing that is inconceivable. Now what happens is that, by virtue of an apodeictic practical law, these Ideas acquire objective reality, inasmuch as they are necessary conditions establishing the possibility of that which the law demands to be *made* the *object* of our pursuit. In other words, we have it enjoined upon us that these Ideas *have objects* corresponding to them, without, however, being in a position to signify the way in which each of them refers to its object. And this state of affairs does not amount to having any knowledge of the *objects in question*, seeing that we are not in the least equipped to make synthetic judgments about them, or to determine, in a theoretical fashion, the manner in which they are to be applied. In other words, it is impossible to make any theoretical use of reason in respect of these objects, this, after all, being of the very essence, so far as reason's speculative knowledge is concerned. Still, the theoretical knowledge (*not indeed of these objects*, but the one possessed by reason conceived of in general terms) comes to be extended in this way, seeing that, in virtue of the practical postulates, these Ideas find themselves *provided with objects*. Thus a merely problematic thought acquires, for the first time, objective reality. What came about, therefore, was not an extension of knowledge with regard to *given supersensible objects*. Still, there was an extension of theoretical reason and [244] of its knowledge as regards the supersensible in general, inasmuch as theoretical reason was compelled to concede the fact *that such objects existed*. On the other hand, it was incapable of determining these Ideas any further, i.e. of extending, through its own efforts, this knowledge of the objects, because the knowledge with which it finds itself now provided is one which rests on practical grounds, and moreover, is intended to be employed solely for the purposes of practice. And so it comes about that, as regards the said augmentation in insight, pure theoretical reason (from whose point of view all these Ideas are transcendent and without an object) owes the additional insight which it gains wholly to reason's pure practical faculty. Within the domain of the latter, these Ideas become *immanent* or *constitutive*, inasmuch as they are grounds rendering possible, and *bestowing actuality* upon, that which is an *object necessarily* pursued by pure practical reason. That object is the *summum bonum*. Apart from this, the aforesaid Ideas of speculative reason are *transcendent* and have the status of merely *regulative* principles, speculative reason, for its part, not being required to presuppose an additional object lying beyond the confines of experience, and its sole concern is that, when these Ideas are employed within the field of experience, this should be done in such a way as to secure approximation to a state of completeness. But then, once reason finds itself in possession of the augmentation of its scope, it will, in its role as speculative reason (properly speaking, it is only the safeguarding of reason's practical employment which is here kept in view), deal with these Ideas in a purely negative manner, not aiming at any increase of knowledge, but merely at exhibiting the Ideas in their purity, reason's purpose being, in the first place, to ward off *anthropomorphism*, the fountain of *superstition*. (Ak136) (The form which the latter takes here is that, on the basis of an alleged experience, a claim is made for an extended use of the said concepts.) And secondly, it aims at warding off *fancifulness*, which promises to obtain such extension through a power of supersensible intuition [245] or feelings of a similar sort. Now these things are, indeed, one and all, obstacles standing in the way of the practical use of pure reason. And as regards the process by means of which these are guarded against, it does indeed amount to an extension of our knowledge, in respect of its practical purpose, while yet there is nothing self-contradictory in confessing, at the same time, that by such an extension reason has made no gain whatever, as regards its speculative purpose.

Whenever reason is employed in respect of an object, no matter of what kind, it is required that pure concepts of the understanding, that is to say, *categories*, should come into operation, in the absence of which no object allows of being thought at all. Now, as far as the theoretical employment of reason is concerned, the said concepts are, in the case of the type of knowledge here in question, capable of having application, only on condition that intuition (which is never anything but sensible in character) is resorted to as forming their basis. In other words, they can be employed, only if one's purpose be that an object of possible experience is to be represented by their means. But then, as regards the *Ideas* deriving from reason, what, in their case, I should have to conceive of in thought, through the instrumentality of the categories, for the purpose of gaining knowledge of it, are entities whose nature is such as to render it impossible that they should be given to us anywhere within the field of experience. On the other hand, what is likewise to be taken into consideration is that what is pertinent in the present case is not the obtaining of theoretical knowledge, in respect of the objects towards which these Ideas are directed, but merely this circumstance, that they should have objects at all. As for the reality pertaining to them, this is supplied by pure practical reason, while theoretical reason, for its part, has no further business to perform than to *conceive* the objects in question *in thought* through the instrumentality of the categories. And we have made it evident in other places that this point is perfectly feasible, seeing that no intuition either sensible or non-sensible is required for the purpose in question. [246] The reason for this being the correct account of the matter is the following. Independently of, and prior to, any intuition, the categories have their seat and their origin solely in the understanding as such — looked upon as the faculty of thinking —, the reference invariably being to an object conceived of in general terms, *no account being taken of the manner in which the object in question may be given to us*. Now it is indeed impossible to supply for the categories, in so far as they are to obtain applicability to these Ideas, an object given in intuition. Still, the fact remains that there *actually is such an object*, and that, in the present instance, the category in operation is not to be looked upon as a mere form of thought, being empty of content, but that, on the contrary, it has meaningfulness, this being a circumstance which, through the instrumentality of the concept of the *summum bonum*, is indubitably established by practical reason. And so it comes about that the *concepts* required for the purpose of making the *summum bonum* possible have sufficient guarantee of their *reality* provided for them, while yet, as regards the said augmentation, it does in no way have the effect of extending our knowledge, inasmuch as the latter proceeds in conformity with theoretical principles.

(Ak137) If the next step taken be that one sets out to determine these concepts of God, of an intelligible realm (*viz.* the Kingdom of God), and of immortality, by virtue of predicates borrowed from our own nature, this must not be taken to mean that one proposes to impart a *sensible character* to those Ideas which originate in pure reason, that is to say, that there is a tendency to deal with them anthropomorphically; nor does it mean that the Ideas are looked upon as providing knowledge of a kind transcending experience, and concerned with *supersensible* objects. For the predicates in operation here are no other than those of [247] understanding and will, the relation subsisting between them being considered solely in respect of what it has to be conceived of as being for the purposes of the moral law: this implies that the use to which they are put is one which pertains to the field of practice.

As regards all the remaining features attaching to the concepts in question in a psychological sense, that is to say, in so far as these faculties of ours are, *in the way they are exercised*, made the objects of empirical observations — as regards these, I say, they are abstracted from in the present case. (For example, there are the following features: that man's power of understanding is of the discursive type, and accordingly, that the representations pertaining to it have the character of thoughts, not of intuitions; that these representations succeed one another in time; that man's will is invariably bound up with a condition of dependence, i.e. the contentment found by him in the existence of the object which he pursues — all these features being inapplicable to the supreme being.) Now the result of the abstraction mentioned above is this: that, as regards the concepts whereby a purely intelligible being is conceived of in thought, nothing remains but precisely what is required for the possibility of conceiving of a moral law in thought. Hence, although a piece of knowledge about God is indeed present here, it is one having application exclusively to the domain of practice. This has the consequence that, if we make the attempt to extend that knowledge in such a way as to impart a theoretical character to it, what we are left with, should we seek to represent such a being to ourselves, is a power of understanding, placing reliance not on thinking but on *intuiting*, as well as a will directed towards objects in such a way that, when it comes to finding contentment, it is not in any way dependent on the existence of these objects. (I need not mention here the transcendental predicates, as for example, that predicating a magnitude of existence, i.e. duration, which, however, is not to be an occurrence in time, while, as against this, that is the sole means we have at our disposal for the purpose of representing existence to ourselves as something exhibiting magnitude.) [248] Now these are, one and all, properties of which we cannot form the least conception, such as would be adequate to our gaining *knowledge* of the object. And this teaches us that the aforesaid properties can never be used for the purpose of any *theory* concerning supersensible entities, and that they are thus, for their part, incapable of serving as the foundation of speculative knowledge. On the contrary, their employment is strictly limited to the sphere whose whole concern is with the moral law and the way in which it is carried out in practice.

As regards the last point, its truth is manifest and allows of being clearly demonstrated by a simple appeal to the facts. One may thus confidently offer this challenge to those alleged to be *learned* men (a singular expression indeed) about *God* and his *natural* attributes,[20] that over and above the merely ontological predicates, (Ak138) they were to name a single property of their object, with regard to which it could not be incontestably demonstrated that, [249] once everything anthropomorphic had been separated off, one was left with a mere word, without there being the least possibility of connecting it with any concept capable of giving rise to the hope that it would lead to an extension of theoretical knowledge. As regards the field of practice, on the other hand, there still remains to us, so far as the attributes pertaining to an understanding and a will are concerned, the concept of a relationship upon which objective reality is bestowed through the instrumentality of the practical law, the law being precisely that which determines the relationship in question in an *a priori* manner. And once this has happened, reality is supplied for the concept referring to what is the object of a will determined by morality, that is to say, for the *summum bonum*, and along with this, for what are the conditions of the possibility of there being a *summum bonum*, i.e. for the Ideas of God, of freedom and immortality — as regards these, the sole reference is to the way in which the moral law is to be carried out, no speculative purpose coming into consideration.

In view of these reminders, there is no difficulty in arriving at a correct solution of this important problem: whether the *concept* of *God* is one *belonging* to the *domain of morality, or* whether it belongs to the domain of *physics*, and, accordingly, likewise to that of metaphysics, seeing that the latter contains nothing except, in their general signification, the pure *a priori* principles which form the basis of physics. If, in being called upon to offer an *explanation* of the arrangements found in nature and of the alterations they suffer, our method is that of having recourse to God, as the Author of all things, this is, to say the least, not a physical explanation. What, in fact, it amounts to is a confession that one's philosophy has come to a dead end. There can indeed be no doubt that this is so, seeing that what

[20] The expression "learning" refers, strictly speaking, only to the sum-total of the *historical* sciences. Consequently, it is only the man who is a teacher of revealed theology who can be called one *learned about God*. If, on the other hand, the title of a man of learning is likewise to be applied to those versed in the rational sciences, i.e. mathematics and philosophy (although this would be contrary to the proper meaning of the word, which attributes to "learning" only that which emphatically requires that one should know it because one has been taught it, it being impossible, accordingly, that one should, by means of reason, come to discover it by oneself), the philosopher, with his knowledge of God looked upon as a positive science, would cut too poor a figure, on account of what he had to offer, to let himself be spoken of as a *man of learning*.

we are here compelled to do is to presuppose the existence of a something [250] regarding which we have otherwise no concept at our
disposal to account for its nature, the aim of it all being that we
should come to comprehend the possibility of a thing which we have
lying before our eyes. Moreover, there is this reason why we cannot,
in reliance on metaphysics, start out from the knowledge we have of
this world in such a way as to be enabled to arrive at the knowledge
of God, being in a position to furnish proof of his existence, *under
the guidance of secure inferences.* In the case supposed we should need
to have knowledge of this world as constituting the most perfect
universe possible, and to enable this end to be accomplished we should
be under the necessity of possessing knowledge of all possible worlds,
so as to be able to compare them with it. (Ak139) In other words, we
should have to be omniscient, to be able to make the assertion that
there was no possibility of this world coming into existence except
through the agency of a *God* (according to the proper signification of
the said concept). And to top it all, if we set out to gain knowledge of
this being, placing reliance on mere concepts, that is an undertaking
which could not possibly be successful, on the ground that every
existential proposition (which asserts, with regard to a being of which
we form a concept, that such a being exists) is a synthetic proposition. In other words, it is a proposition of such a kind that, in enunciating it, I go beyond the said concept, asserting something more,
with regard to this being, than what was thought of in the concept,
namely, that, over and above the concept residing *in the understanding,* there is to be posited a corresponding object having its place
outside the understanding. Now this circumstance is incapable of being
elicited by any kind of inference. Hence reason is left only one way of
proceeding so as to obtain the knowledge in question, namely, that it
should determine its object, by way of starting out from the pure principle governing its pure practical employment (this employment being,
in any case, concerned solely with the *existence* of something thought of
as resulting from reason). [251] But then, what becomes evident here, as
reason proceeds with the task which it cannot escape from, (i.e. that it
was bound to direct the will to go in pursuit of the *summum bonum*), is
the necessity of its presupposing the existence of such an original being
— and the pertinent point here is to establish the possibility that the
aforementioned good should be encounterable in the world.

Yet there is something else which happens, (and this is the strang-
est feature of all, and something which was entirely lacking, when
reason proceeded upon its path by way of natural investigation)
namely: that there emerges a *concept pertaining to the said original*

being which is *determined with precision*. Since it is only a small part of the world which is known to us, while the possibility of our being able to compare it with all possible worlds is still more remote, we may indeed infer from the order, purposiveness and magnitude which it exhibits that it derives from a wise, benevolent, powerful, etc. Author. Yet no conclusion may be drawn concerning his *omniscience*, his being endowed with *supreme benevolence*, his *omnipotence*, etc. Moreover, it may indeed be conceded that we are fully entitled to supplement this inevitable shortcoming by having recourse to a legitimate and perfectly reasonable hypothesis to the effect that, if wisdom, benevolence, etc. shine forth in so many respects whenever things come to be presented to us for closer acquaintance, the position will be the same in all other respects, its being reasonable, accordingly, to presume that the Author of the universe should have all possible perfection attributed to him. However, what is operative here are not stringent *inferences*, entitling us to pride ourselves on the knowledge we possess. On the contrary, their nature is that of concessions indulgently granted to us, while, on the other hand, if we are to be able to make use of them, they stand in need of a recommendation from some other source. As far as the empirical [252] method is concerned, that of physics, the concept of God, predicating perfection in respect of the First Being, remains a *concept failing to be determined with sufficient exactitude*. Accordingly, it is impossible to hold it to be adequate to the concept of a deity, while, as for metaphysics, in its transcendental branch, it is incapable of accomplishing anything whatsoever.

(Ak140) If, then, the experiment we undertake next is to refer to the object of practical reason as the standard whereby the object in question is to be measured, we find that the moral principle grants this to be an admissible concept, only on the supposition that there exists an Author of the world endowed with *supreme perfection*. He must be *omniscient*, so as to have awareness of the disposition of my mind, to its very core, in every conceivable circumstance and into all future. He must be *omnipotent*, so as to be in a position to apportion the consequent effects appropriate to what my conduct has been. In the same way, he must be *omnipresent, eternal*, etc. In other words, what is being accomplished here is that, through the instrumentality of the concept of the *summum bonum* as the object of pure practical reason, the moral law determines the concept of the original being as signifying *the supreme being*. And that is a result which reason was incapable of obtaining either by placing reliance on any method coming within the domain of physics, or at a higher level, a metaphysical one. In other words, this result did not allow of being attained to by any procedure lying within the compass of speculation. And what becomes apparent from what has been pointed out is that the concept of God does not, as regards its origin, belong to physics, i.e. it is not intended to be made use of by speculative reason, but that, on the contrary, its proper place is within the field of morality. And the same holds good for the other concepts of reason which we have just discussed, declaring them to have the nature of postulates, and to appertain to reason in its practical employment.

[253] In the history of Greek philosophy, we do not, before the time of Anaxagoras, encounter any distinct traces of a theory advocating a purely rational theology. However, this is not attributable to the fact that the older philosophers lacked understanding and discernment to such an extent that, in pursuing the path of speculation, they were incapable of rising to such a level, at least by calling in aid an entirely reasonable hypothesis. What indeed could be easier and more natural than the thought, offering itself to everybody of its own accord, that, in the place of an indeterminate degree of perfection, to be met with in several distinct causes of the world, one was to postulate a single rational cause endowed with *any and every perfection*? Still, it seemed to these thinkers that the evils present in the world constituted objections far too weighty to entitle them to have recourse to such a hypothesis, the truth of the matter being this: that they gave evidence of the understanding and discernment which they possessed, precisely by virtue of the fact that they rejected the hypothesis under consideration. And what they did instead was look about among natural causes, so as to discover whether the property required for something to have the status of an original being might not, after all, be encounterable within the field of natural causes. However, it was after the members of this penetrating nation had progressed far enough with their investigations to reach a point where, even in respect of questions about morality, they dealt with things in a philosophical manner (and this is a matter concerning which other nations had never done anything but engage in meaningless chatter), that there came into prominence a requirement of a different sort, namely, a practical requirement. This did not fail to benefit them, in that the concept of the original being had determinacy imparted to it. As for speculative reason, it found itself compelled to make the best of things in a situation in which, to put it at its highest, it could lay claim to no merit except that it performed the service of lending adornment to a concept which had grown up on a soil other than its own, [254] calling in aid a number of confirmatory points taken from the domain of natural observation, (Ak141) confirmations which

were now, for the first time, brought into prominence. The authority of the concept, seeing that it was already sufficiently established, was lent no support, everything that happened being merely a matter of show, while yet there was a pretence, at the same time, that reason's theoretical insight found itself advantaged in this manner.

In view of the above reminders, the reader of the Critique of pure speculative reason will be able to convince himself how necessary that laborious *deduction* of the categories has been, and how beneficial an effect it exerts upon theology and the doctrine of morality. Indeed, it is only through this deduction having been undertaken that it is possible, when declaring the categories to have their source in the power of pure understanding, that we are prevented from considering them, as Plato did, to be innate, this being attended with the emergence of a host of theories concerning the supersensible, theology having assigned it to the role of a magical lantern, as it were, going in pursuit of mere phantoms of the brain. On the other hand, should the categories be regarded as something acquired, what must be guarded against is this: that one should not, with Epicurus, set out to limit every employment of the categories (even that which pertains to the purposes of practice) to the field of sensibility and to the determining grounds deriving from sensibility. But then, what the deduction shows is that, *in the first place*, it has furnished proof of the circumstance that the categories are not of empirical origin, but that their seat and source is, on the contrary, to be located — and that in an *a priori* manner — in the power of pure understanding. *Secondly*, it has been shown that it is impossible for the categories, having reference to *objects in general* — paying no regard to the way these objects are intuited — , [255] to be the source of *theoretical knowledge* except in application to empirical objects. Yet it is just as true that, when the categories are applied to an object supplied by pure practical reason, they lead to a *determinate conception* signifying *the supersensible*, yet with this proviso — that the said supersensible is determined solely by virtue of predicates such as are necessarily bound up with the *practical purpose* (supplied in its purity in an *a priori* manner), and with the possibility of this purpose. Limitation of pure reason, in respect of speculation, and the extension of its scope, within the domain of practice, creates for pure reason, for the first time, that *balanced relationship* which constitutes the possibility of its being used in a purposive manner. And this example

serves to prove more efficiently than anything else that the road to
wisdom (provided it is to be secure, as distinct from being impass-
able, or leading astray) must, with us men, inevitably pass through a
scientific stage, while, on the other hand, it is possible for us to become convinced that it actually leads to the goal aimed at only after
the science has reached completion.

VIII.

ON THE PHENOMENON OF SOMETHING TAKEN TO BE
TRUE BECAUSE OF A REQUIREMENT, ARISING ON THE
PART OF PURE REASON, THAT THIS SHOULD BE SO.

(Ak142) A *requirement* of pure reason, in its speculative employment, leads only to the forming of *hypotheses*, while a requirement
taking its rise in [256] pure practical reason leads to the emergence
of *postulates*, the truth of the matter being this. What happens in the
first case is that, starting out from that which is derivative, I am, in
tracing back the series of causes, free to mount up as high *as I like*.
And if I require that there is to be a ground which is original, this is
not for the purpose of bestowing objective reality upon that which is
derivative in character (e.g. in the matter of the causal connectedness
exhibited by things, or in respect of the alterations undergone by the
things in the world.) Instead, my sole purpose is that my enquiring
power of reason should, through my positing such an original ground,
come to find itself completely satisfied. To take an example, I have
before my eyes the order and purposiveness encounterable in nature,
and in order to convince myself of their *reality*, I do not have to have
recourse to speculation. On the contrary, it is only when my aim is to
explain them that I *presuppose* the existence of *a deity*, looked upon as
the cause of their existence. But then, as regards any inference drawn
from an effect to a determinate cause (especially when it is one as
accurately and completely determined as is the case when it is God
who is to be conceived of in thought), it can never be anything but
uncertain and precarious in character. This being so, it is impossible
for such a presupposition ever to be rated any higher than taking it
to have the nature of an opinion, the holding of which is the most
reasonable course for us to take.[21] [257] As for a requirement having

---

[21] However, even as things are, we should be in no position to make the plea
that it was a requirement *grounded in reason* which was here in operation, were it
not for the circumstance that a problematic, though indispensable, concept of reason was placed before our very eyes, the concept that is, of an absolutely necessary
being. Now as regards the said concept, it stands in need of being defined; and it is

its source in pure *practical* reason, on the other hand, its nature is this: that it is founded upon a *duty*, the duty that a certain thing, i.e. the *summum bonum*, is to be made the object of our pursuit, its being incumbent upon us that we are to act in furtherance of it by every means within our power. And in setting about this task, we are under the necessity of presupposing the possibility of the *summum bonum*, and, conformably to this, of presupposing likewise that there is a God, that there is freedom, and that there is immortality, as these are the conditions of there being a *summum bonum*. There is no other way in which we can proceed in this matter, seeing that, on the one hand, there is nothing our speculative reason can do for us by way of furnishing proof of the validity of the concepts under consideration, while, on the other hand, there is nothing forthcoming which would have the effect of disproving them. Moreover, it is indeed undeniable that the aforementioned duty is founded upon something wholly independent of the said presuppositions, upon something which is of itself apodeictically certain, i.e. the moral law. And to this extent, then, if the question be that the moral law is to be obeyed, and that there rests upon us an obligation, of the most stringent kind possible, that we are to perform actions of such a kind that they conform unconditionally to the demands made by the moral law, none of this requires that support should be forthcoming from some other source, a support basing itself on some theoretical opinion held (Ak143) concerning the inner constitution of things, concerning some hidden design at the bottom of the world-order, or else, concerning the existence of a ruler presiding over that order, he being what it stands in need of. Still, the subjective effect produced by the law — i.e. the *disposition* of the mind (appropriate to the law, and rendered necessary by it) laying it down, as it does, that the *summum bonum* is to be thought of as something practicable which is to be forwarded — presupposes, to say the least, that the *summum bonum* is something *possible*; for otherwise it would amount to a practical impossibility that one should go in pursuit of a thing signified by a concept which was at bottom devoid of meaning, and did not refer to any object.

this circumstance, accompanied as it is by the wish that reason's scope should come to be extended, which constitutes the objective ground of a requirement having its source in speculative reason. The demand made is that a closer definition is to be provided of the concept of a necessary being, a being that is, which, in reference to other beings, is to serve the purpose of constituting that in which they are ultimately grounded — and, in accordance with this, the means should be found, in some way or other, for specifying the distinguishing characteristics of the being in question. In the absence of such inescapable problems taking precedence, [257] there are no such things as *requirements*, at least, no requirements having their source in *pure reason*. As for those remaining, it is *inclination*s which form their basis.

[258] But then, as regards the postulates set out above, their sole concern is with the physical and metaphysical conditions requisite for the *possibility* of there being a *summum bonum*. Yet this happens not on behalf of an arbitrary intention, but on behalf of an end which, in the field of practice, is necessarily pursued by us, on the ground that it pertains to a will, purely rational in character, a will which, in the present case, does not *choose* according to its own pleasing, but, on the contrary, *renders obedience* to an inexorable command of reason, which has its foundation — and that *objectively* — in the constitution of things, in conformity with the way in which they have, in universal terms, to be judged through the instrumentality of pure reason. The nature of this command is not based on *inclination*, and inclination, for its part, is not entitled to presume, with regard to what we *wish* on purely *subjective* grounds, either the availability of the means for accomplishing it, or to presume the actual existence of the object in question. So what is here at play is a *requirement* referring to an *absolutely necessary purpose*. And as for the said presupposition, and the way it has justification conceded to it, its character is not merely that of a legitimate hypothesis but that of a postulate having a practical purpose in view. Hence, if it be granted that the pure moral law is inexorably binding upon each and every man, as a commandment, and not as a prudential rule, the man of honesty is fully entitled to express himself in terms such as the following: I *will* it that there should be God, that my existence should be such that, over and above natural connectedness, there appertains to me an existence in a purely intelligible world. And finally, I will it that my existence should be one having no end. I adhere to my view and will not let myself be deprived of this faith of mine, because this is the only case (seeing that I have not been given *permission* to detract from it in any way) where my interest inevitably decides my judgment. [259] And as for those who go in for reasonings of the hair-splitting sort, I will pay no attention to them, however little I may be capable of making an effective reply, or of countering their arguments with others carrying greater conviction.[22]

* * * * * * * * *

(Ak144) To avoid misinterpretation in the use of a concept as yet as unfamiliar [260] as is the notion of a practical faith taking its rise

---

[22] The *Deutsches Museum* of February 1787 contains an essay by a worthy and clear-headed man, the late Wizenmann, whose early death must be a matter of regret. What he does there is to contest the validity of an inference drawn from a requirement to the objective reality of the object that requirement is directed to-

in pure practical reason, I may be permitted to make this further observation. It might appear almost that the contention here was that the practical faith in question did itself partake of the nature of a *commandment*, the commandment, that is, that the *summum bonum* is to be thought of as something possible. But then the notion of a faith which is the subject of a command partakes of the nature of an absurdity. So we shall do well to remind ourselves of the discussion set forth above, where the point was what is required to be presupposed in the concept of the *summum bonum*. And in proceeding upon this task, we shall be made aware that the possibility under consideration had the nature of something which did not allow of becoming the subject of any command; and moreover, as regards whether this possibility was to be *conceded*, the practical dispositions of the mind had no bearing upon this matter at all, while, as for speculative reason, it was compelled to give its assent unhesitatingly, without requiring any prompting.

And indeed, this is how matters stand. As regards a condition of being worthy to be happy, to be met with in the rational beings in the world, in a manner appropriate to the moral law, this being connected with the possession of such happiness, in proportion to worthiness, there will be no one prepared to contend that such a state of affairs was *inconceivable*. Besides, as for the first constituent of the

wards. And he illustrates his point by the example of a *man in love*, who, having become infatuated with an idea of beauty, which, in fact, is nothing more than a figment of his own brain, would wish to conclude that the object in question actually existed in some place or other. As for my own view, I am in complete agreement with him, as regards all those cases where the requirement in question is founded in *inclination*, as the nature of that inclination is that it has no right to postulate the existence of its object, not even as something which has the character of necessity for the man who is affected by it, while it is still less possible that it should carry with it a demand which was to be necessarily valid for everybody, the nature of an inclination being, accordingly, that it constitutes a ground of desiring which is purely *subjective*. However, what is in question here is a *requirement* having its source in *reason*, taking its rise in a ground which determines the will *objectively*, i.e. in the moral law, which, for its part, is necessarily binding upon every rational being. and which, accordingly, provides an *a priori* justification of the presupposition that the conditions appropriate to the functioning of the moral law are available in nature. These conditions, for their part, are inseparably bound up with the circumstance that the practical employment of reason is to reach a state of completeness. It partakes of the nature of duty that the *summum bonum* is to be made real, through our exerting our power to the utmost, the *summum bonum* having, accordingly, to be something that is capable of existing. From this it follows that for every rational being in the world there is the indispensable need to presuppose the existence of that which is necessary as the objective basis of the possibility of the *summum bonum*. And this presupposition is as necessary as the moral law, while, on the other hand, it is solely in reference to the moral law that it has validity.

summum bonum, i.e. morality, the moral law simply issues a command, and to call in question the possibility of this constituent would be tantamount to throwing doubt on the moral law itself. But as for the second element in the object under consideration (i.e. a condition of happiness in every way proportionate to the aforementioned worthiness), the general possibility of this may be assented to without calling in any command, seeing that theoretical reason has nothing to bring forward against supposing this. [261] (Ak145) Yet we are still left with a *choice* as to the *manner* in which we are to conceive of such harmony between natural law and laws of freedom. This is because theoretical reason has nothing to adduce on this point with apodeictic certainty, and accordingly, there remains the possibility that the concern for morality should be the decisive factor in this matter.

I have previously drawn attention to the circumstance that, if it is merely the course of nature by which the world is governed, a condition of happiness in exact proportion to moral worth is not to be expected, and must be supposed to be incapable of ever coming about. Moreover, I have pointed out that the possibility of there being a *summum bonum* can, in view of this, be granted, only on the presupposition that there is a moral Author of the world. It was of set purpose that I omitted, for the time being, to impose upon the judgment under consideration the qualification that it had its source in the *subjective* conditions attaching to our reason, as it was my intention to make use of this kind of argument only when the task at hand was to provide more precise definition of the manner in which reason is led to conceive of things representing the truth. Indeed, the aforementioned impossibility is *merely subjective* in character, the position being that reason, from its own point of view, finds it *impossible* to make it comprehensible to itself, merely by relying on the course of nature that there should be so thoroughly purposive a connection between two sets of events in the world occurring in conformity with such different laws. And this holds good notwithstanding the circumstance that, as with every purposive thing found in nature, the impossibility of the thing having come about, in accordance with [262] universal laws of nature, is incapable of being established by way of proof. In other words, there is no way in which reason can with sufficient cogency settle the point under consideration by placing reliance on grounds of an objective nature.

But now there comes into play a ground of decision of a different sort which has the effect of turning the scale as regards speculative reason's state of indecision. The command that the *summum bonum* is to be furthered is objectively grounded in practical reason, while, as regards the question of the general possibility of there being a *summum bonum*, it is likewise objectively grounded — and that in theoretical reason — which, for its part, has nothing to bring forward against such a supposition. However, reason is not in a position objectively to decide in what way we are to represent this possibility to ourselves (whether as one conforming to universal laws of nature, without there being a wise Author presiding over nature, or only on the presupposition that there is such an Author.) And, at this stage, it is a *subjective* condition attaching to reason which enters into consideration, the point at issue being the only way in which, theoretically speaking, it is possible for reason to conceive of an exact harmony between the realm of nature and that of morals. Such harmony is the condition of the possibility of there being a *summum bonum*, while this way of conceiving of the matter is the only one that, at the same time, is conducive to morality, which, for its part, is under the jurisdiction of an *objective* law grounded in reason. Moreover, seeing that the furtherance of the *summum bonum*, and accordingly, the presupposition of its possibility, is something that is *objectively* necessary (although only by virtue of practical reason) — the way we propose to look upon the *summum bonum* as conceivable being left to our own choice, while, on the other hand, a disinterested concern arising from pure practical reason favours the presupposition of there (Ak146) existing a wise Author of the world — the conclusion to be drawn from all this is seen to be the following. The principle [263] which determines our judgment has indeed the nature of a requirement, on its *subjective* side. Yet since it serves, at the same time, as a means of furthering that which is *objectively* necessary, when considered from the point of view of practice, it forms the foundation of a *maxim*, bringing it about that, in consideration of a purpose pertaining to morality, a certain thing is taken to be true. In other words, what is operative here is *a faith having its source in pure practical reason*. A faith it is, but not one which is the subject of any command: on the contrary, its nature is that of a voluntary determination, on the part of our judgment (conducive to the moral purpose and, in addition to this, in keeping with the theoretical requirements of reason), to the effect that the being under consideration is to be presupposed as existing, and that it is to be made the basis of reason's employment in the future. It thus happens that this faith, having sprung from the moral disposition itself, may indeed at times be shaken, even in those who are well-intentioned. But there is never the possibility that it will be diminished to such an extent as to amount to an entire absence of faith.

IX.

MAN'S FACULTIES OF COGNITION
STAND IN A PROPORTION TO ANOTHER
WHICH IS WISELY ADAPTED TO HIS PRACTICAL DESTINY.

If human nature is destined to strive after the attainment of the *summum bonum*, this inevitably carries with it the conclusion that the measure of man's faculties, especially as regards the way in which they are related to one another, is such that it is suited to the purpose in question. But then the Critique of pure *speculative* reason does furnish proof of how very incompetent [264] reason is in providing a solution appropriate to the end it pursues, in respect of the most crucial problems it finds itself presented with. True enough, the Critique does not disregard the hints, natural and unmistakable, which this very reason throws out, nor is it forgetful of what long steps reason is in a position to take for the purpose of approximating to the great goal which it has set before it. However, the fact remains that reason never attains to this goal, not even by calling in aid the greatest possible knowledge which it has at its disposal. And the appearance is thus given that nature has treated us in a *niggardly* fashion when it comes to furnishing us with a faculty required for our purposes.

Now let us suppose that in this matter reason had actually lent a ready ear to us, in respect of what we desire, and had imparted to us the capacity for insight and illumination which we would gladly possess, and which certain people come to *imagine* we actually do possess: what, to all appearances, would have been the consequence of this being the case? Unless our whole nature had at the same time undergone a complete transformation, the *inclinations* (Ak147) (which anyhow invariably have the first word) would have demanded satisfaction, and, attended with reasonable deliberation, should obtain the greatest possible and enduring satisfaction, under the general title of *happiness*. The moral law would have its say only subsequently, for the purpose of confining the inclinations to their proper limits, with the intention even of subjecting them to a higher purpose which pays no regard whatever to any inclination. However, instead of the struggle with the inclinations, in which, as things are, moral disposition is under the necessity of engaging in a struggle (which leaves open the possibility that, a number of initial defeats having been suffered, [265] moral strength of mind should, after all, come to be gradually acquired, the position would be this: that *God* and *eternity*, in their *awesome majesty*, would lie incessantly *before our very eyes* (for that which we can furnish proof of concerning certitude is to us the same as that which we are assured of by our own sight). Transgression of the law would admittedly be avoided; what had been commanded would be done. But since the *disposition* of the mind from which actions are to proceed never allows of being infused by any command, while what in the present case spurs on to activity is ready at hand and is *external* (reason being given no opportunity that it should, first of all, labour on, gathering strength by the lively representation of the dignity of the law, for offering resistance to the inclinations), the inevitable result of the features to which we have drawn attention would be this: most actions which accord with the law would result from fear, only a few from hope, and none at all from duty; while, as for the moral worth of actions (upon which alone there depends, in the eyes of the supreme wisdom, not only the worth of the person but also that of the world), no such thing would exist at all. The conduct of men, so long as their nature remained as it is now, would be transformed into a mere mechanism, where, as in a puppet-show, everything would *gesticulate* effectively enough, while yet *no life* was to be met with in the figures. But then, the state in which we actually find ourselves is wholly different from this, namely, that we have, however great an effort our reason may make, [266] only a very obscure and ambiguous prospect into the future, while the Governor of the world only allows us to conjecture his existence and his grandeur, not to behold them or prove them. And as against this, the moral law within ourselves (not promising us anything with certainty, and not holding out any threat) demands that we should hold it in disinterested respect, while, when this respect has become active and dominant, it is only then, and by virtue of the said circumstance, that it allows us to have vistas into the realm of the supersensible — and that only with enfeebled glances. And so true moral disposition, with an undeviating devotion to law, is capable of coming into existence, and the rational creature can become worthy of that share in the *summum bonum* which, for its part, is in conformity not merely with the actions performed but with the worth of the personality. Hence it would seem that here, too, we have an instance of the correctness of the view which we have been taught, in other connections, by our study of nature and of man: namely, the circumstance that the inscrutable wisdom to which we owe our existence is no less worthy of veneration in what it has denied us than in that which it has vouchsafed to us.

PART II

METHODOLOGY
OF
PURE PRACTICAL REASON

[269] (Ak151) It is impossible that the term "*Methodology* pertaining to pure *practical* reason" should signify the manner (in respect of both reflection and exposition) in which one has to deal with pure practical principles, with a view to obtaining a *scientific* knowledge of them, this being what alone is called method, strictly speaking, in the *theoretical* field. Indeed, what popular method stands in need of is a *special* kind of *style*, while science requires the operation of a *method*, in conformity with *principles* of *reason*, by virtue of which alone the manifoldness of cognitions allow of acquiring the character of a *system*. As regards the methodology which is our present concern, on the other hand, it is to be understood as signifying the manner in which the law, appertaining to pure practical reason, permits of *finding entry* into the human mind and gaining an *influence* over the maxims adopted by that mind — in other words, it is an explanation as to how reason, which pertains to practice in the objective sense, is enabled to play a practical part in the *subjective* sense as well.

Now it is indeed clear that those grounds determining the will — the immediate representation of the law as well as the objectively necessary obedience to it as duty, which alone make the maxims truly moral and gives them a moral value — must be looked upon as the real motive forces of action, because otherwise the effect produced would be *legality* of [270] actions, as distinct from *morality*, on the part of the dispositions of the mind. What is not so clear, however, but on the contrary must at first glance appear a most improbable thing in everybody's sight, is that, even on its subjective side, the representation of pure virtue should be able to exert a *greater effect* on the human mind, and provide a much stronger motive, even for the purpose of effecting the said legality; and over and above this, to bring forth mightier resolutions to prefer the law to any other considerations, merely by virtue of the respect in which it is held. It seems most improbable, I say, that all this should have a greater weight than any allurements arising from our having held up before us dazzling prospects of pleasure, greater weight, that is, than anything classed under the general title of happiness — all this coming about without any threat of our having to suffer pain or encounter evils. (Ak152) Nevertheless, this is how things actually stand. And were not human nature so constituted, the taking of a circuitous route, or any attempt to recommend the moral law by way of making it palatable, would be of no avail in bringing a moral disposition into being. Everything would be sheer futility, and as for the law, it would be hated or even despised, while at the same time, in the event of obedience being rendered to it, the motive would be merely that of gaining one's own advantage: the letter of the law, i.e. legality, would be encounterable in our actions, while, as regards its spirit permeating the disposition of our mind, i.e. as regards morality, there would be no trace of it. Nevertheless, since, as regards our way of thinking, we should still be unable in our judgment to emancipate ourselves wholly from reason, it would inevitably happen that, [271] in our own eyes, we appeared to ourselves as worthless and depraved human beings. All the same, in the event of seeking to compensate ourselves for this mortification before the inner tribunal through taking a delight in these pleasures, a supposedly natural or divine law would come into play, operating like a mechanical contraption, attended — so as to delude ourselves — by a police force. Such a law, in directing its operations, would take into account only what was done, paying no attention whatever to any motives determining the action.

There is, it is true, no way of denying that, if one's purpose be that one should, first of all, act as a guide towards the pathway where the morally good is to be found, it is required (in the case of a mind as yet untutored, or of one which has grown into savagery) that certain preliminary instructions should be laid down, the mind being actuated by a consideration of its own advantage, or alternatively, being deterred by the thought of its coming to suffer an injury. However, no sooner has any effect been produced by this machine-like operation (a way of proceeding which has the character of a leading string, as it were), than it is emphatically necessary that the soul should be brought into contact with the purely moral motive. This imparts to the mind a strength unexpected by the man himself, not only because it is the sole motive which forms the foundation of a character (i.e. a consistent disposition of the mind, in the field of practice, in conformity with invariable maxims), but also because it teaches man to have a feeling of his own dignity, that is, to have the strength to tear himself away from all sensible attachments (in so far as they set out to become predominant) and to find in the independence of his intelligible nature, as well as in the greatness of his soul [272] to which he feels himself to be destined, ample compensation for the sacrifices he is offering. As regards this property of our mind, this receptiveness it has to a concern purely moral in character — in other words, as regards the power of moving us which the pure representation of virtue possesses, when the human soul is brought into sufficiently close contact with it — we propose to furnish proof of all this by way of pointing to a number of observations which everybody is able to make for themselves. For the point at issue is that it is the aforementioned circumstance which constitutes the most powerful, indeed the only force, when what is in question is the persistence and punctiliousness displayed in rendering obedience to moral maxims. (Ak153) It is essential, however, that we should remind ourselves of the fact that, if the observations in question prove no more than the reality of such a feeling — not that moral improvement has been accomplished by it — , this does not in any way invalidate (so that we could treat it as a result from mere fancy) the one and only method in fact available to us, for the purpose of making the objectively practical laws issuing in pure reason subjectively practical, solely in virtue of the pure representation of duty. And indeed, seeing that the method in question has never as yet been given the opportunity of running its course, experience is so far incapable of giving us any indication whether the method under consideration is successful or not. On the contrary, the only proofs which can fairly be demanded here must concern the point that we have a receptiveness for the motive forces of the kind mentioned. And I propose to bring forward such proofs here in brief, proceeding next to sketch out in a few words the method appropriate for the founding and cultivating of genuinely moral dispositions.

In attending to the course taken by conversations in mixed company comprising not only scholars [273] and subtle debaters, but over and above this, men of business, as well as persons of the female sex, one becomes aware that, apart from story-telling and jesting, still another form of entertainment makes its appearance, namely, people giving way to arguing about things. This happens the way it does because story-telling, provided there is to be any novelty or interest about it, soon exhausts itself, while jesting, for its part, becomes easily insipid. Now among all the various kinds of arguing, there is none which evokes such participation (on the part of people otherwise soon affected by boredom, whenever they find themselves confronted with any reasoning of the sophisticated sort) as when the *moral worth* of this or that action is talked about — a certain kind of liveliness thus being imparted to the company — and all done with the purpose of making out what is the character to be assigned to some person or other. Those who, as regards theoretical questions, look upon everything which savours of subtlety, everything having its source in rumination, as being arid and a matter of vexation, soon join in when what is at issue is to make out the moral value of a good or an evil action of which they are told, and they are just as precise, just as much given to rumination, just as subtle in finding devices for tracking down anything which could lessen, or throw suspicion upon, the purity of the intention (i.e. the degree of virtue encounterable in the action); though this way of proceeding is not to be expected of them when it is any other object of speculation that is under consideration. As regards this way of judging things, it frequently happens that it serves to illuminate the character assignable to the people pronouncing judgment upon others, certain persons appearing to be particularly inclined that, in performing their judicial office (principally in respect of those who have departed this life), [274] they ought to defend the good of which they are told, concerning this or that action, against every mortifying imputation of insincerity, and that they ought ultimately to defend the entire worth of the personality against the reproach of dissimulation or hidden malice. Others, again, are intent upon bringing forward accusations and imputations, with a view to contesting that worth. Still, as regards this latter type, we cannot ascribe to them, in every case, (Ak154) the intention that, whenever they are faced with particular examples of what men do, they mean to argue in such a way as to discard virtue altogether, so as to declare it to be nothing but an empty name. Instead of this, there is frequent evidence that what is in operation here is nothing other than a well-intentioned strictness, resorted to for the purpose of determining genuine moral worth, the reference being to a law which is inflexible in character. And it is when a comparison is made with a law such as this — not with particular examples — that self-conceit, in matters of morality, finds itself considerably diminished, humility being truly felt by everybody — not merely taught — in the face of such severe self-examination. None the less, what becomes plainly visible in the champions of purity of intention (concerning examples which are being brought forward) is that, where there is a presumption of honest dealing, they would gladly remove even the least blemish, this line being taken, for fear that, if all examples had their veracity impugned, and all human virtue was denied its integrity, the ultimate effect might be this: that virtue should be taken to have the nature of a mere phantom of the brain, and all striving after it rendered to be of no worth, having the character of an idle affectation and of a self-conceit tending only to deceive.

[275] I do not know how it is that those responsible for educating the young should not long since have made use of this propensity of reason, that, when practical questions come up for consideration, it should, in pursuing its course, find pleasure even in the examination of issues of the greatest possible subtlety. Taking as their foundation a catechism wholly concerned with morals, they might have searched through biographies of ancient and modern times, so as to have at hand confirmatory instances referring to the duties specified, calling into activity the power of judgment to be met with in the pupils chiefly by way of instituting a comparison between similar actions in different circumstances, their pupils being thus enabled to perceive the greater or lesser moral content to be met with in actions. Moreover, what will turn out likewise is that even the very young, too immature for any kind of speculation, will soon acquire that acuteness, showing an interest by no means inconsiderable, in virtue of which they will come to feel the advance which their faculty of judgment has made. The principal point, however, is this: that the prospect of a sure hope is aroused, through the frequent practice of getting to know good conduct in all its purity, through coming to applaud it, while taking note, with regret or even contempt, of the slightest deviation from the right course — such a sure hope, I say, is aroused (even though up to now it is all merely a game engaged in occasionally by the faculty of judgment in which children can compete with one another), namely, that a lasting impression of high esteem and detestation respectively will be left, while actions, which merely by the force of habit, [276] are looked upon as praiseworthy or blameworthy, serve as a sound foundation leading to (Ak155) uprightness in the future conduct of one's life. Still, my wish is that the pupils should be spared having set before them *noble*, i.e. suprameritorious, actions (of the kind which are thrown about in such quantities in our writings of the sentimental brand) and that everything should be made to hinge on duty and on that worth which man can, and in fact must, assign to himself, by virtue of the consciousness he has, in his own eyes, of not having transgressed duty. This is the only way possible, seeing that everything which amounts to having empty wishes and longings after transcendent perfection has no other effect than to produce heroes of romance, who, priding themselves on their feeling for greatness surpassing all else, exempt[23]

---

[23] It is perfectly appropriate to give praise to actions which reflect a disposition of the mind, magnanimous, disinterested, and sympathetic in character, or which give evidence of the humanity which shines forth from them. However,

themselves, in return, from the observation of commonplace and everyday obligation, which, placed as they are, appear to them trifling and insignificant.

[277] On the other hand, if it be asked what is the *real* character of pure morality, by reference to which, as to a touchstone, the intrinsic moral worth of every action has to be measured, I must confess that it is only philosophers who can raise a doubt as to how this question is to be decided. And indeed, as regards reason as it is encountered in the ordinary man, the issue has been settled long since (like the distinction between the right hand and the left) — not indeed by way of abstract general formulae but by its use in common practice. So what we propose to do, first of all, is to exhibit the criterion of pure virtue, by way of having recourse to an example; and we shall suppose that this criterion is being put before a boy (let us say, ten years of age), the point at issue being whether he must, of his own accord, come to judge in a certain way, without receiving direction from his master. Let him be told the story of a man of honour whom certain people seek to induce to lend his support to the slanderers of some person or other, innocent indeed, but otherwise having no power (say, Anne Boleyn, indicted by Henry VIII, King of England). The man is offered advantages, e.g. large presents or high honours. He rejects them. This will only have the effect of evoking applause and approbation in the soul of the listener, because they constitute gain. The next thing people set about is to threaten loss. [278] (Ak156) The slanderers, counting among their number his best friends, now proceed to renounce their friendship. There are close relations of his threatening to disinherit him when he himself is without fortune. There are powerful men able to persecute him and worry him in many a place and in all sorts of circumstances; there is a prince threatening him with loss of freedom, even loss of life. Then, to fill up the measure of his suffering, and to cause him to feel that

---

what one has to attend to here is not so much the *elevation of the soul*, which is very fleeting and transitory, as the *subjection of the heart* to *duty*, which can be expected to leave a more lasting impression, on the ground that what is implied here is the presence of a principle, while it is only impulses of the moment which are operative in the former case. One need reflect but a little to discover, in every single case, that what has happened is that a man has incurred an indebtedness to the human race in some way or other (and be it only the circumstance that, owing to the inequality of men under the civil constitution, he is in enjoyment of certain advantages, on account of which others are obliged to suffer want to a correspondingly greater extent). And reflecting upon this state of affairs will have the effect of preventing the thought of *duty* from being supplanted by the fancy of something *meritorious* which, in fact, springs from self-regard.

pain which only the morally good heart is capable of feeling with true intensity, let us suppose that there is his family, threatened by extreme distress and want of support, *imploring him that he is to yield.* Let us picture the man himself, who, although indeed a man of honour, does not on that account find himself equipped with organs sufficiently hardened or insensitive as to make him incapable of feeling sympathy as well as his own distress. Let us imagine him at a moment when his wish is that he should never have seen the day exposing him to such indescribable pain. Let us suppose him further as remaining, in spite of it all, faithful to his resolution that he is to conduct himself in an honourable manner, never faltering or even doubting.

Now as regards the youthful listener of whom we have spoken, what will happen to him is that he will find himself raised by degrees from mere approbation to admiration, and finally to the greatest veneration, attended with a lively wish that he himself could be a man such as this (although indeed not in his situation). Nevertheless, virtue is here worth so much, not because it brings any profit, but because it costs so much. All the admiration, and even the endeavour to bear resemblance to such a character, rests here [279] wholly on the purity of the moral principle which allows of being set before our eyes with appropriate clarity, precisely by virtue of the fact that everything which men class as happiness has been eliminated from the motive forces of the action. And so the truth of the matter must be this: that the power morality exerts over the human heart must be the greater the more purely it is represented. It follows further that, if the law of morality, and the depicting of holiness and of virtue, are to exert any significant influence over our souls, they can do so only in so far as they are laid to heart as motive forces in their purity, and wholly apart from any consideration for the agent's wellbeing. This cannot be otherwise, for it is in suffering that they are most gloriously manifested. Now when the position is that the removal of something strengthens the effect exerted by a moving force, the force in question must have partaken of the nature of an obstacle. Consequently, all admixture of the forces moving to action which derive from consideration for one's own happiness constitutes an obstacle standing in the way of procuring for the moral law an influence over the human heart. My further contention is this: even in the case of the aforementioned action which was the source of admiration, provided it was the high esteem in which the agent held his duty which supplied the motive for its being performed, (Ak157) then it is this respect for the law which exerts the greatest power over the mind of the spectator — not any pretended claim to being endowed with an inward magnanimity, or a noble-minded and meritorious way of thinking. The conclusion to be drawn from all this is that it must be duty, not merit, which, when seen in the true light [280] of its inviolability, exerts not only the most definite but the most forcible influence over the mind.

To draw attention to this method is more necessary that it ever was, in these times of ours, when men expect to make a greater impact on the mind through feelings of the melting and soft-hearted sort and through high-flying and overweening pretensions (which have the effect rather of shrivelling up the heart than of strengthening it) — all this, I say, will make a greater impact on the mind than to have recourse to the sober and earnest representation of duty, this latter course being better suited to human imperfection and to the way progress is made in goodness. To put certain actions, declared to be noble, magnanimous and meritorious, before children as a model, in the belief that one will predispose them in their favour, instilling in them an enthusiasm on their behalf — all this amounts to a procedure which is wholly absurd. And indeed, since they are still so backward in the observance of the most ordinary duties, and even in the correct estimate of them, the policy here pursued means that, in no time at all, one comes to transform them into characters chasing after mere fancies. On the other hand, even with the better-instructed and more experienced portion of humankind, the moving force supposed to be in operation, in the present case, although failing to be actually harmful, has at any rate no genuine effect on the heart, this being the very thing one meant it to accomplish.

All *feelings*, especially those supposed to call forth the making of an unwonted effort, must exert their effect at the moment when they are at their height, and before they come to evaporate. Otherwise they accomplish nothing at all, [281] the heart returning, in the ordinary course of events, to the moderate level of vitality natural to it, and then falling back into that languor characterizing it at an earlier stage. This is bound to be the truth of the matter, owing to the circumstance that the heart, although being brought into contact with something by which it found itself stimulated, was not brought into contact with anything giving it strength. *Principles* must be founded on concepts. On any other basis, nothing can emerge but mere whims, such as are incapable of imparting any moral worth to the person, incapable even of engendering that confidence in oneself, in the absence of which consciousness of one's moral disposition and of one's being in possession of a character of the kind here in question — the highest good to be met with in man — does not allow of ever being brought into existence. Now if the said concepts are to become practical, in the subjective sense, we must not stop at the objective laws of morality, bestowing our admiration upon them, and holding them in high esteem, but instead we must consider the representation encounterable in them, in reference to man and his existence as an individual. And what happens then is that the law does indeed present itself in a form making it (Ak158) worthy of the highest respect, though not in so pleasing a form as if it belonged to the sphere to which man is naturally accustomed. On the contrary, he will discover how the law compels him, on many an occasion, to leave his natural sphere — not without a great deal of self-denial — and to rise up to a higher sphere, where he maintains himself only with an effort, while having to be constantly anxious that he will suffer a relapse. In other words, what the moral law demands is that obedience should be rendered to it from an awareness of where one's duty lies, not as the result of predilection in its favour, which neither can nor, in fact, ought to be presupposed in any way.

[282] Let us consider next, by having recourse to an example, whether there appertains a greater subjective driving power, as a motive force, to the representation of an action as noble or magnanimous than is the case when the action is represented merely as a duty, and in reference to the law of morality and the solemn character exhibited by the latter. The action performed by someone, when he seeks to rescue others from suffering shipwreck, exposing his own life to the greatest danger and finally losing it — such an action, I say, will indeed be thought of as partaking, on the one hand, of the nature of a duty, while, on the other hand, it will be looked upon as having, for the most part, the character of a meritorious action. Still, the high esteem in which this action is to be held will find itself considerably diminished by virtue of there being a certain *duty towards ourselves* which is incumbent upon us, this duty suffering some impairment in the present case. However, a more decisive importance will be attached to the question of making a magnanimous sacrifice of one's own life for the preservation of one's country. And yet there remains some doubt that it is so unquestionably our bounden duty to dedicate ourselves to such a purpose, of our own accord, and without being commanded. And as for the action, it lacks the full force of a model impelling towards imitation. If, on the other hand, it is an inexorable duty which is in question, i.e. that duty whose transgression violates the moral law itself (no regard for the welfare of human beings coming here into consideration), a transgression, that is, which

tramples underfoot the moral law and the holiness appertaining to it (such duties being commonly referred to as duties towards God, on the ground that we conceive of him as the ideal of holiness embodied in a substance), then the true state of the case is the following. When obedience is rendered to the moral law, a sacrifice being made of everything that is of any value [283] from the point of view of our dearest inclinations, then we bestow upon such conduct the highest and most complete esteem. And by such an example, we find our soul strengthened and uplifted as we discover that, by means of it, we are enabled to convince ourselves that human nature is capable of lifting itself high above any moving force, capable of being summoned up by nature for the purpose of offering opposition. Juvenal sets forth an example of what is in question here by building up a climax, with the result that a lively feeling is evoked in the reader of the strength of a motive appertaining to the pure law where duty is spoken of as duty:

> *Esto bonus miles, tutor bonus, arbiter idem*
> *Integer; ambiguæ si quando citabere testis*
> *Incertæque rei, (Ak159) Phalaris licet imperet, ut sis*
> *Falsus, ed admoto dicet periuria tauro:*
> *Summum crede nefas animam præferre pudori,*
> *Et propter vitam vivendi perdere causas.*[24]

If anything of a flattering sort, anything which makes us think of merit, is allowed to have a bearing upon our actions, then the motive force is already somewhat mixed up with self-love, thus receiving some assistance from the side of sensibility. Yet to make everything else take second place, by comparison with the holiness of duty alone, and to become conscious that one *is capable* of doing so, on the ground that our reason acknowledges this as a command laid down by it, declaring that it *ought* to be done — as regards all this, I say, it amounts to our raising ourselves, as it were, entirely beyond the world of sense. Moreover, this feeling of elevation is inextricably bound up with the very consciousness of the law as playing the part of a motive force, in respect of a faculty *exercising the mastery over sensibility,* [284] notwithstanding the fact that success may not be forthcoming in every case. Indeed, as regards the question of success, frequent concern

---

[24] "Be a good soldier, a good guardian and an impartial judge. Should you, at any time, be summoned to bear witness on behalf of a dubious and questionable cause, then, even though Phalaris himself should order you to be false and, having his bull brought along, command you to commit perjury, consider it the greatest of all crimes to prefer life to honour, and to ruin, for the sake of keeping alive, all that makes life worth living." – Juvenal, *Satire,* viii. 79–84.

with the motive in question, as well as the attempts — slight at first — to make use of it, arouse the hope that the affect will be accomplished, with the result that, by degrees, there is produced in us the greatest concern about this matter, although, on the other hand, it is a concern which remains purely moral in character.

The method employed, then, takes the following course. Our *first* concern is merely this: that pronouncing judgment, in accordance with moral laws, should become a natural occupation, accompanying all the actions we ourselves perform and, over and above this, the free actions performed by others, this way of looking at things acquiring, as it were, the character of a habit. Moreover, to sharpen our power of judgment, we must first raise the question whether the action is objectively *in accordance with moral law*, and if so, with which of these laws. And the point to be taken into consideration here is this: how a law which merely supplies *a ground* of obligation is to be distinguished from what happens when the law in question is actually *obligatory* upon us (*leges obligandi a legibus obligantibus*). For example, there is a law concerned with the question what the *needs* of men require of us, in contradistinction from the law laying it down what the *right* possessed by men requires of us, the latter kind describing essential, the former only non-essential, duties. In this way we learn to discriminate between various duties coming together in one and the same action. The second point to which attention is to be directed is the question whether the action has, also on its subjective side, been done *for the sake of the* [285] *moral law* — in other words, whether it has not only moral correctness as a deed performed, or whether, the disposition of the mind being taken into consideration, it has moral worth also, to be looked upon as affecting the disposition of the mind, by virtue of the maxim prompting that disposition. Now there is indeed no doubt that this exercise, and the consciousness of gaining in culture by virtue of it, which arises on the part of our reason (whose sole concern here is to pronounce judgment upon what falls within the domain of practice), is bound gradually to have the effect that a certain special interest is taken in the law originating in reason, and conformably to this, taken in morally good actions. (Ak160) And, in the end, we come to acquire a liking for the things the contemplation of which makes us feel an extension of scope in the use of our cognitive powers, that extension being promoted principally by that in which we encounter moral correctness. All this is attributable to the fact that reason (along with its faculty of determining what ought to be done, in obedience to principles and in an *a priori* fashion) can rest satisfied only when it

finds itself placed within the compass of an order of the type aforementioned. After all, even an observer of nature eventually comes to
like objects which, to begin with, offended his senses, as he discovers
the high degree of purposiveness exhibited by the way in which these
objects are organized, his reason delighting itself in observing them.
And there was Leibniz, sparing an insect which he had carefully examined under a microscope, and taking pains to put it back on the
leaf where it had been, because of the instruction he had received through
viewing it, and because it had, as it were, bestowed a benefit upon him.

However, this occupation, on the part of our faculty of judgment, which awakens in us a feeling that pertains to the state in
which our cognitive powers find themselves, [286] does not as yet
amount to having a concern about the actions themselves and their
moral character. All it accomplishes is that we are led to like entertaining ourselves with such a type of judging. And to virtue and a
disposition of the mind which conforms to the moral law, there is
imparted a form of beauty which, while being admired, is not yet, on
that account, sought after (*laudatur et alget*)[25]. The same holds good
for every case where the contemplation of a thing gives rise, on its
subjective side, to a consciousness that our powers of representation
are in harmony with one another, our faculty of knowledge (i.e. the
understanding and the imagination) feeling itself, in its entirety,
strengthened in this way. What is produced is a delight capable of
being communicated to others, while yet it exhibits this feature: that
the existence of the object remains to us a matter of indifference,
because this object is looked upon merely as an occasion for our
being aware that, as regards the nature of our aptitudes, we have the
capacity of being elevated above the level of mere animality.

Now the next step is that the *second* kind of exercise comes into
play, consisting in a lively representation, by way of adducing examples of the nature of a disposition of the mind determined by
morality, the point at issue being to draw attention to the purity of
the will. It is a purely negative perfection of the will which comes up
for consideration, in the first instance, the circumstance, namely,
that in the case of an action proceeding from duty, no motive forces
which have their source in inclinations exert any influence over the
will as determining grounds. Still, this has the result that the pupil's
attention is kept alive to the circumstance that consciousness of *freedom* is to be met with in him. And although the renunciation
aforementioned initially excites a feeling of pain, still the pupil,

---

[25] ["*probitas laudatur et alget*" — "virtue is acclaimed yet freezes" — Juvenal,
Satire, i. 74. Editors' tr.]

by finding himself relieved from the constraint which is characteristic of all needs, even genuine ones, has proclaimed to him a liberation from the manifold forms of discontent [287] in which he finds himself entangled through all these needs. The mind is thus made receptive to a feeling of contentment from other sources. (Ak161) As for the heart, it finds itself freed from a burden, after all, and is given relief when, by reference to purely moral resolutions (examples of which are being set forth), there is disclosed an inner faculty not properly known to man in any other respect. This is the inner freedom through which he has to emancipate himself from the vehement importunity of the inclinations. The extent of this reaches so high a degree that none of these inclinations, not even the most highly favoured, exercises an influence any longer in respect of a resolution that, as things now stand, is supposed to be formed through our making use of our reason. In a case where it is *known only to myself* that my cause is unjust, and where a free confession of the injustice and an offer to make restitution would conflict most markedly with vanity, with self-interest, as well as with an antipathy — not otherwise unjustified — to the man whose right I am infringing: in such a case, I say, if I can nevertheless find it in me to be able to disregard all such considerations, this implies the presence of a consciousness of my finding myself in a condition of independence of inclinations and external circumstances, as well as a consciousness of my being sufficient to myself. This is a state of affairs which is in every way salutary to me in other respects as well. And so the law of duty, obedience to it making us feel the positive worth appertaining to it, finds easier access to the mind, this coming about through the instrumentality of the *respect* which, in the consciousness of our freedom, we gain *for ourselves*. [288] Every moral disposition permits of being grafted onto this self-respect when it is soundly established that a man dreads nothing more, on examining himself, than to appear worthless and contemptible in his own eyes. For this attitude is the best, indeed the only, custodian that can prevent ignoble and corrupting influence from gaining an influence over the mind.

The sole purpose of the remarks I have made has been to draw attention to the most general maxims governing that methodology whose concern is with moral cultivation and the practice appertaining to it. To consider the multiplicity of duties would demand special definitions of each kind, and this would amount to a lengthy business. Hence the reader will tender me his forgiveness if, in a work such as this, which is purely propaedeutic in character, I let matters rest with the general outline I have supplied.

CONCLUSION

There are two things which imbue the mind with a feeling of admiration and reverence, ever renewed, and ever on the increase, the more frequently and the more perseveringly our thoughts are occupied with them: *the star-clad sky* there *above us, and the moral law within ourselves.* There is no need that we should search after them, or merely surmise them, as hidden in obscurities, or as having to be placed in a transcendent region beyond our horizon. [289] (AkI62) We see them before us and connect them directly with the consciousness we have of our existence. The starting-point of the former is the place which we occupy in the external world of the senses, and as for the connection in which we find ourselves placed, its dimension is widened to an immeasurable extent, with worlds upon worlds, systems upon systems, and moreover, limitless times, in respect of their periodic motions, their beginning and their continuance. The starting-point of the latter is our invisible self, our personality, and exhibits us as having our place within a world which has true infinity, while, on the other hand, it is only the understanding to which it is discernible. And as for our way of being connected with this world (and along with this, with all the aforementioned visible worlds), we recognize it as a connection which does not, as happened in the former case, exhibit a merely contingent character but one which is universal and necessary. That which engaged our attention first — the sight, that is, of a countless multiplicity of worlds — annihilates us in importance, as it were, inasmuch as we are *animal creatures*, obliged to give back to the planet (a mere speck in the universe) the matter from which it came, these creatures having been provided for a short time — one does not know how — with a vital force. As regards the second characteristic, on the other hand, it infinitely raises our value; we are thought of as having the attribute of being *intelligences*, and that by virtue of our personality containing within it the moral law which reveals to us a life independent of animality and even of the whole world of sense. Such is the truth of the matter, at least as regards anything which may be gathered from what happens when a purposive destiny is assigned to our existence through the instrumentality of this law, [290] a destiny not restricted to the conditions and limits of this life, but which, on the contrary, reaches out to infinity.

However, although admiration and respect can operate by way of stimulating enquiry, they are incapable of making good the want of it. What, then, is to be done for the purpose of conducting this enquiry in a manner profitable and appropriate to the sublimity of its subject matter? As for examples, they may here perform the role of providing a warning. Yet they may also be resorted to the purpose of calling forth imitation. The contemplation of the universe began with the most splendid spectacle conceivable capable of being presented to the human senses, our understanding being challenged to undertake the venture of tracing it out to the widest extent possible. And what it ended in was — astrology. Morality began with the noblest attribute of human nature, the development and cultivation of which holds out the prospect of infinite utility. And what it ended up with was a state of enthusiastic exaltation and superstition. So it goes with all attempts as yet rude, where the principal part of the business is to determine the way in which reason is to be used, a result which does not just turn up (as is the case with the use of the feet) by itself, as the outcome of frequent practice. (Ak163) And this is especially true when what is in question are properties such as do not permit of being exhibited straightaway and directly in common experience. But after the maxim had come into vogue, albeit late, that every single step which reason proposed to take should be deliberated upon carefully in advance, and that one should not let it proceed on its course except by the path of a well-considered method, [291] a quite different direction was given to the way in which the nature of the universe was judged, and along with this, an incomparably more promising prospect of meeting with success. The fall of a stone, as well as the movement of a sling, reduced to their elements and to the forces to which they give expression, on the occasion of their coming into operation, and, over and above this, being dealt with mathematically — all this finally produced a clear insight into the structure of the universe, an insight incapable of suffering alteration at any future time, and one giving rise to the expectation that, as observation continues, this insight will find itself steadily extended, there never having to be any fear that it will be obliged to retrace its steps.

That we should pursue such a course in treating of the moral capacities of our nature is a way of proceeding which the example just set forth may rightly commend to us, and the hope is aroused that a good result of a similar nature will be accomplished in this field. After all, there are examples of reason pronouncing judgment in moral matters which we have at hand. Now if we analyze these into their elementary concepts, and if, for the purpose of *separating* off the empirical and rational elements encounterable in them, we have recourse, in the absence of *mathematics*, to a procedure not unlike that adopted in *chemistry* (where man's ordinary understanding is made the subject of frequent experiments), this will enable us to exhibit both elements in their *purity*, and to signify with certainty what each can accomplish by itself. In proceeding in such a manner, we shall, on the one hand, preclude the emergence of errors such as follow from judging things in a way as yet *crude* and unpracticed, and, on the other hand, we shall preclude — this being a much more pressing matter — the emergence of *flights of genius*, the result of which (as is customary with the adepts of the philosopher's stone) is this: that in the absence of all methodical enquiry, [292] or any proper knowledge of nature, a promise is made of visionary treasures being obtained, while the true ones are being thrown away. In a word, it is science (critically pursued and methodically directed) which is the narrow gate leading to the *doctrine of wisdom*, provided what is to be signified by the latter is not merely what is to be *done*, but what is to serve as a guide to *teachers*, for the purpose of laying out well and clearly the path leading to wisdom which everyone is to tread, while guarding others against the danger of straying from the way. And as regards this science, it is philosophy which, at any and every time, must remain its guardian, while the general public, having no share in its subtle investigations, is yet obliged to take an interest in the *doctrines* propounded which become properly comprehensible to it only after such a laborious enquiry has been undertaken.

INDEX

aberrations of which philosophers have been guilty 76f

admiration 93 95 194 196 201

aesthetic of pure theoretical and practical reason 111

analogy 11 67, cf 111 147

analytic of pure practical reason 7; critical evaluation 110; of pure speculative reason 16 47f 110f

analytic and synthetic method 9; judgments 13; unity (connection) 139; knowledge 141

Anaxagoras 178

"Ancients" 25 77 134f 139 145 159 178

animality in man 12 73 93f 160n 199, cf 201

anthropomorphism 165 172f 175

antinomy into which pure speculative reason falls 1 32 134 143 168; to which practical reason gives rise 142ff; resolution of this a.143-150; of mathematics and empiricism 13

appearances (distinct from things-in-themselves) 4f 5n 31f 56 62 117 123 127 133 143; determinable in time 117, cf noumena

a priori (distinct from empirical) 11f, cf 59

archetype 36 102 161n 162, cf 49

Aristotle 161n

arrogance 105, cf 11 16 30 59 89

Author of the world 163 177 184f (cf 127, Governor 187); of nature 144 185; of all things 162 165 175; of the universe 177

automaton materiale and *spirituale* 120, cf 125

autonomy of the will or of pure practical reason as the highest principle of morality 37 48 49f 87 158 162; arising from freedom 37 137; of choice 41; cf heteronomy of choice 37 41

badness of a man's character, amateur vs. true scholar 95

border-line between morality and self-love distinctly marked 40

blessedness, state of 26 149 155n 162 165n

calamity 71ff (*see also* well-being)

catechism moral 192

categories (1) determination of 4; of nature 79; of causality 63 129; of understanding 172f; their deduction 179; division into mathematical and dynamical 128f; criteria pertaining to the pure understanding 8n; making experience possible 53

(2) of freedom 78f; their table 80

causality, causal laws (1) of nature 1 5n 30 48 55 78 82 116ff 144 180 (= mechanism of nature 5n 120); psychological and mechanical 119; contested by Hume 12 59ff

(2) empirically unconditioned c. of the will or of freedom 1 5n 15 16 19 20 51 55f 78 80 82f 116ff 123 128ff 142f 157; intellectual (causal efficacy) 89 129

cause and effect (see causality)

character defined 189; moral 155 195f; how it arises 120f 122 123; illuminating the c. of the judgmental 191

chemistry, procedure of, applied to the moral ground 114 202f, cf 28

choice presupposed 123, see autonomy, heteronomy of

Christian religion, its teaching (doctrine) 155n, 160f; its moral precepts 160nf 162ff, cf 102f 105 (*see*

within pure theoretical (speculative) reason 129, cf 133f

dignity, immediate through obedience to moral law 44; of humanity 108; of the moral law 187; essential d. appertaining to duty 109; of man 189 (*see also* value, worth)

disposition of the mind, moral 86 102f 145f 186f 190 etc

divine voice (see reason)

doctrine of method
   see Methodology

doctrine of Christian morality 160f 162 (*see also* Christian religion)

doctrine of morals (in stark contrast to doctrine of happiness) 114 164

doubt (see scepticism, universal)

dynamical laws 48, cf 128

duty defined 36 41 99; formula in respect of 7 7n; classification of 7n 10n 80; the only feeling which deserves to be called moral 45; the concept utterly destroyed if treated as an object of sentiment 45; the supreme principle in life 105; distinct from a requirement 158; distinct from an affection spontaneously felt 103f 147 192 193n; acting from d. distinct from acting in conformity with d. 99; essential dignity of d. has nothing to do with enjoyment of life 109; and moral restraint, i.e. obligation 100, cf 103; true end of moral cultivation 147; and *summum bonum* 158 163 181 183; recognized as divine commandment 163; d. vs. merit 195; Kant's apostrophe to d. 106 (*see also* holiness)

education, principles of 46 123 (use of examples in 192f 195)

empirical = belonging to world of sense 31f, cf 81f

empiricism, system of universal 12f

60ff; its foundation in feeling 13; guarding against e. in matters of practical reason 85; more of a threat than mysticism to morality 86; its threadbare superficiality 116

empiricists, concept of freedom stone of stumbling for all 6f

end in itself (man as end in himself) 107 166

enthusiastic exaltation, enthusiasm 86 103, cf 154f 202; moral 104 105, cf 67 195

Epicurus 24 46 145 151 179; followers of 108 139f 159f

eternity, awesome majesty of 186

evil distinct from misery 70f; distinct from the unpleasant 69; good and evil sole objects of practical reason 69 75 111f; table 80; e. principles voluntarily adopted 124; cf 43 70f 74 78 81 85 92 124 160 178 191(*see also* good)

existential proposition 176

experience defined 48; distinct from reason 11 28 41; distinct from necessity (see Hume) 59f; possible e. 48 51 63f 172; common e. 202; Hume's criterion 13

exposition (distinct from deduction) of the moral law 53

fact of pure practical reason 5 34f 48 49 (distinct from empirical f. 34); moral law given to us as a f., as it were 54; freedom as a f., as it were 113; f. and causality 130

faith having its source in pure practical reason 182f 185 (*see also* rational faith)

fancifulness 172

fatalist (cf Priestley) 122

First Being 177

fatality, actions ruled by 125

feeling, all f. sensible in character 92 147; or pathological 91; distinct from understanding 21; distinct from principles 195; of pleasure and pain 26ff 69 74ff; moral f. 45 92f 97f 111 (cf sensation 69f 73ff 92 96; cf sense (moral), respect, f. of)

Fontenelle, B. 93

form (distinct from matter) of intuition 13n; of universality 39; of legislation (law) 27 28f 30f 34 84; of the intelligible world 49f; of thought 79; of the will 28; of the pure will as distinct from f. of intuition 79; subjective f. of principles and objective f. of law 34; mere or universal legislative f. (see legislation)

formal laws determining the will 22; cf 35 45; f. practical principle of pure reason 47

freedom (1) only in a comparative sense 118 125; in psychological sense 116ff; through inner representations 118 = freedom enjoyed by a turnspit 120

(2) transcendental 1f 31 119f; (2a) its first conception is negative in character 31 37 48 55 96 = independence of any desired object 37; of nature 119; of the inclinations 147f; of the sensible world 167; (2b) the second conception positive in character = autonomy of pure practical reason 37 96; f. with absolute spontaneity 56 122; as causal efficacy pertaining to a being 80 96 130; type of a law of f. 84; inasmuch as it belongs to the intelligible world 167; law and f. 167 cf 47f 122f; gives other Ideas objective reality 2ff 168f; its rel. to the moral law 2 2n; cf 31f 37 54f; re unconditioned practical law 31; as coping stone of system of pure reason 2; its categories 78ff; its productiveness 128; its difficulty 5f 54f 119;

its indispensability 6; incomprehensibility of the concept 6; its possibility admits of no further explanation 53; instrumentality of 116; as a regulative principle of reason 57; as fact 4f; f. and natural necessity (see necessity) 116ff; practical f. = independence of the will of anything except the moral law 116; consciousness of practical f. 48 199; method to salvage it 118 124f; reconciling Idea of f. with sensible existence 124; postulates of 167ff (see free will)

free will 31ff 34f 38 48 50ff 65ff 88 120 122 142 163

fundamental law issuing in practical reason 33 = moral law 35

fundamental powers or faculties 54

genius, flights of (in contrast to methodical enquiry) 203

geometry, pure 33 see mathematics

God concept (Idea) of, not conditioned by the moral law but only by the will's relation to the *summum bonum* 2 168; as containing the ground of the complete agreement between happiness and morality 157f; only Idea or postulate 2 11n 67 156ff; presence of a piece of knowledge about God 174; morally necessary in subjective sense to assure his existence 158; concept of God belongs to domain of morality, not domain of physics 175ff; posited as a concept outside the understanding 176ff; author of nature (universe) 144 157f, cf 175 i.e moral 177 184; ideal of holiness embodied in a substance 197, cf 95f; all-sufficiency 34 124; self-sufficiency of 149; infinite 155; wise and all-powerful apportioner of happiness 162f, cf 155; but no basis of our

r.15f; its purpose wrongly or rightly used 73f; its relation to sensibility 72f 111; to will 65ff; to the sciences 112; takes concepts in their entirety 9n, cf 112 (*see also* limitations)

also: conditions attaching to r., obj. and subj. 184f, cf 164f; knowledge by means of r. = knowledge *a priori* 11; employment of r. 11f 202f; in ordinary affairs 61 112f; of pure 15; of theoretical 15 19 49 62 158; of practical 15 39f 112; of theoretical (speculative) and practical 16 58ff 66 150ff 169ff; transcendent and immanent 56 169; scientific 61; theosophers and mystics imposing their monstrosities upon r. 152; being deaf to the divine voice of r. 39

receptiveness of the mind to a concern purely moral in character 190

relation of practical categories 80

religion defined 163; the step towards r. from morality 164, cf 155 (also religious teaching 155n 160); how to prevent enthusiastic exaltation in r. 103, cf 154 163f 165n

repentance thought of as a feeling of pain 121f

requirement (need) of pure (speculative) reason (= subjective necessity) 3 112, practical req. 178; req. referring to an absolutely necessary purpose 182; cf 158f 180ff; cf 182nf 185

respect feeling of, defined 98; the only feeling *a priori* 89 96; is termed moral feeling 91f 98; neg. and pos. 90f; sole motive force operative in moral matters 95; for persons 92ff 99n; for the moral law 89 101 167 196 etc; as distinct from love 101f

rule, practical, diff. from law 18, cf 18ff 81ff; division 80; rules of skill 27 and imagination 60; general vs. universal 41

sacrificing oneself for one's country 196

sanctification 155n

scepticism, doubt, universal, 1 13 60ff 63 128

schema defined 83 cf 82; distinct from law 83; to be applied to a law itself 83

science and philosophy 11 61 134f 203; and wisdom 135 180 203; and rational knowledge 112

self, the invisible, our personality 201

self-conceit, moral (*philautia*) 89f 92 94f 101 106f 135 191 (cf humility)

self-constraint (sacrifice) 102

self-esteem 89

self-interest 64 200

self-love (opp. morality), principle of rational 21 22 27 39 40 43 89f 91 92 101n 104 105f 197

self-regard (*solipsismus*) 89f

self-respect 200

self-satisfaction (*arrogantia*) 46 89

sensation (see feeling)

sense, inner 22f 69 98 121 (and external 119); illusion of 146; distinct from the understanding 22; moral 44

sensibility, realm (domain) of 16 23f 36 64 69 71 74 75 81 82 89 92 93 96ff 111 122 156 160n 179 197 (cf reason, sense, inclination)

sensible see entries under feeling, intuition, world of sense, nature; *also* supersensible, freedom

sensible character 173

sensible world (see world of sense)

sentimental educationalists and writers of romance 105, cf 192f

Kant's criticisms of the present age

(a) *the present age:* syncretistic, compromising, dishonest, superficial 25

(b) *modern philosophy, scholars, men of learning:* recourse to venturesome definitions 8n; dogmatic course 9n; men otherwise acute 22; ignorant men desirous of dabbling in metaphysics 24; inconsistency 25; petty juggling about words 118, cf 78 140; try to embody repentance within syncretistic system 122; arrogance of title of philosopher 135; those learned about God 174nf; meaningless chatter about morality 178; theology pursuing phantoms of the brain 179; *as distinct from ordinary understanding* : speculations confuse the mind 39; universal doubt, scepticism affects only the learned, tending to destruction of all knowledge 61f, *see also* critique of all philosophy 45, 76f; question re nature of *summum bonum* gone out of fashion with the moderns 77

(c) *sentimental educationalists and writers of romance:* create unsubstantial, high-flying dispositions and moral exaltation 104f; present noble, suprameritorious actions 192f; feelings high-flying and melting 195

EXAMPLES AND ILLUSTRATIONS USED BY KANT

(a) proper and improper use of examples 202; common man and example 84; setting example 94 100; limited use 191; in contrast to those setting up noble, suprameritorious actions 192; style as distinct from scientific method 188; Kant's own use of rhetoric: peroration to Duty 106f; law, duty, dignity 186f; the star-clad sky above us and the moral law within ourselves 201

(b) *list of examples*: orator and poet coining new words 10n; no insult tolerated without revenge 18; precept of saving for old age vs. imperative against lying promise 20; degrees of pleasure, quality of delight determining actions 23; gold worth the same from mountain or from sea 23f; designing a mill in order to eat (theoretical principle) 27; yawning when others yawn 27; keeping deposit money of another 29; marriage partners bent on one another's ruin 30; King Francis I's arrogance towards Emperor Charles V 30; mastering desire of alleged irresistable lust and desire of life itself 32f; justifying false testimony and stealing for refined ends 39f; cleverness and cash, cheating for profit 42f; Stoic in pain 72; teasing people and receiving a deserved beating 72f; considering oneself justified in committing fraud, or suicide, or in being unloving 84; "Love yourself above everything, and love God and your neighbour for your own sake" 101n; avoiding the lie to avoid contempt of oneself 107f; wishing to tell a lie when confronted by the moral law (chemical precipitation) 114; theft viewed to be in conformity with the law of natural necessity (comparative freedom) 118; avoiding the accusing conscience in vain 121; displaying a malicious disposition from childhood, which advances, notwithstanding receiving an education 123; Vaucanson and the puppet show 125; cf 187; man in love imagining that the object of his infatuation exists (Wizenmann) 183n; the dinner party's "moral" conversation 190f; the innocent slandered (Anne Boleyn) 193; shipwreck and sacrifice (merit contrasted with duty) 196; atoning for my unjust action of which I alone am aware 200